Drawn Down the Way

Drawn Down the Way

A journey along the Camino Francés in sketches

AUSTIN CLIFFORD

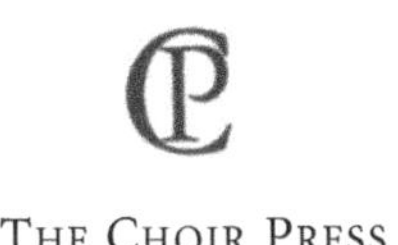

THE CHOIR PRESS

First published in the United Kingdom in 2016 by
The Choir Press

ISBN 978-1-910864-79-1

For Finley and Layla, for being Finley and Layla
My wife Ann for letting me walk my two Caminos
Caroline, her stoicism, my inspiration

Acknowledgements

To all those Pilgrims with whom I was privileged to share laughter, aches, pains, blisters, vino tinto, and an all to brief friendship; thank you.

To Nicola, whose example taught me so much about the spirit of the Camino and whose friendship I cherish.

Thankyou too to those of you who encouraged me to publish this book, Caiã, amongst the first, if not the first.

To Annalisa and Roberto, Ann Marie, Caiã and Raquel, Chris and Geraldine, Christy, Geesje, Hyon and Koongang, Jan and Terrill, Monty, Natalia, Pia, Roland, Tracey, all of whom have kindly let me use their photographs, thank you.

To DC, my GP for 30 years, Sandwell and New Cross Hospital's Cardiology Departments, whose combined skills have kept me ticking!

To Munir and Brigitte for their generous advice on publishing.

Contents

Preface

The Camino Francés is an historic Christian Pilgrimage. Walked by countless Pilgrims for over one thousand years along what had been a Roman trade route known as *la voire lactė,* the Milky Way. Stretching some 800Km from St Jean Pied de Port, nestling in the foothills of the French Pyrenees, over the Route Napoleon to Roncesvalles, Pamplona, Burgos, León, and eventually Santiago de Compostela.

More than half a million Pilgrims are reputed to have travelled to Compostela in the 11th. And 12th. Centuries, twice the number than in the years I walked, 2014, and 2015.

I do not recall exactly when or how I heard of the Camino. I was brought up as an Anglican, in retrospect, low, although I was unaware of the distinction at the time. I remember only one lady parishioner in the congregation, who used to genuflect. Even as a choir boy, and server, when crossing the aisle, we only turned toward the altar cross and lowered our heads in respect. So unlikely I would have known of the Camino from childhood.

I suspect I was in my fifties, probably from some TV travel programme. The romance, probably, the adventure too, caught my imagination, and the history and architecture chimed with my interests. I guess I initially thought it would be a nice idea, which as time passed became an ambition to walk it.

When I finally got to do my first Camino, it seemed natural for me, as I have enjoyed sketching on high days, and holidays, to record my journey in sketches.

As I walked, and sketched along the Way, I met numerous Pilgrims who either assumed I was preparing a book for publication, or thought, and encouraged me to do so. And thus the seeds of this book were sown.

Introduction

The book records my progress along the Way, with sketches, and anecdotal text relating to the drawings, villages, towns and Cities I passed through on both of my Caminos. It is not a guide book, there are excellent ones available. It is about the joy I found, the friendships I enjoyed, and the love I shared, with people and places, on the moving community that is the Way.

Although originally intended as a personal memento, my hope is it will be enjoyed equally by those who have made their Camino, those who will, and those for whom it will ever remain a dream. For Pilgrims, I hope it will evoke fond memories of places visited, and for those considering walking, give further inspiration to do so.

A Note About The Drawings

All the drawings were made insitu, along the Way. They are not necessarily the view of choice, or are they the iconic image of a particular subject. They were affected by, and in many cases determined by, tiredness, maybe a step to sit on, or a wall to lean against, whether in the sun or in the shade. Shelter too, from the little rain I was fortunate to experience, and occasional early morning chill, when I'd been to weary to draw the previous evening. And not the least constraint, time, or lack of it! As such, I hope the sketches convey something of the flavour of the Camino.

Preparation

When my passing interest in the Camino blossomed into an ambition I hoped to fulfil in retirement I thought it prudent to try and learn enough of the language to get by, as I had read that in the remoter areas of the Way only Spanish was understood.

I was in my mid-sixties by then, and although of a generation when English grammar was still taught, I struggled with Spanish grammar and verb conjugation. I had not done a Romance language, having done only German at school, and that unused and mostly forgotten.

We holidayed along the coast from Barcelona, and I thought it would be a good opportunity to practice. On one occasion I had wandered through a maze of narrow streets and become disorientated and could not remember where I'd left my hire car. I scanned the deserted street and as I did so an elderly lady came out of a shop. I see everyone around my age as elderly, except me! Fortunately I had noted the name of the street, and so enquired in the best Spanish I could muster the street's whereabouts.

She gave me a blank stare, and I repeated the query. Still no comprehension, but she took my arm, and virtually dragged me into the shop she had just exited. A lengthy conversation followed with the young woman behind the counter, punctuated by the occasional glance in my direction. Eventually leaning across the counter she asked in English what I wanted. I repeated again my query in Spanish. After the briefest of pauses she burst out laughing. Was my Spanish so awful, I thought, until she turned to the elderly lady, saying between chuckles, *"él está hablando español "*

I learned from that I wouldn't get much Spanish practice in *Catalunya* .

Towards the end of our holiday, we were walking back to our hotel in the evening, when we heard a bird chirrup, *do de doo a, do de doo a, do de doo a,* We stopped and looked up into the tree to see the bird. We stood gazing upward for some time, and then movement and a Great Tit hopped into view.

My knowledge of bird song and calls is pretty limited. I can recognise Blackbirds, Robins, and I thought, Great Tits too! Great Tits known as the *teacher bird* from their call *te da, te da, te da, te da, teacher teacher teacher!* Odd I thought, and then it struck me, *do de doo a,* or *profesora!* It was practically the only Spanish I'd heard on that holiday!

Ironically, I need not have troubled, as I found the lingua franca of the Way to be English.

Retirement arrived, and I talked in rather vague terms about a Camino. I think family and friends thought it was a pipe dream that would never be realised. I vacillated between walking, and cycling, eventually settling for walking, and then circumstances seemed to contrive to delay my plans. I had had Angina since my early fifties, thankfully drug controlled, until out of the blue, I got off a tram, walked a few yards at my normal pace, and wham! I was brought to a rather sudden halt, and progress then was slow with frequent rests. I had a triple bypass at Eastertide 2009. Fortunately I'd recovered sufficiently by August to walk up Snowdon by the Pyg Track, and down via the Miners.

I made plans through 2011 to walk in the Autumn of 2012, until my Son announced marriage plans for June of that year. From then it seemed to be frocks, and hats, and none for me!

After the Wedding, I had plans for the autumn of 2013, you have probably guessed, our first Grandchild was due in the September, and I couldn't be away on such a momentous occasion. So Spring of 2014 it was! I was seventy-one and a half!

In preparation I walked five miles before breakfast, at least five mornings a week. As time went by, in an attempt to acclimatize shoulder and back muscles, I carried my rucksack weighted with odds and ends and books. I spent the day prior to my departure packing, and re-packing my rucksack, trying to identify and cull unnecessary items. My one concession to weight reduction was to replace a specially purchased A3 sketchpad, with an A4 size. To be honest, only because the A3 pad would not fit in the sack!

When finally I swung the sack onto my shoulders, I realized the weights I'd used for training, were hopelessly optimistic. As I'd booked my flight home I'd kept the overall weight to just below 15Kg. but still harboured doubts at my ability to manage it.

April 2nd arrived, departure day, although my wife maintained it should have been the day before! Coming down stairs bare foot, to make some tea, I carelessly trod on a nosing, slipped onto my back, and bumped down the remaining half a dozen steps. I lay in a heap at the stair bottom not daring to move. I had nightmarish flashes that cancellation loomed. Slowly I inched into a sitting position, and then cautiously stood ..... nothing worse than friction burns on my hip!

Journey to SJPdP

The first drawing of my Camino which I felt to be appropriate was to be the *Tour St Jacques,* Paris. The tower, all that remains extant of *St-Jacques-de-la-Boucherie,* destroyed during the Revolution. In the middle Ages, it was the traditional starting point for Pilgrims, who after attending Mass would set off, cheered, and accompanied the short distance to *Notre-Dame* by well-wishers. From there onward to Etamps, Orléans, Tours and eventually, Spain and Santiago.

I had chosen to travel overnight by Eurolines to Paris Gallieni. Not the best decision I made along the Way! And on the evidence of that journey, not one I would wish to repeat. It arrived getting on for three hours late, which meant taking the Metro direct to Montparnasse for the TGV to Bayonne.

So no *Tour St Jacques* sketch!

Most of the passengers were already seated as I boarded the TGV, and I could see that the luggage area adjacent to the entrance lobby was stacked full which meant my sack was destined for the rack above my seat. As I began to weave down the aisle to my seat, which was well down the carriage, conscious of my poles and mono-easel protruding and not wishing to catch anyone. I had taken but a couple of steps, adjacent to the first seats, when a tall Scandinavian guy stood and said, "Let me help you" He did not appear to be that much younger than me, but before I could answer he had grabbed the sack, and was headed down the aisle to my seat.

I thanked him as we reached my seat, saying I could manage from there. I removed the poles and easel to so the sack would fit onto the overhead luggage rack and laid them under the seat. As I stooped to grab and swing my sack up, the young lady sitting opposite jumped up saying "Let me do that" I just about managed to beat her, thanking her none the less.

I sat in my seat. The TGV began to glide smoothly out of the station, it felt like the adventure was beginning. I smiled wryly as I thought, here I was about to embark on an 800 Km. walk, and apparently I looked so feeble, young women feel obliged to assist me!

The TGV drew in to Bayonne on time. There had been a landslip on the narrow gauge line to SJPdP and a replacement coach service was provided. My fears that this would delay my arrival at the albergue I had booked were unfounded as the coach dropped us off at the station a few minutes ahead of the train schedule.

I consulted my notes on how to walk to the albergue and as I did so realised I had not confirmed my booking on the proposed arrival day as had been requested. It was now about seven in the evening and a light drizzle began to fall dampening the paving to match my dampened spirits as I worried if my reservation had been held.

Walking up the Rue de la Citadelle I found *L'esprit du Chemin* and avoiding the old rucksacks and boots decorating half the stone step I pushed nervously at the heavy dark timber door. The hall rang with excited chatter and laughter, a young Brazilian lad sitting closest to the door on the bench, sprang to his feet and greeted me. Soon I was swept up by a *hospitalera,* Geesje, who showed me upstairs to my dorm. It was a small room with one double bunk on one wall with clothes and belongings carelessly laid out, and opposite a single bed, a decorated card with my name on, and a sweet lying on the cover,

I so enjoyed the company of the Pilgrims I met briefly during my two night stay. Some left on my rest day, so were ahead of me, others, as Phil his partner Kim and her sister, I caught up with in Roncesvalles. The Brazilian lad who had welcomed me, I came upon in Burguete pushing his bicycle as the drive mech had failed. Apparently there were no cycle repair shops until Pamplona, so he faced a two day walk rather than a short day's ride. I saw him again in Pamplona with bicycle repaired, with my room mates, Nigel and Bruno.

Sadly, different schedules, walking speeds, injuries and my tendency to stop two nights in Cities meant that I saw none of those Pilgrims I'd shared my first two nights with, after Pamplona. Names I did not catch or are lost, some faces I can dredge up from the dim recesses of memory with clarity, whilst others are just out of reach. They were my introduction to the Camino, and in a strange way they will always remain with me.

My one regret of my stay at *L'esprit du Chemin* was having arrived late, I was swept up in the fun, food and chatter, that it was only after I had left that I realised I failed to get my passport stamped, and of course the following year it had changed ownership and name.

Rest day prior to walk 2014

My rest day in St-Jean-Pied-de Port dawned grey and wet. After breakfast I headed down Rue de la Citadelle to the Pilgrim's Office to get my Passport. From there, I had an exploratory walk. The greyish mauve stone of the town walls sodden from the overnight rain contrasted with the glistening sets of the Citadelle paving. The persistent light rain meant I had to find shelter, if I was to draw; not necessarily for me, but the page as cartridge paper is vulnerable to water, and the water colour paint would run.

I found sanctuary in the *église Notre Dame du bout du Pont*, at the bottom of the hill. An open Church! Sadly there would be few along the Way. I sat in the pews on the South of the aisle looking up at the corner of the Apse. When I left the church, the rain had stopped, sky was lightening, sun was breaking through white clouds, and patches of blue gave the promise of a pleasant day ahead.

Although the weather was improved it still seemed prudent to draw with quickly accessible shelter against the intermittent light showers. I found handy niches in the South wall of the church afforded cover when needed, and the capping of the stout stone embankment retaining wall lent support for my pad, for a sketch of the bridge.

A number of people passed by, some local, walking the dog, some obviously tourists, and a few pilgrims standing on the bridge taking in the view before starting their Camino, and

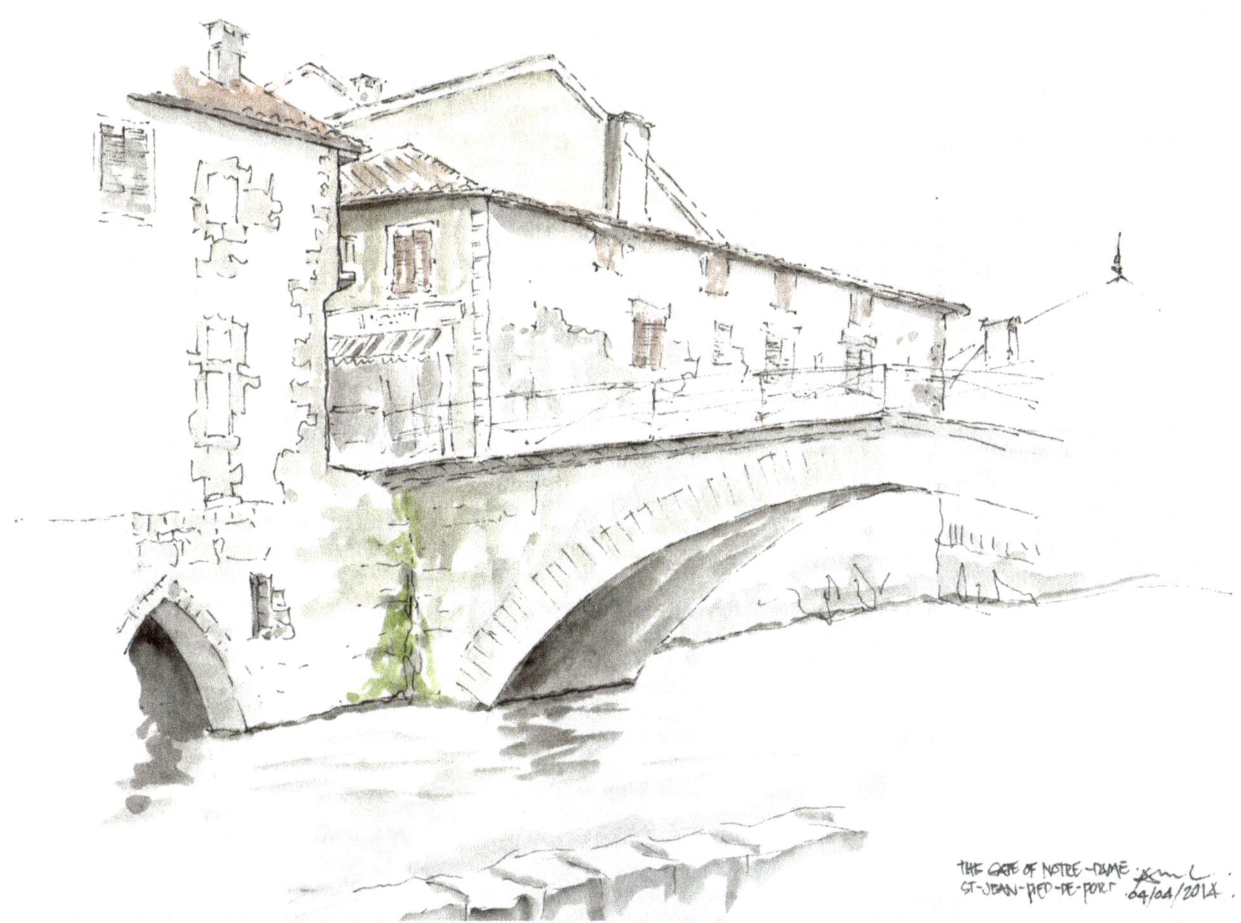

heading off up the testing, steep, breath catching ascent to Orrison, or maybe beyond, over the Pyrenees to Roncesvalles. Then I noticed an extremely attractive young woman standing on the bridge looking in my direction. She then strolled along the embankment, slowly passing by, turned at the little footbridge, up river, and walked back again. You will have gathered at this point my attention was not wholly on the drawing! As she came close, I confess, I was willing her to stop and talk. Sensibly, she chose not to! Now with the benefit of hindsight, or am I imagining, in my mind's eye, this beautiful young lady was Nicola, whom I would meet days later, outside the *Café Iruña* in Pamplona.

Later I moved from the niches to another sheltered position, a little ways up the hill, under cover of the arcaded shop next to the Church. The shop within it was closed, too early in the season, so I was able to draw with a splendid elevated view of the Church tower and the Gate of Notre Dame, sheltered from any showers. It too, was also just far enough away from two young men, their dog, and their bottles, who inhabited the Church Porch, and with cider fuelled bonhomie engaged every passer-by in banter. Had they not been there, then perhaps the porch would have been a subject for a sketch. It has a plain tympanum, over a flattish multilobed arched lintel, but the corbels, or *ménsula* in Spanish, are fun, as are the gurning faces to the adjacent capitals.

The church is 14C. Simple Gothic, with a semi-circular Apse, and galleried interior, typical, I am told, of the Basque region. Church and tower, and the stone buildings within the Citadel appear to have been built in the same local schist, as the Town walls, although dressed. Although still showery, the sun, and breeze had dried out the surface of the stone, and it now glowed pinky mauve, in contrast to the early morning sodden dull grey.

Whilst drawing, Geesje the *hospitalera* who had booked me in the previous evening spotted me. She seemed charmed that I was drawing, and said she loved the drawings. As she appeared to like them so much I offered to scan and email a copy on my return. She smiled and said "Can I kiss you!" "Do you often kiss strange men in the street?" I replied. We laughed, and protesting that I was not a strange man, she continued her walk to the church to light a candle in prayer.

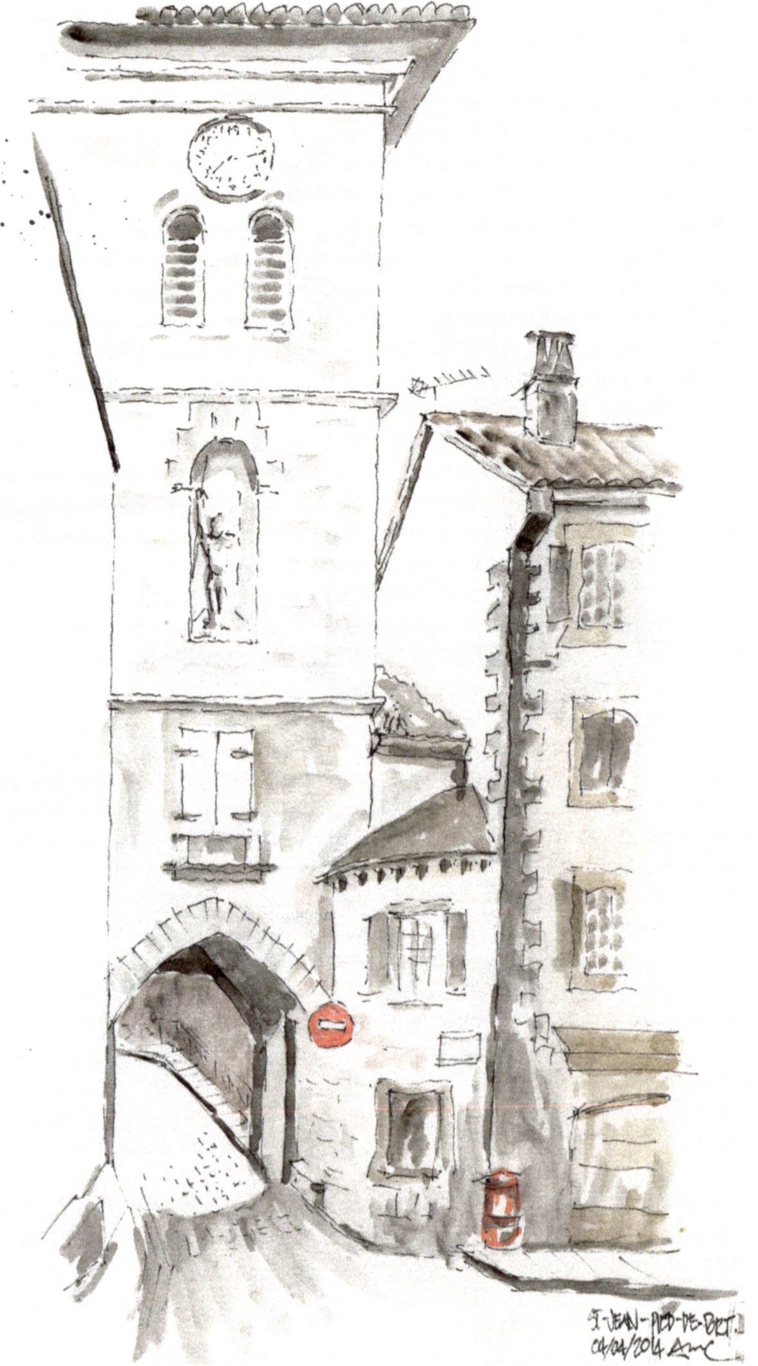

I recalled that moment with a smile, as I walked the Way. And albeit a doubting, or searching Anglican, I lit an occasional candle, silently offering the hope that Geesje's candle-prayer would be answered.

A fun, and ice breaking ritual of the albergue's communal dinner was a game of throwing an imaginary Basque ball, across the table from pilgrim to pilgrim. The recipient then introduced themselves, giving a brief explanation of why and what brought them to the Camino. Reasons varied, from the amusing, to the movingly heart-rending, as a recently retired Paediatric Nurse from the USA, who was walking to put to rest all those children, she had had to say goodbye to, throughout her career.

My turn came, as a leavening from so poignant a moment. I introduced myself as normal. "Austin, like the motorcar." I saw a mass of blank uncomprehending faces, and was about to explain, when the lady who had spoken previously said she knew what I meant, her husband had had an Austin Healey sports car which he'd reluctantly had to exchange for a more suitable vehicle when their two boys were small.

I learnt from that to introduce myself as Austin, as in Texas! No problems.

Frankly I hadn't a coherent reason to offer, other than I was glad I'd decided to draw down the Way, as it apparently attracted young ladies to kiss me in the street! I recounted the episode. Poor Geesje coloured, but enjoyed the joke; the room was full of laughter, probably fuelled by the free flowing rustic wine. Kip, the other lady *hospitalera*, asked to see my sketches, I showed her of course, but only after exacting a kiss. More laughter! And an instant convert to drawing from a guy in my dorm!

Oh yes, I'm happy to relate, to those who may doubt candle power, that I heard from her in the New Year, announcing with great joy, that her Daughter-in-Law had had a baby boy they had prayed and longed for.

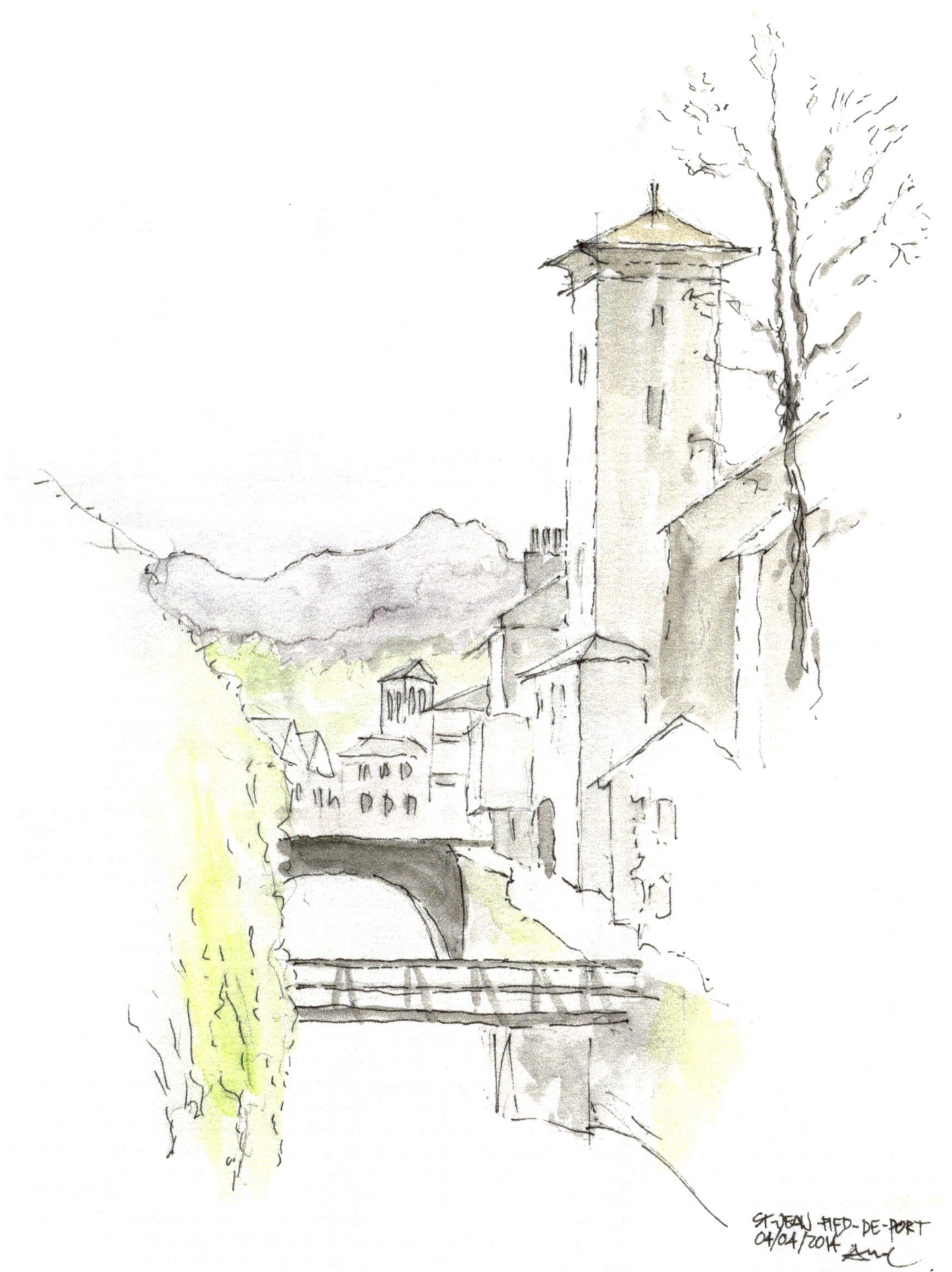

Rest day prior to walk 2015

On my second Camino in 2015, I flew into Biarritz and caught the bus into Bayonne, where I spent the night as a guest in the apartment of a wonderful lady I had found by chance on the web. She would not charge, and so I took small gifts, and the following morning I treated her to a simply delicious hot chocolate, at a café a French friend had recommended, *Chocolatier Cazenave.*

Afterwards she took me to her beloved Cathedral, where the Verger with evident pride showed us into the Sacristy to see the hidden gem of the South doorway. Protected since the enclosure of the North leg of the Cloister to form the Sacristy, the intricate carving to the tympanums (It's a double door separated by a mullion) and archivolts rising from a hooded impost with a figured freeze below, all remain crisp.

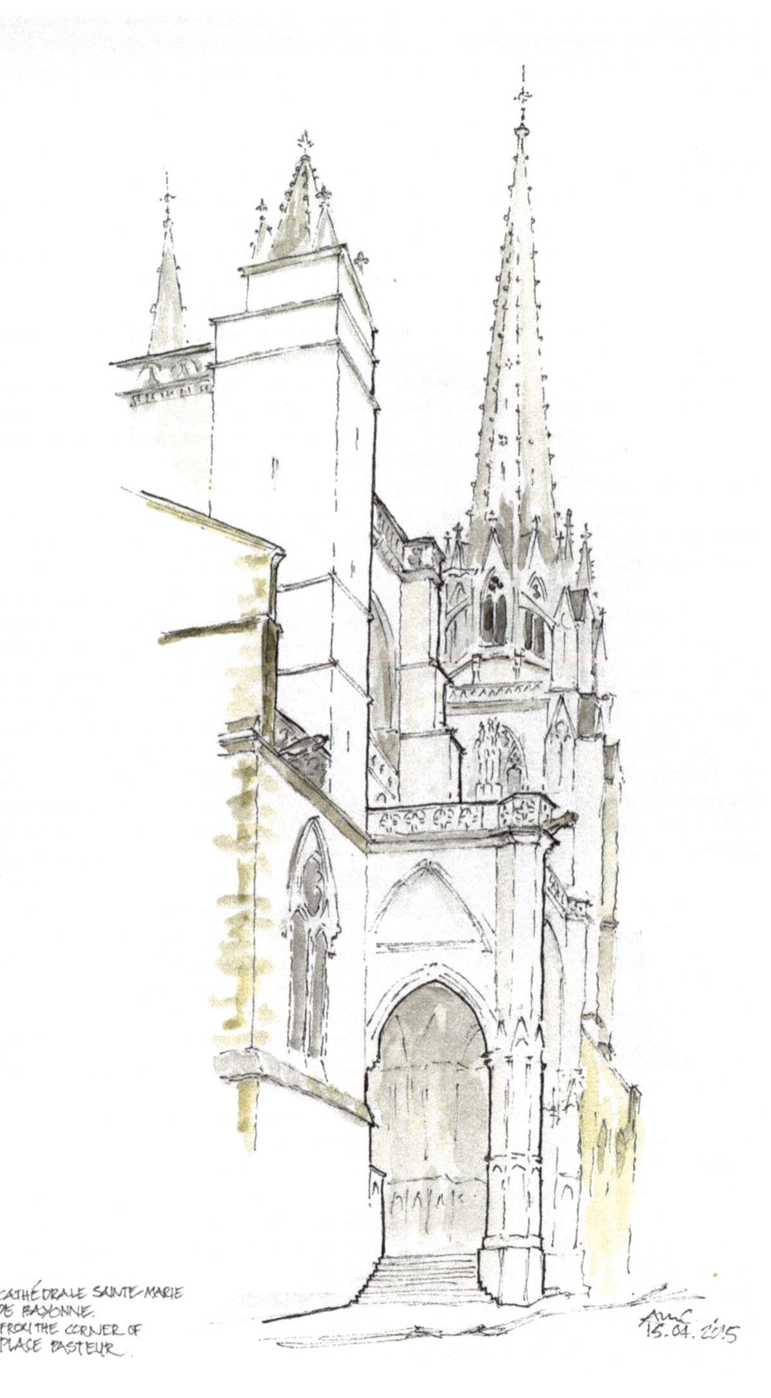

Later whilst drawing I saw a young couple passing by, the man with both back and front packs, something I planned to do. I called out to them, and fortunately they were American, so had quite reasonable English! It was interesting hearing his positive experience, and it confirmed my intention to wear my day pack, complete with sketchpad and drawing kit, as a more easily accessible front pack.

In the evening I collected my things from where I'd stayed and walked out of the old Town across the Pont Saint Esprit to the station, where I'd arranged to meet my Son Simon off the TGV from Paris.

As in 2014 we caught the train replacement's bus to St Jean and the same albergue that I'd stayed in previously, although now named *Beilari* but this time there were no young ladies wanting to kiss me in the street!

It was a particular joy for me to have Simon walking with me for the first three days to Pamplona, before he had to return to home and work. As he commented, with his young family, and my increasing years, this would most likely be the last time just the two of us would walk together, A poignant moment for me to savour.

St. Jean Pied de Port to Roncesvalles

The following morning, I said goodbyes to the hospitaleros, slipped a packed lunch into my rucksack, and set off on my first day's walk. I had spent the day prior with my nose in my sketch pad scribbling, and only as I left the albergue did I realise I didn't know which way to turn! I hastily consulted guide book, info I'd picked up from the Pilgrim's Office, and something I'd collected in the albergue. I digested, or rather confused the jumble of information, turned down the hill, passed the church, through the Gate of Notre Dame, over the bridge; up the street, and through Porte d'Espagne at 9.00am. And again at 10.30am!! Not the most auspicious of starts for the route Napoleon.

Once through Porte d'Espagne the second time I saw the sign I had missed earlier with my head buried in three sets of information!

The relative lateness of my start meant that I was alone, for most of the way. I walked briefly with an Australian lady until we reached Orrison, where she decided to stay. I spoke with some pilgrims I had met the previous evening, apparently, a Scottish couple were the only recent walkers ahead of me. Before commencing their Camino the following day, they were just going for a pipe opener as far as Pic D'Orisson, before returning by taxi. I walked by them, as they viewed the Statue of the Virgin.

A short while later a taxi passed me turned at a junction just ahead, and picked up a local lady who had been waiting. The taxi returned heading back to Orisson, and staring out from the rear was a face I would see repeatedly along the Way.

I reached the wayside cross, below Pic de Leizar Atheka, left the metalled road and crossed the high pasture skirting the Pic to the Spanish border. Dense Beech woodland fell away steeply from the contoured path on the Spanish side. The mountainside slope met the path still covered with 18 inches of last week's snow. Long stretches of the path lay more than shin deep in snow that had slivered down the slope. Stretches where no snow lay were bounded by fantastic snow sculpted waves, precariously undercut by the thaw. Rivulets of melt water trickled onto the already sodden, sticky, squelchy, boot sucking mud.

A February fill dyke in April! Progress was slow, a choice of trudging through the snowy bank, or sticking, sometimes literally to the path, slithering ankle deep in mud.

At the Col de Lepoeder I stepped on to the road. Above the Beechwood the sun low in the sky as twilight beckoned over the hills of Navarre beyond. Tiredness or exhilaration, or maybe both, at that moment I forgot the warnings and advice in the guide books, to take the slightly longer, but safer metalled road to Ibañeta in such conditions. I saw the Camino waymark ahead, and in my mind's eye, saw the images of the Monastery at Roncesvalles through the Beechwood……. Wrong! Oh so wrong! What lay ahead was over 4kms of steep, sodden, squelchy slippery, mud path, winding steeply down through tall Beeches in the gathering dusk!

I almost made it to within hailing distance of the Monastery, when mud caked on the soles of my boots met the mud on the path, propelling me on a surprisingly rapid ungainly mud skate, narrowly avoiding the splits, I landed softly on my back. I progressed luge-like downwards, rising up the embankment at each bend in the path, and shooting down again, with what seemed to me increased momentum. Thankfully, one acute bend brought me to a precarious halt part way up the embankment. Stranded as upturned turtle with my 15Kg rucksack, I laughed aloud at each failure to gain purchase, until I finally managed to ease out of my rucksack, and grabbing, now with both hands at the exposed tree roots, pulled myself up.

With light fading fast he path was now even gloomier, the sky virtually blocked out by the tall Beeches, gingerly I picked my way, until the welcome sight of the Monastery.

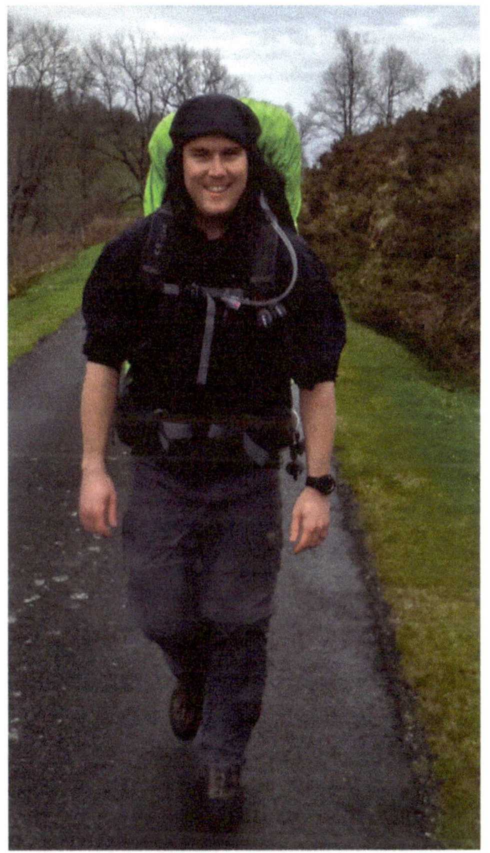
Simon walking up to Orrison

Muddied, I arrived too late for dinner; all I wanted though, was water and sleep!

Walking to the wash room in the morning, my step was lightened by what I assumed to be a CD of a sonorous bass, singing Gregorian chant. I thought what a splendid wake up call, and as I turned the corner, was met by the *hospitalero* who had booked me in the previous evening, in full flow. Wonderful.

Having arrived too late to draw on arrival and with a long day's walk ahead; the Monastery at Roncesvalles became the first omission, of my loose list of to draws. On my second visit, in 2015, this time with more time to look, the bleak, austere exterior did not offer an inviting sketch, or maybe the company off my Son, who walked with me for the first three days, to Pamplona, was more of a draw!

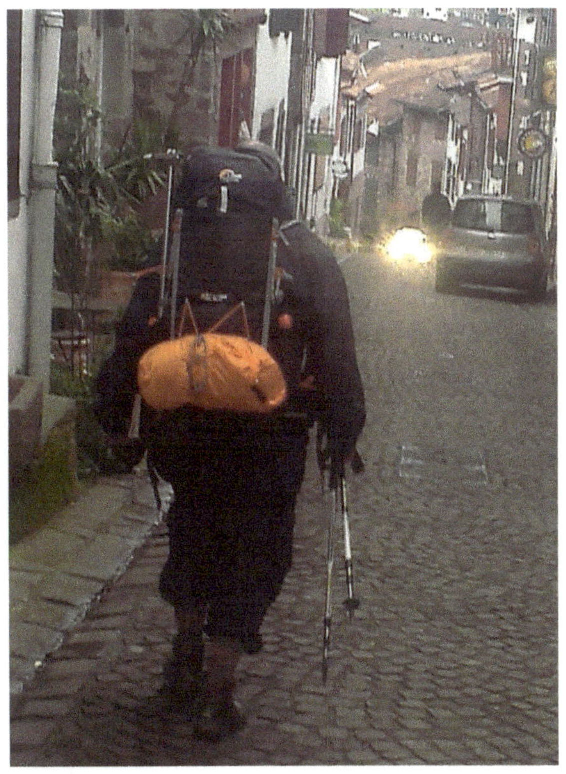
GEESJE KIP
Setting forth 2014

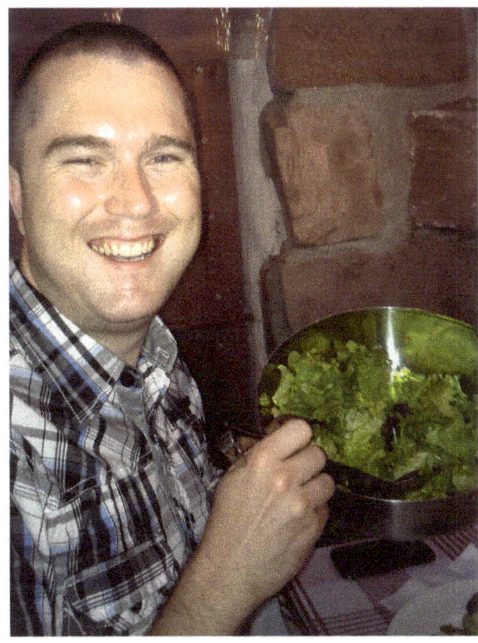
Simon serving the communal dinner at Beilari

Roncesvalles to Pamplona

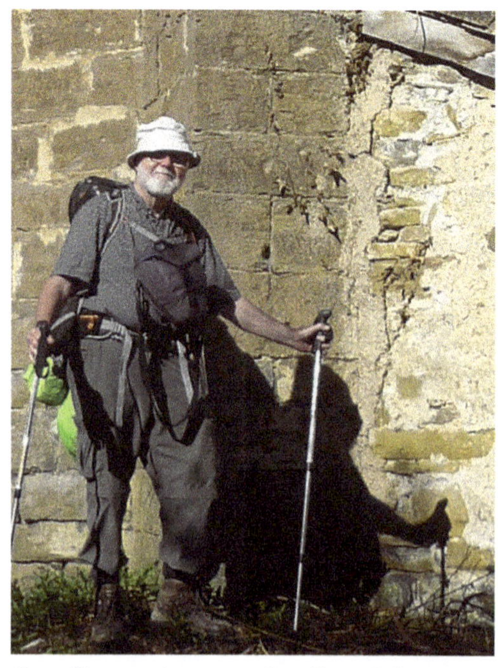
Standing against a useless French buttress.

Shortly after leaving Rocesvalles about fifteen minutes along the wooded path that runs alonside the road into Burguete a mature lady came jogging along the path towards me. By her dress and backpack she was evidently a Pilgrim and I joked “Are you heading in the wrong direction, or am I?” Rather breathlessly she said her daughter had left her laundry at the albergue. I wished her well, as apart from the splendid bass, it seemed to me the rest of the hospitaleros ran the place for their conveneince, and although I had little to compare with at that stage, now having walked two Caminos and despite its excellent facilities it was the most unwelcoming and least friendly of all I met with. So I suspected she would have little joy trying to raise and gain entry to collect the laundry, before the appointed opening time.

Just before breakfasting in the friendly bar in Burgette that Brierley mentions, I passed the Brazillian lad pushing his broken bike. After breakfast I set forth again in sparkling green countryside and a vivid blue sky meeting the snow capped Pyrenees to the North. So sometime had passed since meeting the jogging lady as I reached Espinal. I could see the modern church across the rough pasture, and a kitten was summoning the courage to jump from an open first floor window onto the logstore roof below. I turned the corner and saw a lady Pilgrim looking back, was this the daughter I wondered,I spoke briefly with her, yes she was awaiting her friend to return and had walked slowly from Burgette, so my fears would seem to have been confirmed.

As I walked on I often wondered if she did eventually suceed and also why she didn’t leave her backpack; but as I write, of course she neededd it to put the clothes.in.

Walking from Zubiri to Pamplona, I came upon an interesting church that I hadn’t noted in any of the guides that I’d seen. It had Romanesque features, but difficult to date with so scant a knowledge of the Region. The buttresses at the quoins were set diagonally, a feature which briefly appeared in England in the 14C, and known as a French buttress. They were found to have no structural purpose, so were purely decorative, a factor which might explain the crack down the East end which seems to indicate roof spread. As I looked a guy came out of the adjacent small attached cemetery. I asked in Spanish for information, but he looked puzzled, and said “Do you speak English!” It turned out he was South African.

Neal had, after a struggle, managed to buy the then redundant church. The *Abadía Ilarratz/Eskirotz*, (I think it’s called). At first he had met with opposition from the local Priest, but eventually got to see the Bishop, who had more than 200 redundant churches in his Diocese, and was happy to sell.

His plan was to convert it for use as a dwelling. He showed me around the interior, he was making inroads, but has a mammoth task ahead. The original Camino runs through his property, so he had long term plans for a Pilgrims rest and information area.

Sadly when I passed by in 2015, it was locked. Little evidence of progress externally, so I hope he is making headway on the interior. I wish him well, he really has a formidable task!

Further along the way, as my Son and I walked through Zuriáin, we took the option signed to the Medieval *Iglesia de san Milan*. We crossed the road and climbed the steep narrow path to the church, set on the highest point of the village, we walked alongside the South aisle, to the green fronting the West face and entrance to the church.

A lady dressed in a grey woollen cloak stood in the porch beside a stone bench. The door was open, and I could see into the dimly lit interior. As I approached she spoke to me. She was one of four Sisters working in the village, and greeting pilgrims. She had come there, some eight years previous, from Gothenburg. Although Swedish, she had excellent English, telling me of her work there, during a brief guided tour of the Church. On hearing I was from Birmingham, she beamed, and was evidently pleased, as she had, she told me, a dear friend, from her days in Sweden, who was called to Birmingham; to become a Bishop. Did I know him!?

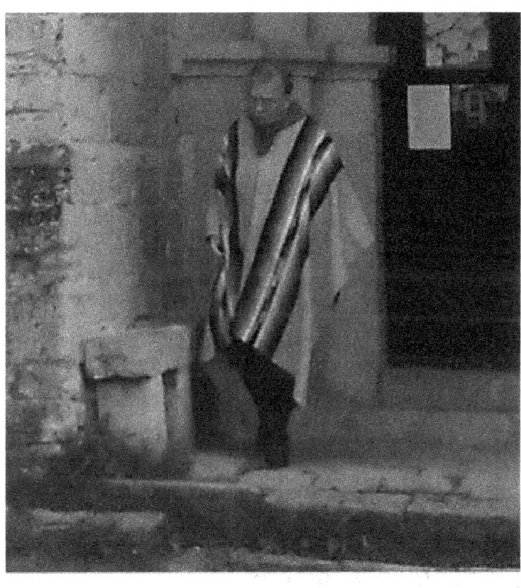

No! I don't move in such exalted circles!

Walking through Arre and into the outer, and poorer suburbs of Pamplona, I Passed a sad looking apartment block, moms chatting sociably at the entrance, and a dozen or so kids, boys, girls, four year olds, to teenage, all playing happily together. A couple of the older lads spoke to me in slow, deliberate, and seemingly thoughtful French, which they were evidently learning at school, and keen to practice. They were visibly disappointed that I was English, but soon recovered their good humour and I was greeted with *"Heeello" "How are yooou" "Goood moarning"* to a chorus of laughter from the younger children. I smiled with them too, their English could have been learned from the TV comedy 'Allo Allo'.

Within sight of the neoclassical twin towers of the cathedral, the obvious poverty of the area, the pinched, drab, dull, dingy, buildings, the run down *alimentación;* contrasted with the busy affluence I was to find in the centre with fashionable stores, their windows displaying smart and expensive goods. For the visitor to Spain, the Spanish economy is puzzling, such an apparent wide disparity between the haves, and have nots!

I stopped on the Puente Magdalena admiring the view. A black guy, in working garb trundled towards me, his wheelbarrow filled with his tools. He stopped, and surprised me by speaking in perfect English. He was equally surprised to find I too replied in English. Originally from Nigeria, but had lived in Pamplona for eleven years. Until then, the only Pilgrims he had previously met were German, and had assumed that the Camino was a peculiar German custom!

Pamplona

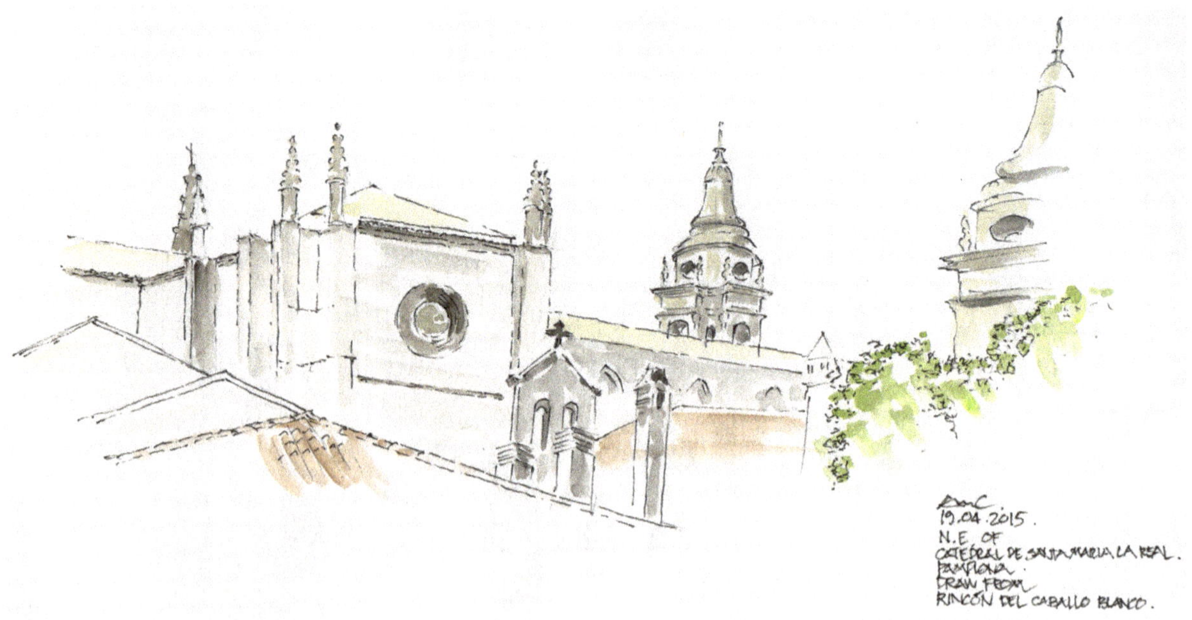

Being a City, I had pre-booked an albergue. As I walked up the ramp beside the town walls, I stopped, consulted my notes for directions. A guy in a business suit and large brief case, hurried across to me, asking where I was looking for, and then insisted on walking with me, showing to the door. An instance of the many kindnesses shown to Pilgrims along the Way by locals. An instance of the many kindnesses, shown by locals to Pilgrims along the Way.

I walked around, reconnoitring drawing possibilities for the following morning, before dining alone in the *Café Iruña* off the *Plaza del Castillo*, where I drew a sketch in 2015. I had almost finished my meal when Pilgrims I had met in SJPdP, Nigel and Jenny came in and up to the bar. She spotted me and came over to speak; she was with a group of their friends, drinking at the tables outside. I finished my meal, forsook my desert, and joined the party outside, with the best part of the bottle of *Bodega Irache*

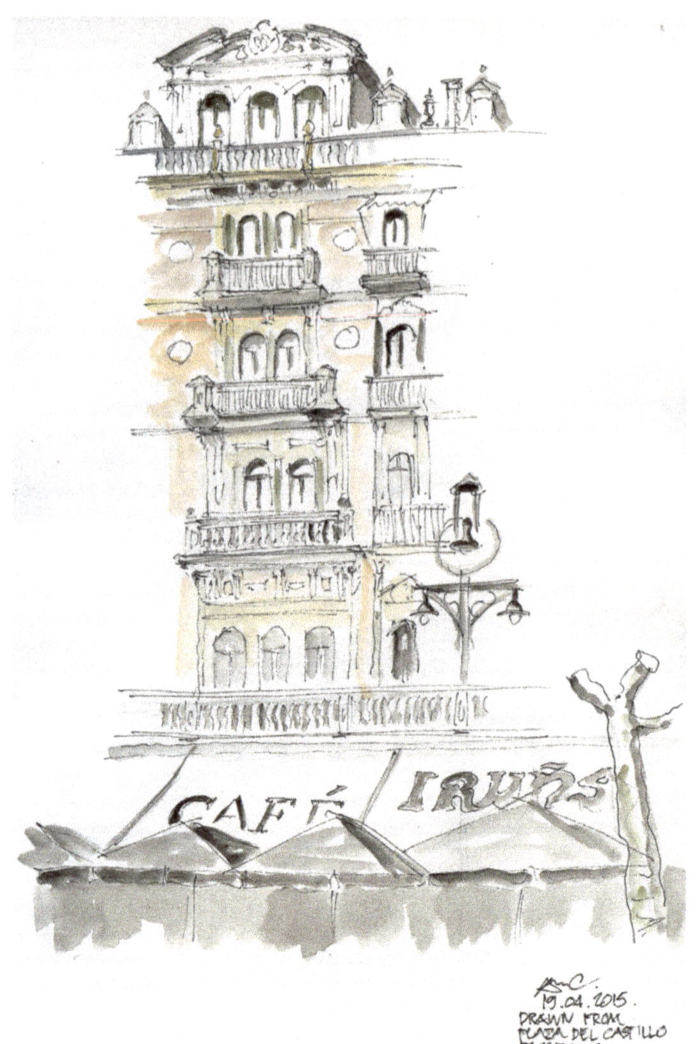

wine. Some around the table were known to me, and others new, but one in particular, the mystery lady I'd seen in SJPdP, and willed without success for her to stop and speak! Lovely Nicola, spoke this time! She had seen me in SJPdP drawing, but had not liked to interrupt. I so enjoyed her company, as we walked dined, laughed together whenever our paths crossed, as we progressed along the Way.

The following day, after drawing in the morning, I made my way back to the Cathedral to escape the fierce afternoon sun. I passed through the door leading off the South Aisle and into the cloister. Slowly circuiting, I settled in the Southwest corner looking across the garth to the Southeast corner, laying my kit out, and sitting on the low plinth. I was soon engrossed in my sketch, when in my peripheral vision, I became aware of movement. An attractive English lady came, and did what Nicola had failed to do in SJPdP, she spoke to me. She was interested in drawing, and had brought her kit to sketch, but so far had lacked the confidence to start. I encouraged her to do so, chatting about developing a thick skin to overcome feeling self-conscious about drawing in public. Whatever I said, I don't recall exactly, but it seemed to have worked, as I was to see her the following day in a meadow above the church at Eunate.

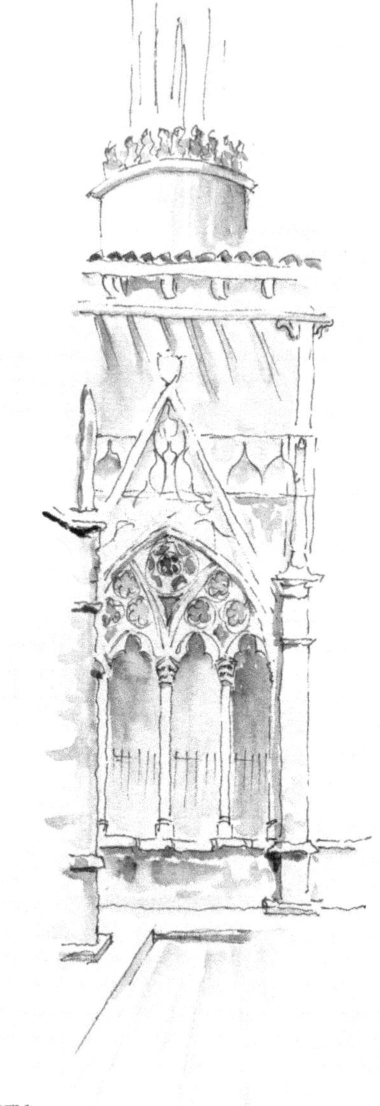

CLAUSTRO
CATEDRAL DE PAMPLONA.
04/04/2014.

On my return to the albergue, I met Phil, an Australian guy I'd sat next to at dinner on my first night in SJPdP. Unless I'd anything planned, he suggested dining together. So at the prescribed time we set forth. First he said he had to go to a phone shop to buy some data, no I didn't know what that was either! We traipsed through the old town, and into the commercial district, passing many phone shops, but apparently, not the right ones! Eventually he settled on a huge corner premises, where through the plate glass windows, as we approached, I could see by the queues that at least a quarter of Pamplona's population had decided this was the place to pass an hour, or two!

Undeterred, Phil entered and wandered around through the crowds for several minutes, before concluding what had been obvious to me from 50 yards!

He came out muttering that he would find another outlet some other time. Then he said he'd arranged to meet with a New Zealand couple at a restaurant by the Bull Ring. A quick consultation of the Tourist Map confirmed we were, by chance, quite close.

I checked my watch, and asked what time we were meeting, he'd forgotten. On arrival at the Bull Ring, I looked down a long run of shops opposite, most of which were Restaurants. "Right, which one are we looking for?" I asked. A restaurant, but he couldn't remember its name!

I felt that this was not a unique experience for him, and he'd spend the best part of the evening looking to meet a couple whose names he didn't have, at an unremembered time and place in a City of a quarter of a million souls! For me, on the other hand, the novelty of this rather pointless pursuit soon palled!

I decided I, or we if he cared to, would eat where I'd dined the previous evening, at the Café Iruña. Phil had an *ensalda mixta* for his first course. It made his day! A lover of salads, it was he said the best meal of his Camino. On the way back to the albergue, the mystery New Zealand couple were walking towards us. Oddly, I had met them previously too! They were accompanied by a very fair haired German guy, who I'd seen at various points, though not met. He was noticeable, as he appeared to be the only Northern European not to have heard of sun blocker, and consequently glowed bright red. I winced whenever I saw him.

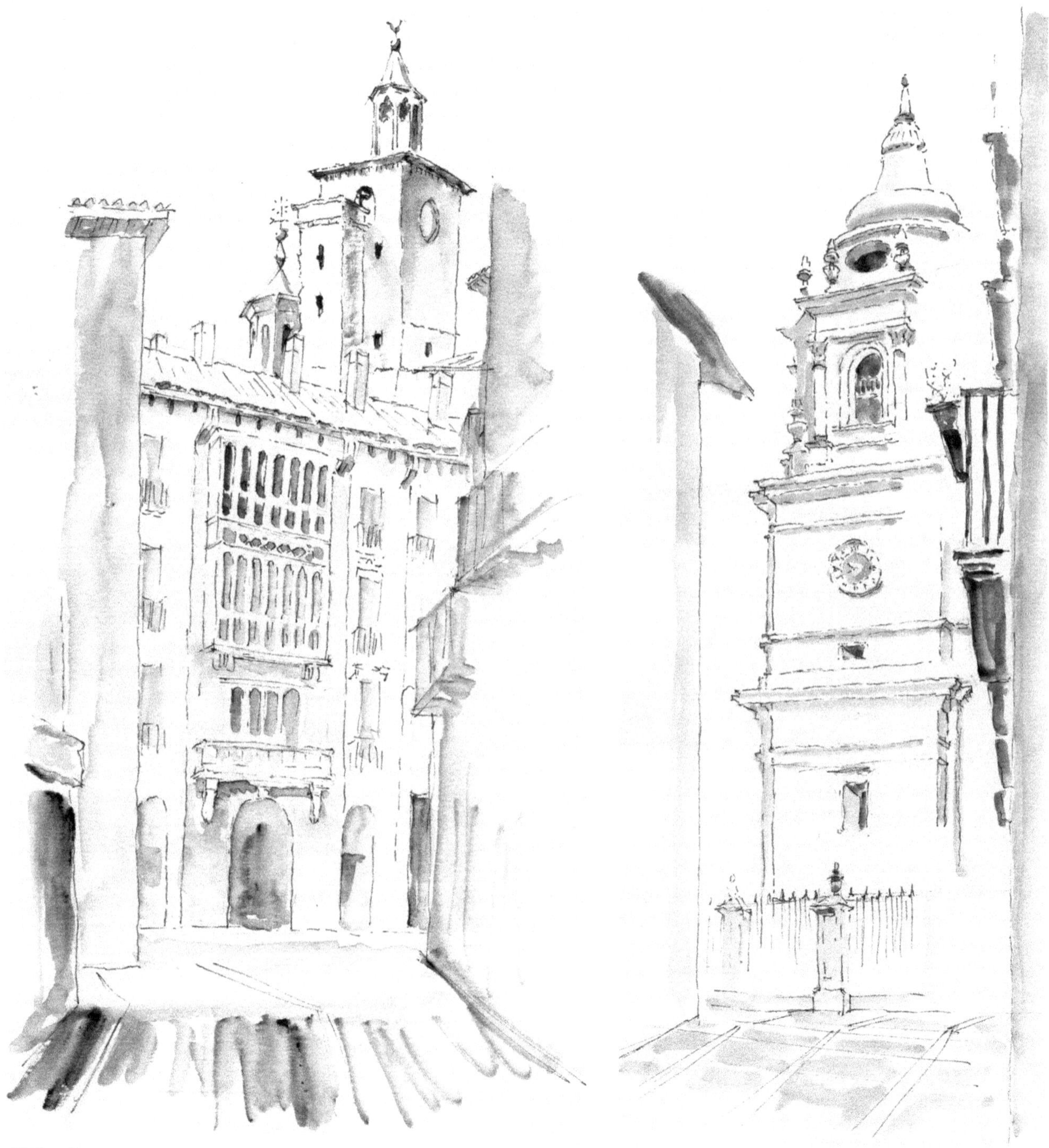

Leaving Pamplona for Eunate

I walked out through the suburbs with a young man and his Son, who was about 10 years old. He was scooting along on a skate board, and I joked with him, that it wasn't fair! Both he, and his Dad, were avid fans of the film, "The Way" They had watched so often, they knew the script verbatim! I left them just before the paved section gave out. I didn't see them again, but felt sorry for the lad, as it would be Logroño before scooting was an option again!

When I reached Muruzábal, I took the detour for Eunate. It was somewhere I had looked forward to seeing, and well worth the little effort. I crossed the road and followed the sign pointing down a narrow metalled track, which served as vehicular access to the church, small albergue, and the deserted rough stoned car park. As I approached I could see to my dismay, the gate in the boundary wall was closed. I read the information board, and the opening times. I was fortunate, as it was just ten minutes to four, and more by luck than judgement, I had arrived ten minutes before it was due to open.

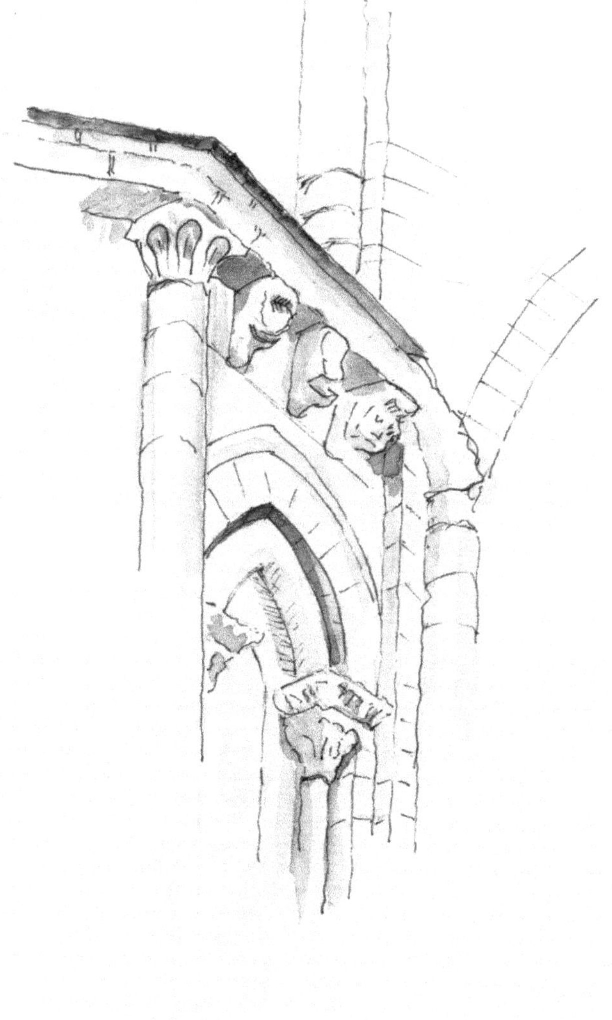

At a quarter past four, a lady drew her car up alongside the gate, unlocked it, and gestured me to follow her between the arched perimeter wall, and the octagonal church, to the West door, which she also unlocked, before leaving me, and driving off.

Alone in the church, I rested my kit on the bench at the rear, looked around, admiring the beautiful Romanesque simplicity. The heavy, rustic plain vault ribs, the silence.

It was not easy, eyes not fully adjusted to the low light, to see in any detail the capitals, and they certainly lacked the exuberance of those on the encircling colonnade, and seemed, mainly, simple variations on an acanthus design. The exception, the two on the right of the Apse arch. I think I could see a face peering down!

I had set myself just thirty minutes for the sketch, as I planned to stay in Puente la Reina that night, and didn't want to arrive too late. Whilst looking up, and sketching the corbels along the Apse eaves, a German couple arrived by car. They wandered around, closely inspecting, and photographing the capitals along the arched perimeter wall. At some point they must have entered the church, as, after my set time limit, I ceased drawing, and went back to pack and collect my kit from where I'd left it. The German guy was in the aisle. Expensive camera mounted on a heavy tripod, reflectors and equipment bags littered the benches.

I packed my drawing kit away, fastened my rucksack, and before lifting and swinging it onto my shoulders, I grabbed my water bottle, stood, and raised it to my lips. JABBBER JAB! A voice from somewhere, loud as adjacent thunder, pierced the silence. The German guy who was stooping over his camera, shot bolt upright, and like me, looked around, both of us, I think, wondering if we'd witnessed the voice of God! We could see nothing to indicate where the sound had come from, or what had caused it. We looked at one another, shrugged, and slowly returned to what we'd been doing.

In my case, it was attempting to take a drink. I slowly raised the bottle to my lips again, JABBER JAB JABBER! Even louder! Startled we both looked at one another and shrugged. Slowly, we both set about continuing, I paused, watching the German guy mess with his equipment. Light meter reading, setting, focus, depressing the remote shutter release which emitted a satisfying Ker-chunk, across the silence. Obviously, I thought, photographing did not bring down the wrath of the Gods! Raising my bottle, you've guessed. Louder than ever!

Further down the Way, I recounted this episode to a fellow pilgrim. She too had visited Eunate, smarter than I, she had noticed a 'No Photography' sign and detected where CCTV cameras were located, so carefully positioned herself to be out of view, whilst taking her photos. It would seem unnecessarily! It's ironic, it would seem OK to ignore signs, and photograph, but Pilgrims beware of taking sips of water!

I took one last admiring view of the church; it did not disappoint, and set off for Puente la Reina. I passed the boundary wall, and the rear of the small albergue, took a brief look at the notice board, and as I did so saw a figure in the meadow above the church. It was the lady who had spoken with me in the cloisters at Pamplona the day before. As I walked up to greet her, I could see she was sitting on the grass, on her head a frilly bonnet sunhat, sketch pad on her lap, the grass around her littered with water-colours and drawing kit, looking quite the Edwardian English rose!

As I walked on following our brief conversation, I admit to preening myself! Whatever I had said had obviously encouraged her, if away from public gaze, but I hoped now she had started, she would continue, wherever, and whenever, she wished.

By curious happenchance, three weeks later, I would learn more of her.

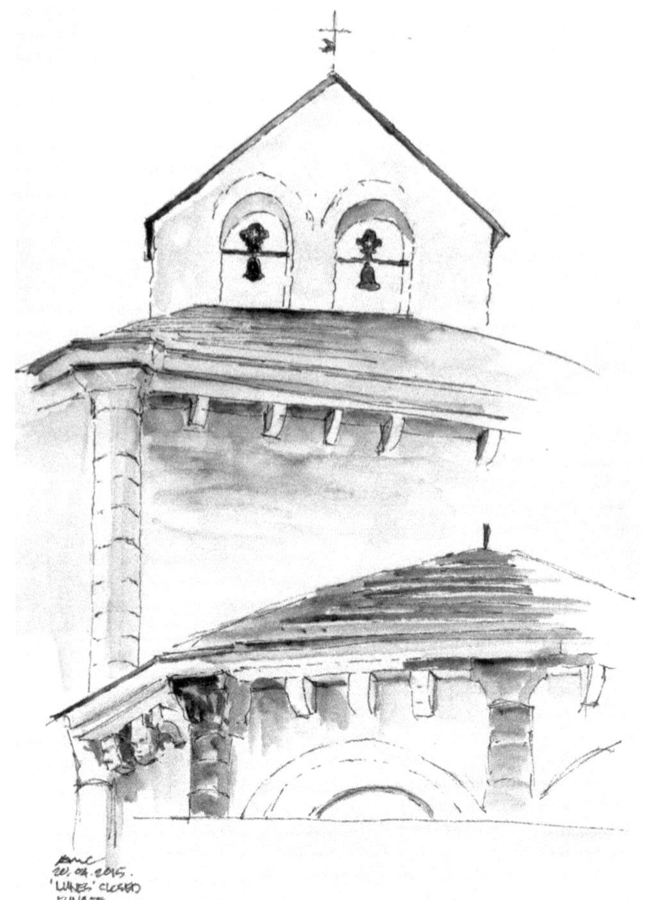

In 2015, I again detoured to take in Eunate. Sadly, I had forgotten the day, and as sod's law would have it, it was a Monday. The church, as do Museums, Galleries, and like institutions, in Spain, remain closed on Mondays.

I thought of hopping, well scrambling over the boundary wall, which appears to be invitingly low in places, until you check the drop on the inside! That would have enabled me to get close enough to sketch the capitals to the encircling arched wall; which had been my intention.

Having incurred the wrath of God previously, for just trying to quench my thirst, I decided discretion was the better part of valour; and sat on the grass bank outside the boundary wall.

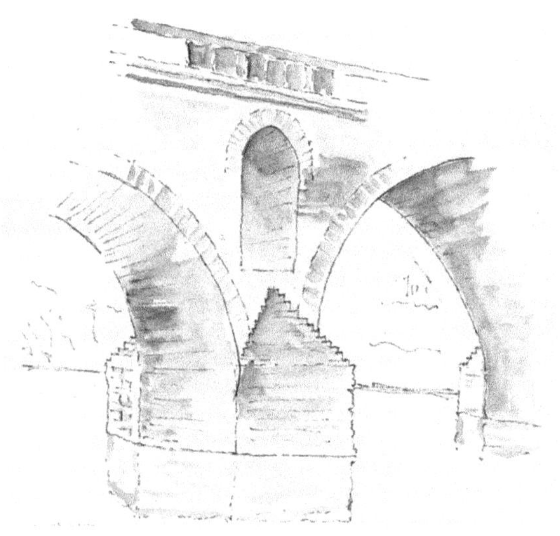

Puente la Reina

I booked into the first albergue one comes to, on the edge of Puente la Reina, and ate dinner at the adjacent hotel. Looking across the restaurant, I could see a couple seated at a table. The face looked familiar, but I just couldn't place it. It continued to puzzle me as I made numerous trips to the buffet, and *vino tinto* tap! What a splendid idea! At the end of my meal, as I sat twiddling the wine glass by the stem, it came to me! He was the face that had stared from the taxi window, as I walked to Roncesvalles. I was to see them at points down the way. I rarely if ever saw him walking, he always it seemed, managed to arrive ahead of me, and when we met, he was always seated in the sunshine on a bar terrace, 'sitting comfortably'.

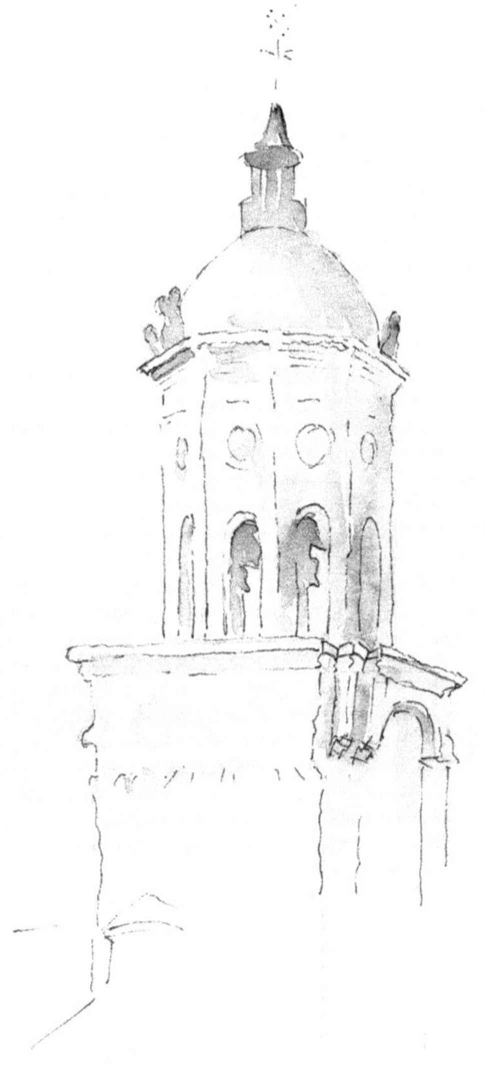

IGLESIA DEL CRUCIFIJO
PUENTE LA REINA
10/04/2014 -

Leaving the alburgue the following morning, I headed along the straight road into town, passing newly built apartment blocks to my right. As I approached what seems to have been a ceramic plant the first of two splendid church towers pierced the skyline. Looking through railings of the gated yard I could see an an array of interesting sculptures, and the plaque on the gatepost confirmed it to be an artist studio.

I reached the crossroads at the *Alburgue de Peregrinos,* and missed the Way which goes around the church and between the South Door and the Seminary. However it was fortuitous, as a little further along the stone boundary wall at back of pavement, thickened, and offered a fine view of the *Iglesia del Cruifijo,* across some lovingly tended smallholdings.

I laid my kit out on the wall, and rested the pad and sketched in relative comfort, apart from the morning chill. As I drew, a guy with a hand held motorised cultivator, carefully ploughed, back, and forth, revealing rich earth furrows in meticulous straight lines.

It didn't strike me at the time, but later as I walked in 2015, it occurred to me that I'd seen and admired numerous such smallholdings. All beautifully tended, neatly laid out with staple, and seasonal vegetables. I'd seen men working on them, women working on them, couples, small groups; and they all had something in common. I never saw one, not even at a weekend, who was younger than me! All in 70's, 80's, and who knows, maybe beyond! It posed the question in my mind. These small holdings are such an attractive, and I guess important feature of the area, and generally across Spain; what is to happen when this generation dies out?

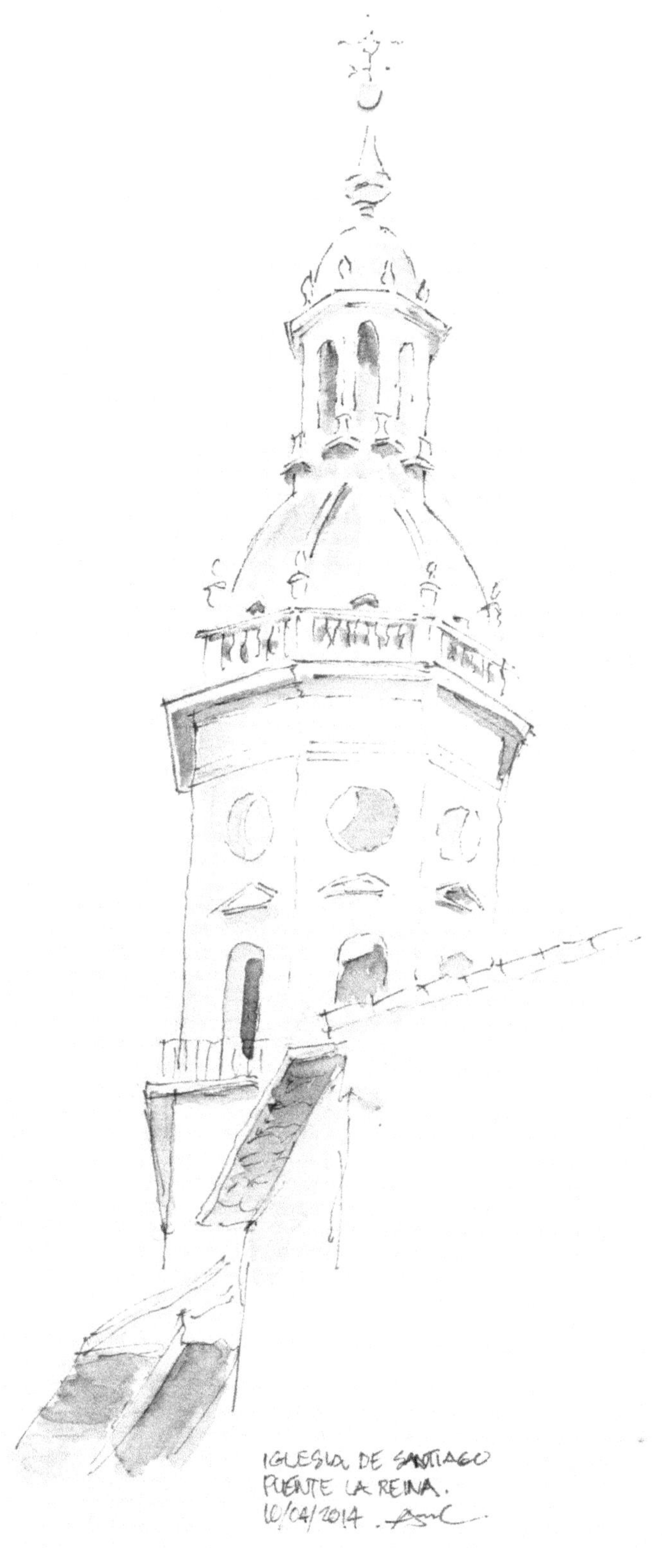

I walked on, through the town, pausing to sketch the *Iglesia de Santiago,* and admiring the South portal, with splendid *Mudijar* multi-lobed arch, wishing I'd time within my schedule to stop and draw.

As I looked, I saw a guy, sitting on his back pack, leaning against the Porch plinth, head lowered, and peaked cap pulled well down. He appeared dejected, and to be begging. I by contrast was on a high. Still early mid-morning, two sketches done, flushed with fresh pastries and strong Café solo, I searched for some Euros and was making towards him, when I noticed his walking pole against the wall. Embarrassment avoided. Or was it, the idea of a mendicant Pilgrim did not occur at the time. But, I was to see this guy again in León.

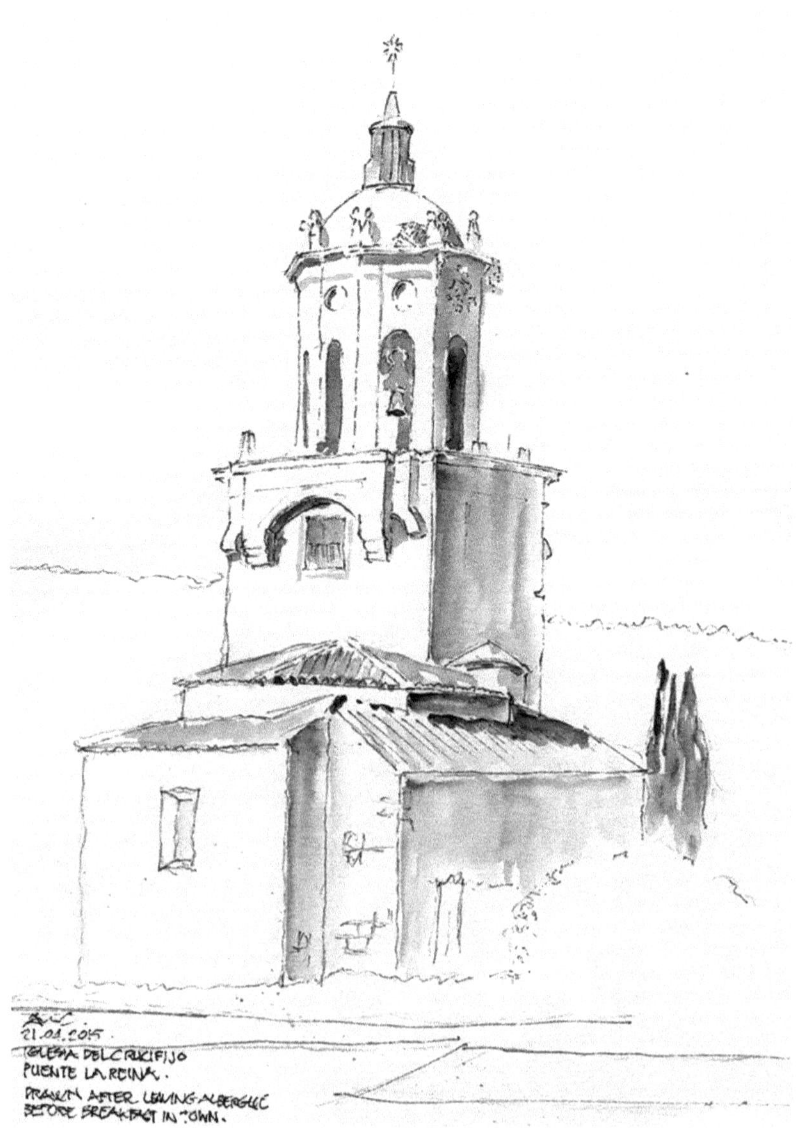

Puente la Reina became one of my favourites from what I had seen, and featured on my "to draw" wish list for 2015. That year I decided to carry a small folding stool, figuring the pain of the extra weight was more than compensated by the relative comfort, and increased aspect choice, for drawing. So walking into Puente la Reina, and arriving at the *Iglesia del Crucifijo*, gave me the first opportunity to use it. I sat prominently, in the middle of the minor road, at the junction. Though with very light traffic, and acres of width, I felt quite safe. Whilst drawing a guy with a smock came and spoke with me. He was the sculptor from the studio nearby.

Afterwards, I made my way to the South portal of the *Iglesia de Santiago*, a sketch high on my wish list! I set up my stool again, within the Precinct of the church, my back to the low plinth wall and iron railings. My view was obscured from time to time, as people gathered in animated chattering groups, gathering for what I concluded must have been a Memorial Service. This crowd eventually drifted into the church, and for a while I had a clear view, with only the odd curious local for company.

As I progressed, wave after wave of Spanish tourists arrived. Groups stood in front of me, sometimes shepherded away by more thoughtful friends, and finally I had finished. Concentration relaxed, I became aware that my bottom had pins and needles, and my legs felt stiff as I stood to stretch and pat my backside into life! I paced around a little to loosen up, glanced down at the sketch from the vantage of a little distance, and checked it against the portal, making mental notes of what I needed to tweak. My backside, now with feeling! Legs moving freely, I sat, or plonked down on my stool. CRACK! A leg snapped. The stool, not mine! I went rather heavily flat on my back; the collapsed stool beneath me.

I hadn't time to catch breath, gather my thoughts, or move, when hands descended on me from all directions, grabbing legs, arms, clothes, seemingly anything grabbable, and before I knew it, I was hoisted to my feet, surrounded by a host of anxious faces; locals, tourists, men, and women. I was very grateful for their concern, and mouthed embarrassed thanks in all directions as I was dusted down, whilst others were picking up bits of my kit and water-colour pans, which had flown into the air as I hit the deck!

It must have been an amusing spectacle, and yet as I looked at those kindly worried expressions, I seemed to be the only one suppressing laughter.

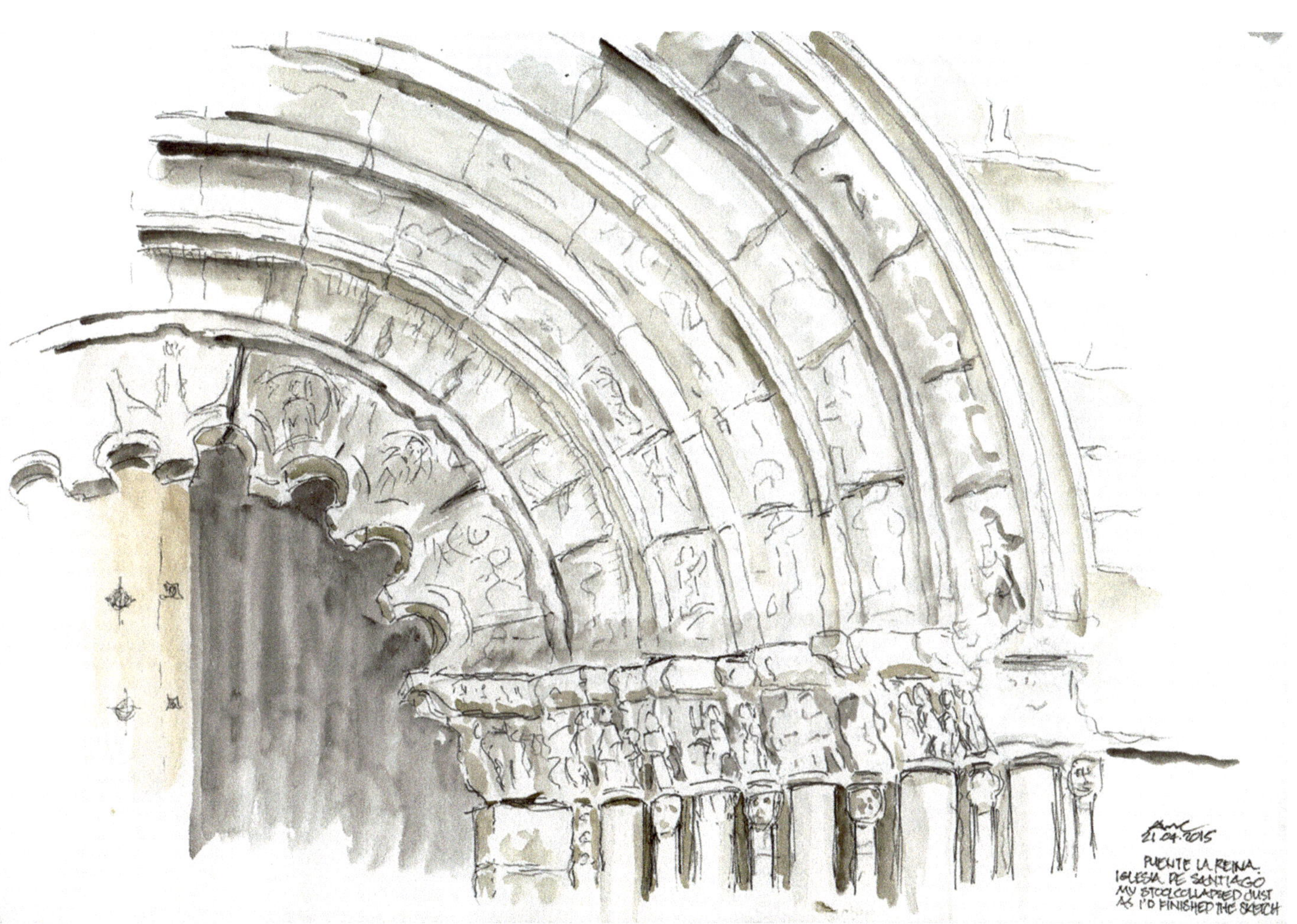

Estella

In 2015, after spending time enjoying Puente la Reina, I stayed in Lorca, about 8 Kms short of Estella. I had remembered the alburgue from the previous year, when I'd called for lunch. I recognised the young guy booking me in, but I couldn't see, and enquired of, the lovely Korean girl, who had made my lunch. The guy blushed, and said with pride they were now married! It was her day off.

Whether it was the nice things I'd said about his now wife, without knowing of his relationship, or whether just taking pity on an old man, but he gave me a room, with only two single beds, just to myself!

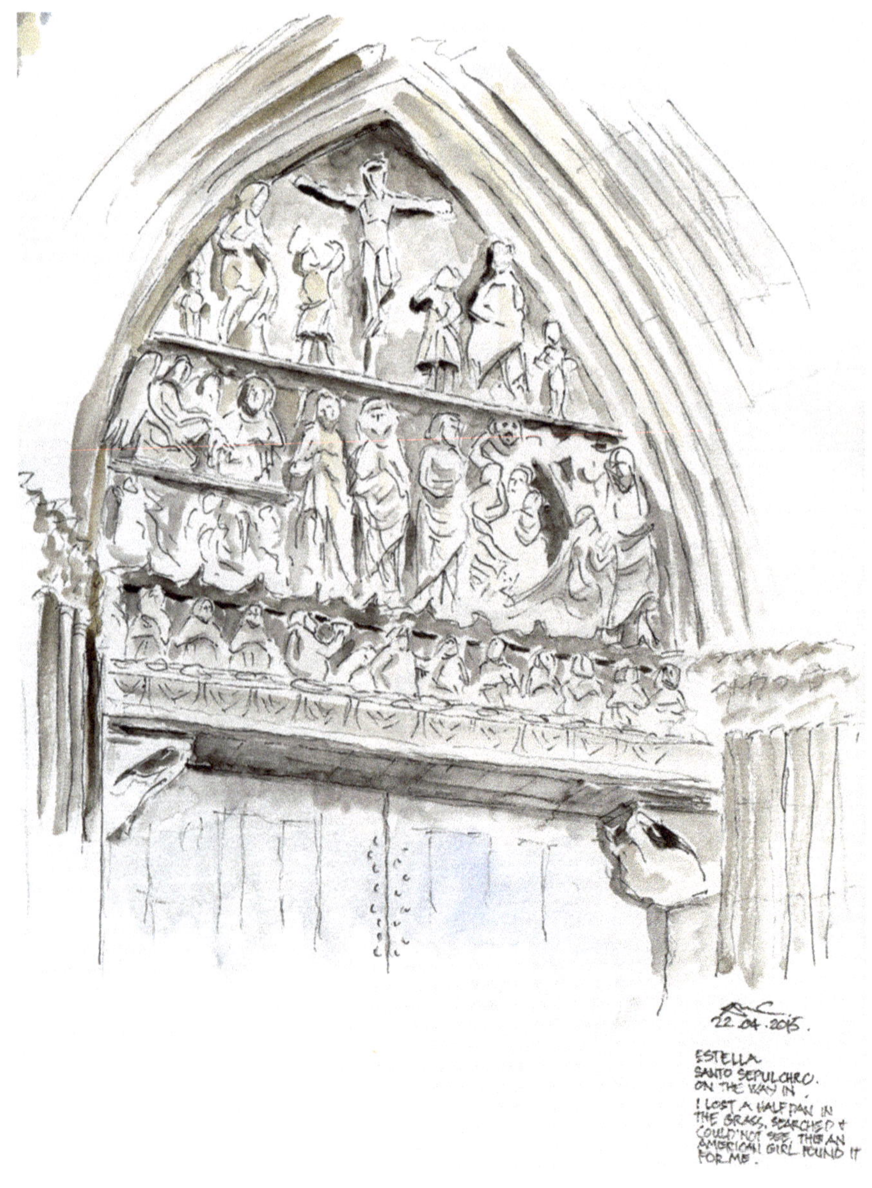

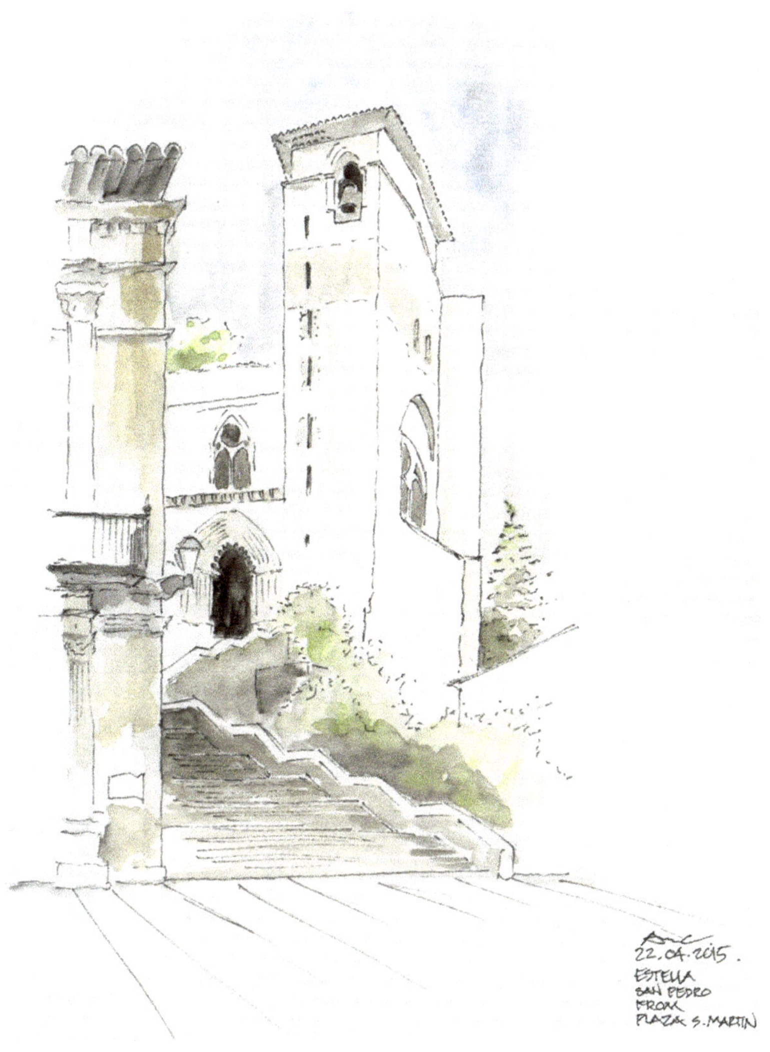
22.04.2015.
ESTELLA
SAN PEDRO
FROM
PLAZA S.MARTIN

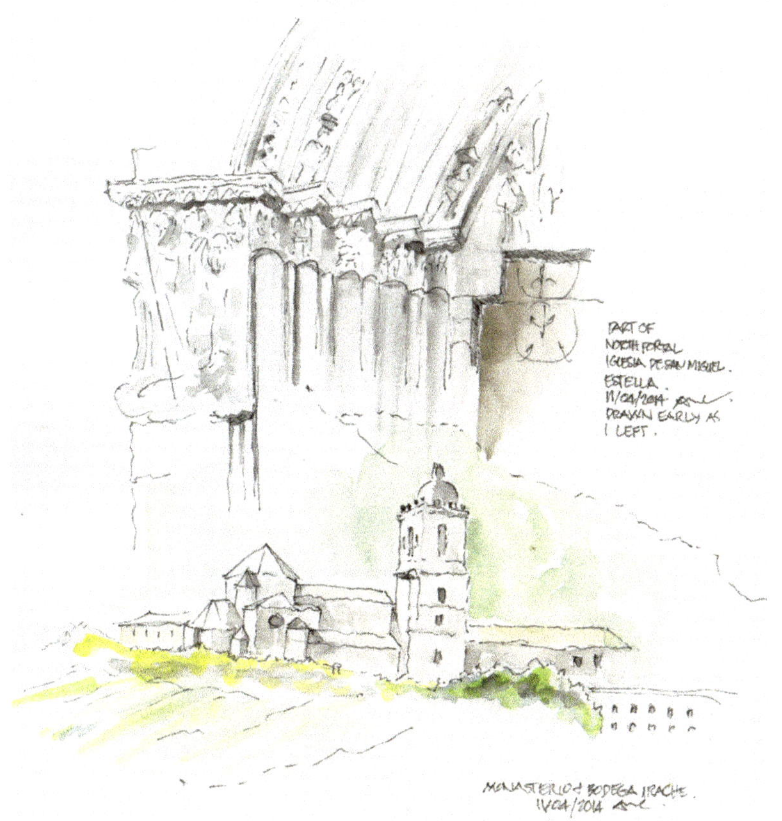
PART OF
NORTH PORTAL
IGLESIA DE SAN MIGUEL.
ESTELLA.
11/04/2014.
DRAWN EARLY AS
I LEFT.
MONASTERIO + BODEGA IRACHE.
11/04/2014

If that were not sufficient luxury, I had the company of two charming Italian young ladies over dinner. And we breakfasted together in Estella where Roberta was ending her current Camino section. Annalisa, young and fit would disappear well ahead of my pace, covering prodigious distances daily, newly graduated she had had difficulty in finding a nursing post at home, but was offered one in the UK. Lucky NHS!

As a consequence of staying in Lorca, I was able to arrive in Estelle relatively early, allowing time for exploration and drawing. I had remembered the *14th.-C Iglesia de Santo Sepulcro*, which was on my wish list. So after a wander around, I walked back and stood on the grass, across the road and opposite the North Portal with its fine Tympanum.

As I was drawing, watercolour box balanced on the edge of my pad, it inevitably slipped, scattering the half pans across the turf. I found all but one, and looking for it, quartering the area semi-stooped, staring intently at the ground, I must have presented an odd sight to anyone passing by. So much so, curiosity lead one young American Pilgrim to ask what I was doing, I explained, and bless her, her young eyes spotted it almost immediately.

Whilst sketching later, a local lady artist spoke to me. She was going to the picture framer, carrying a fine ink and mixed media painting of the *Fuente de los Chorros*, the fountain at the centre of the Plaza where I was drawing. It's always a joy to meet strangers with similar loves, and passions, even when the conversation is conducted in Spanglish.

Just off the Plaza, passed the steps up to the church, is a sign, for the *ascensor* to the *12thC Claustro*. I went up the narrow alley leading off the street, to a superdoop glass lift, with a sculptural winding stair, leading up to the level of the Cloisters. It's a free ride, with splendid views, but of course the Cloisters were closed! That's Spain!

Leaving the following morning and dropping down a hill in Estella's suburbs a splendid vista of the *Monasterio de Irache* opened up. I found a terrace come parking area to an apartment block with a metal balustrade guarding the sheer drop which came in very handy to rest my sketchpad.

Although still early morning as I passed the *Bodega*, it would have been churlish not to have a little *vino tinto*. Had it been towards the end of the walk, I confess I would have sampled more than a sip!

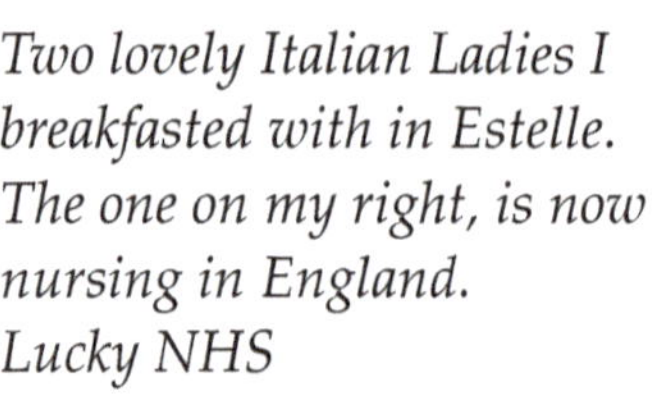
Two lovely Italian Ladies I breakfasted with in Estelle. The one on my right, is now nursing in England. Lucky NHS

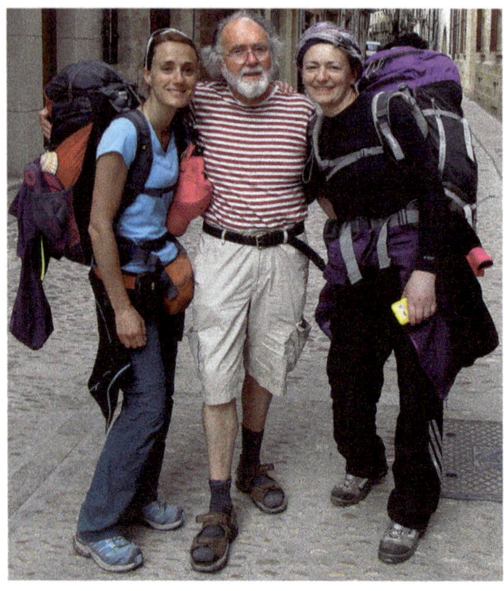

ANNALISA POMERO

Los Arcos

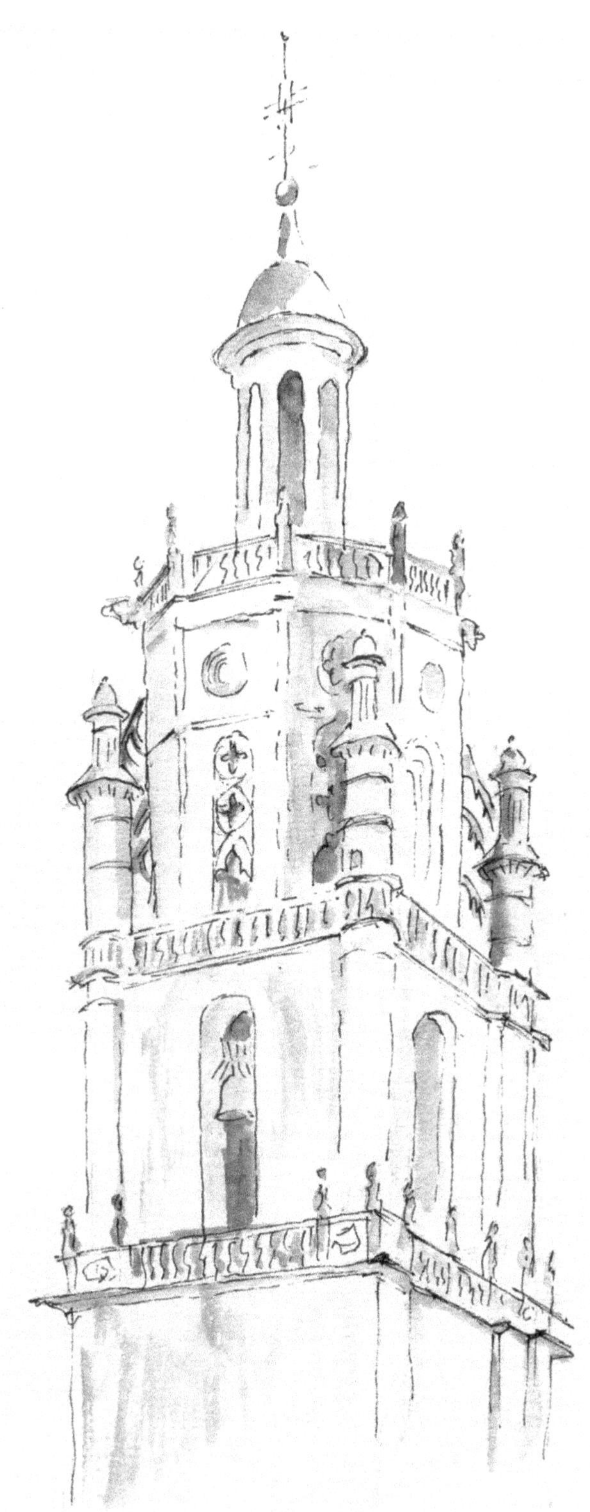

Walking into Los Arcos I came upon a tall American guy, (Monty) and we walked into town together. He was about to peel off at the first albergue we came to, so I wished him farewell, as I had made notes from the excellent *Eroski* site, and was looking for *Casa Abuela's.*

Impressed with my notes he came along too, and that is how we came to "sleep" together! as he jokingly put it. The dorm was small, just three bunks, he had one low, and I had the adjacent low. On the third, opposite, lay a young German lady I recognised, as she had passed me like an express train earlier on the Way.

In the evening, Monty saw me scribbling in the Plaza, he had just taken up drawing, mainly bridges, and it became a bond between us. I offered some advice, but mainly encouragement.

Whilst I stood with my back propped up against a pier to the arcade, sketching the superbly elegant late 16thC tower of the *Iglesia de Santa Maria de la Asunción;* where Monty had seen me. I was initially intrigued, and amused by an old guy who popped out of his door behind me. Well, he was quite young really, about my age! He walked round me, peering at the drawing, shaking his head, muttering, before disappearing back into his doorway. A short while later, he came out again, walked slowly around me, head shaking and muttering and returning once more to his doorway. He did this several times, each time, circling closer, until finally after a lengthy glower in my direction, he walked to the middle of the road, and loudly addressed, both me, and numerous

Pilgrims enjoying the evening sunshine at bar tables laid out in the Plaza. His message was, in gesture, and Spanish that even I understood, that I was *"Loco! Pérdida de tiempo"* Apparently I was stupid and wasting my time, I should take a photograph!

Unlike Monty, and I, the German lady rose early next morning, whilst still in the dark, and spent interminable head-torch flashing minutes, before exiting, returning, exiting, returning! I think you get the gist. It seemed she had finally left, and figuring the streets were now aired, I got up, and a little later, Monty also. We were just on the point of leaving the dorm, when I spotted a pink jumper the torchlight had failed to illuminate. I had it in my hand to take down to Reception, as we walked toward the door, when in burst a very red faced German lady. (I should add she was one of a very few Germans met, who had little or no English) Dredging up my 60 odd year old unused school German, I understood, *"Das fräulein hat ihr Geld verloren!!!!!!"* Her money was missing.

Monty and I raised eyes to heaven, in unison, and with the prospect of imminent arrest, we searched high and low, scrabbling around under bunks, turning the mattresses. Oh such fun!

Eventually, long childhood afternoons staring out of *'das fenster'*, whilst seeing how long I could balance on the back legs of the iron framed school chair, paid dividends!!!! I calmed, and persuaded her to unpack her rucksack, and not surprisingly really, tucked in, at the bottom of her *Schlafsack* was her purse!.......... Relief all round.

Leaning on a wall of a building drawing in 2015, a Spanish lady came and spoke with me. It was difficult for me to follow her conversation, since she apparently commenced by asking if I had eaten dinner! Oh Lord, she thinks I'm begging, I thought. I shrugged and fiddled with my pen, as if to continue. Undeterred, she nodded in the direction of the Portal Castilla, and said her house was over there. I shuffled and looked around, hoping for an interruption, none came. Next, I thought she was asking if I would like to go with her to her house! She would give me dinner! In the embarrassed pauses, between, what seemed to me, unrelated phrases, I realised I had not uttered a word, English, nor Spanish as I struggled to make sense of the situation. Finally she gave an exasperated shrug, and walked off.

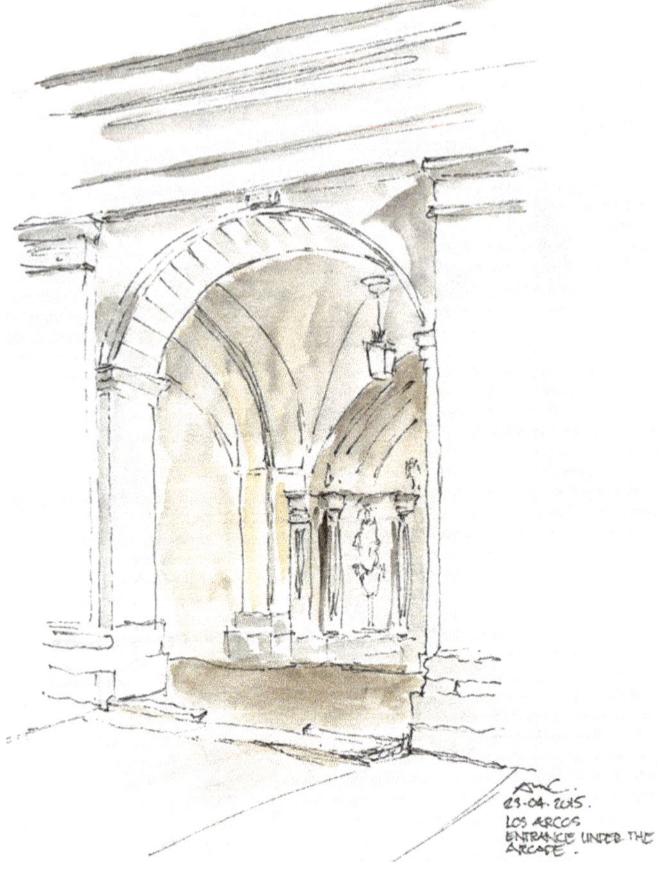

I remained leant against the wall, for some time before starting to draw again. In the meanwhile, I ran the conversation over, and over, in retrospect. Like early morning mist, driven off by the strengthening sun, the jumble of disconnected conversation began to resolve into some semblance of sense.

It seemed I had missed one vital phrase at the beginning, *"Quisiera un dibujo de mi casa"* Consequently the following conversation seemed bizarre. I wished I had had a better grasp of Spanish, as I think the gist was, she was very proud of her house, and wanted a drawing of it, and by way of payment, she would give me dinner! I looked around, but she had disappeared. I was both disappointed, but mainly relieved, as I was not wholly sure of my translation!

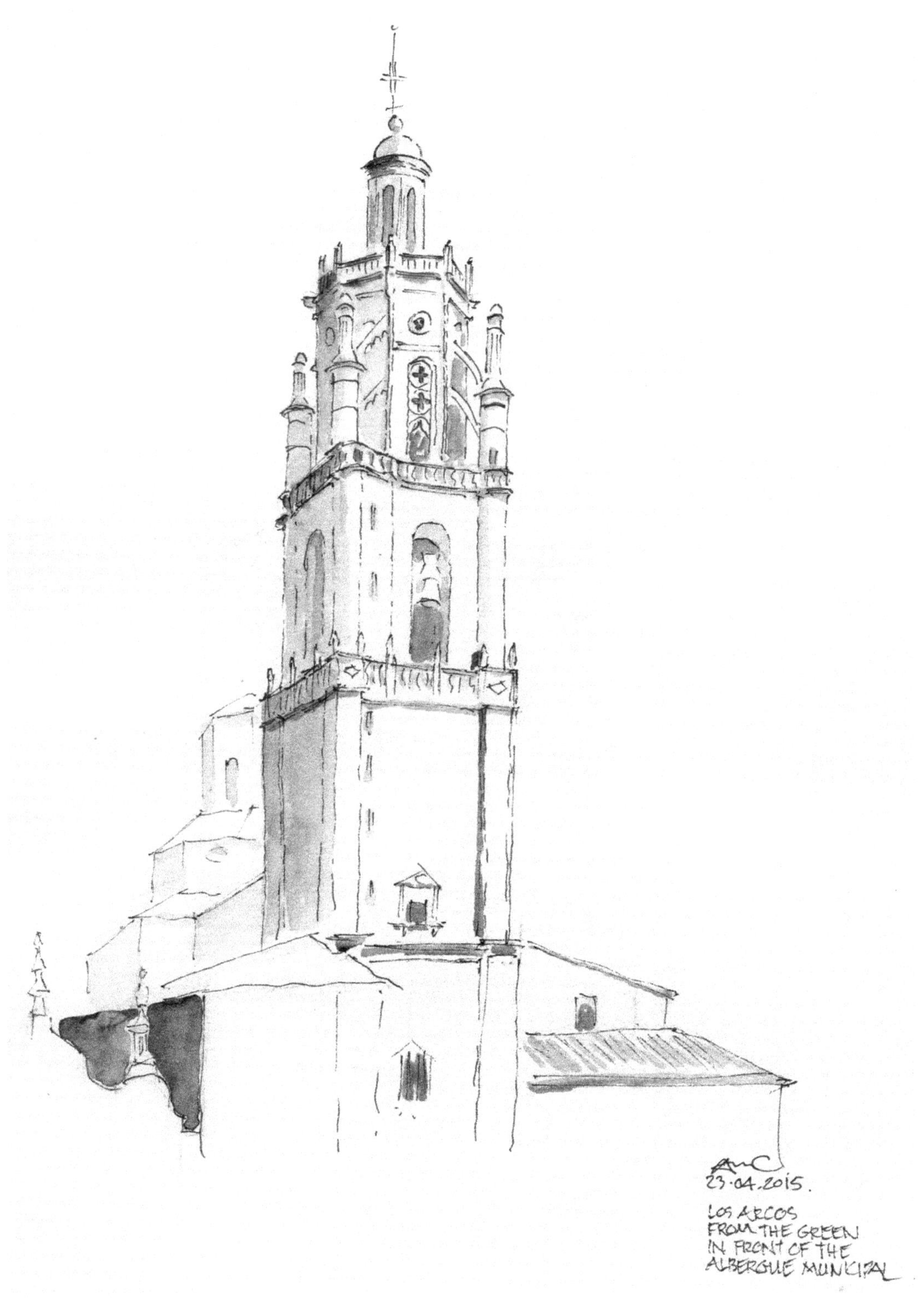

Walking from Los Arcos

In 2014 as I passed through Torres the church was open. It was a long day's walk to Logroño, if I was to maintain my schedule, and I chose to walk on. As I write, I find it difficult to understand my mind-set at the time.

The 12th.C churches octagonal plan, similar to Eunate, many believe, suggests it may have had associations with the Knights Templar. My Gitlitz and Davidson speculate it too may have been a funeral chapel, whatever, a splendid building and on my list in 2015.

I was pleased to see the church open as I arrived, but decided to sketch first. I sat on a doorstep next to a laundry, the steam and laundry smell drifting on the morning air. I finished the sketch and collected my things together, packed them into my sack, looked up, aaaagh! The door had closed. I looked at my watch, 12 noon. I never learn!

That night I stayed in Viana, so was able to explore and draw bits of what I'd seen as I passed through the year before.

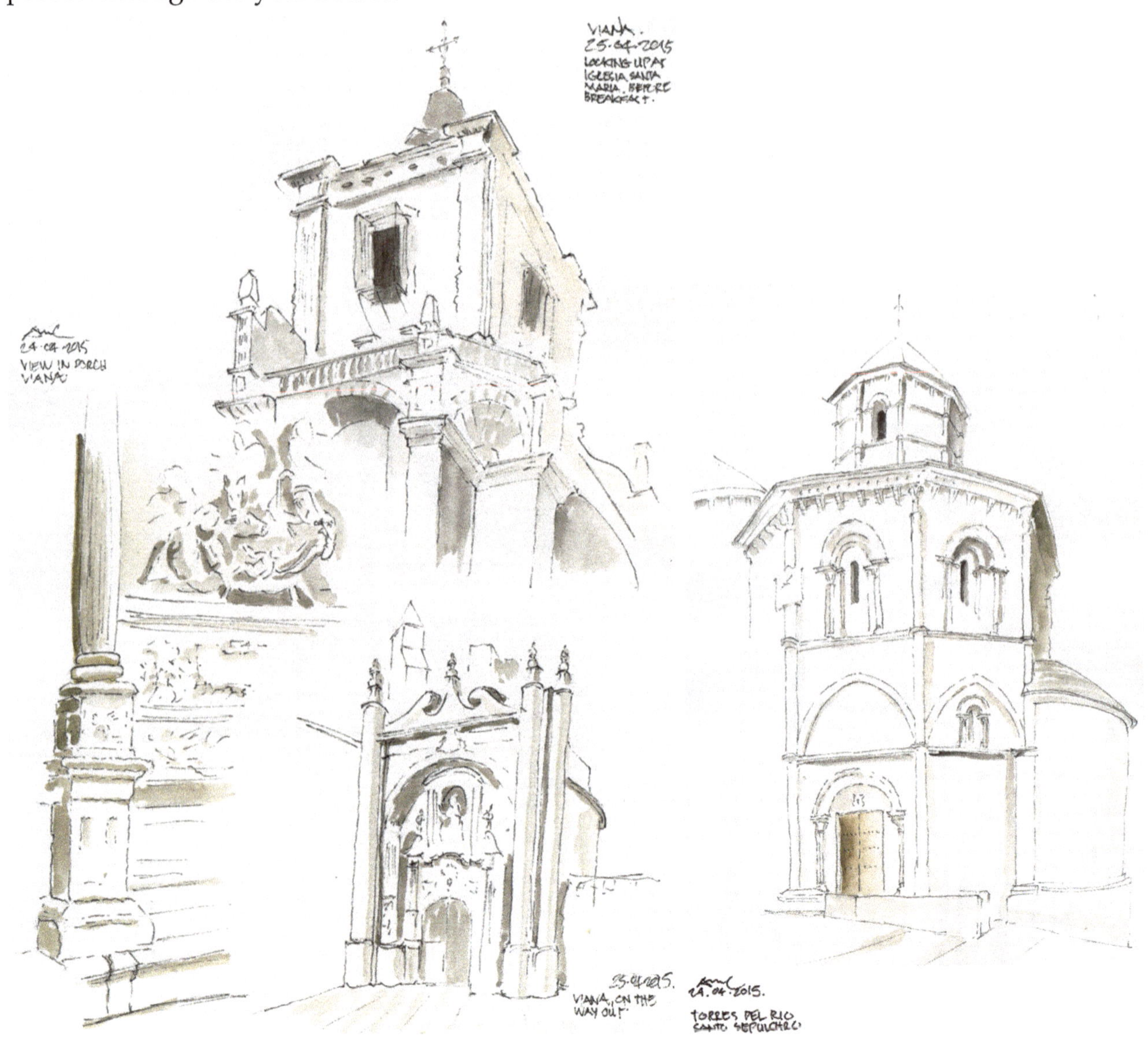

Logroño

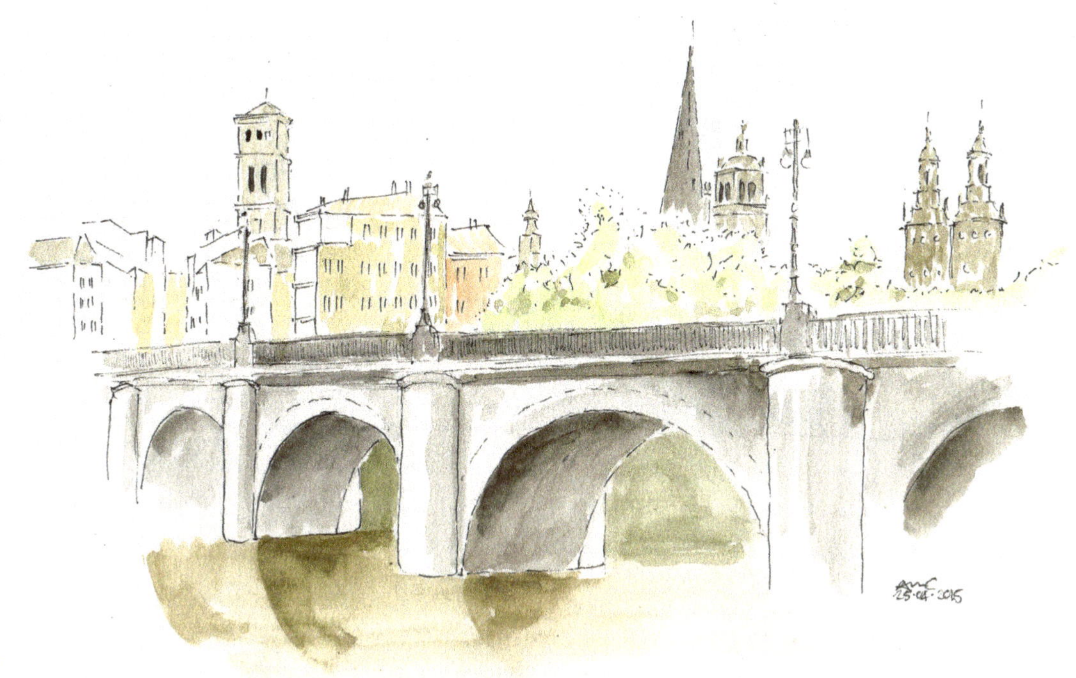

As I walked into Logroño, passing some well-kept allotment gardens, coming to life in the late afternoon sunshine, crossing the road, to join a mature treed path, parallel to the river; I could see through gaps in the trees, what must be one of the most beautiful approaches, to any town along the Way.

It was Saturday evening, as descending the hill on the outskirts of Logroño I heard the distant boom boom drumming, of some band practice. The following morning, *Domingo de Ramos* (Palm Sunday) I left the alburgue early, and walked through the deserted streets. I found a bench on Calle Portales, sat and drew the *Catedral*, or to give it it's proper title, *"Concatedral de Sta María de La Redonda"* The *con,* (with) indicating that uniquely, it shares a Bishop with Santa Domingo de Calzada.

Whilst drawing the street gradually came to life, the odd pilgrim passed, shop shutters clattered as they rolled up. The Chino store behind me laid out fruit and vegetables, more folk walked by, some now sat in the morning sunshine on the benches opposite.

From where I sat I could see more and more folk gathering around the South Door, many carrying sprigs of greenery, Palm leaves, which was being sold on every corner by street vendors. Taller palms swayed above the heads of the assembling Fraternity. A purple banner *(Estandarte)* held high at the head. The Fraternity men, women, and children, all dressed in rich purple cassocks, *(Tunicas)* white sashes tied around their waists, were now in loose formation, awaiting arrival of other brotherhoods.

Another Fraternity in deep burgundy passed by as I walked down to the Plaza Mercado. I stood with the crowds, as a group of *Peneitentes* (Those following) in pure white cassocks, with sashes, trims, and flowing satin cloaks *(Capas)* in bright cobalt blue, emerged from the

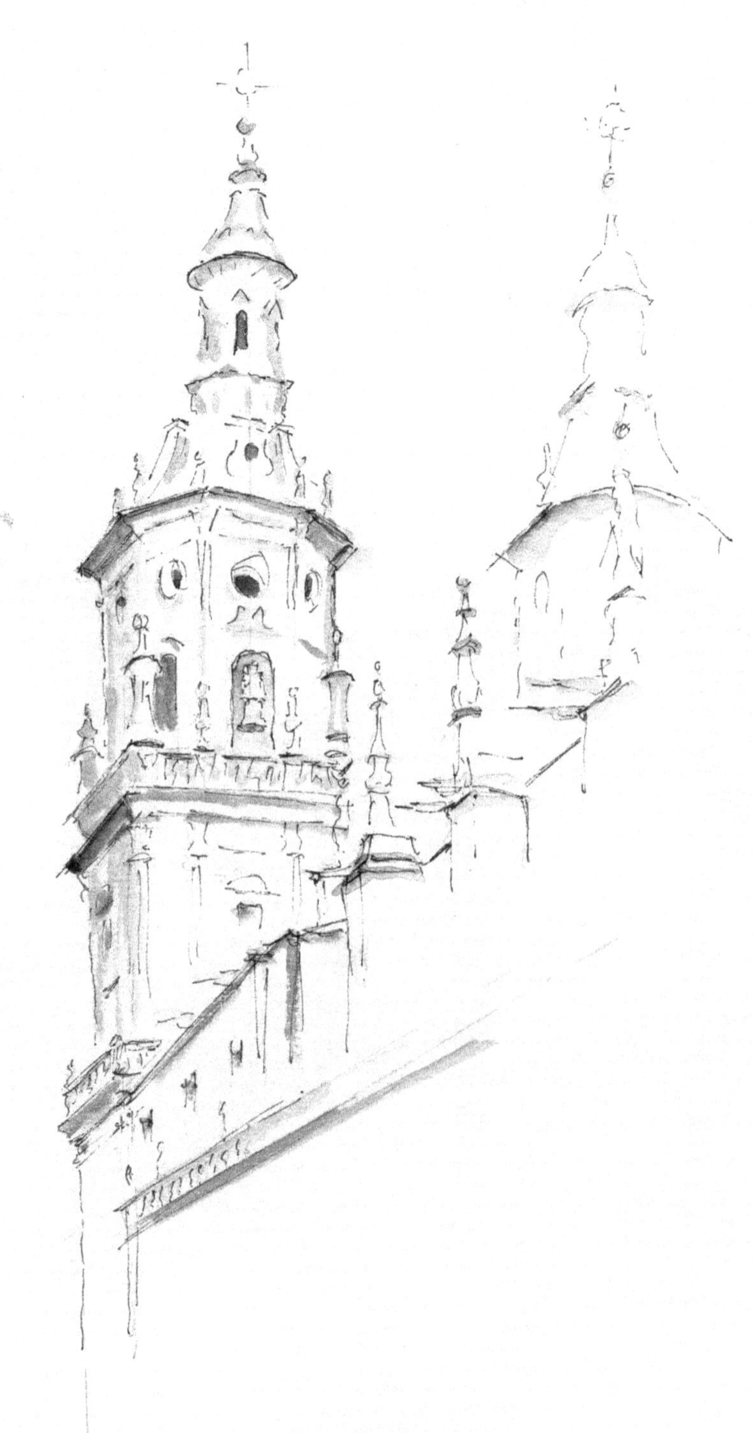

CATEDRAL SANTA MARIA DE LA REDONDA · LOGROÑO
13/04/2014.
PALM SUNDAY.

West door, joining there colleagues'. Cloak less the *Costaleros,* waited patiently in formation, shoulders at the ready beneath the upholstered hardwood shafts which carried a life-size tableau of Christ, riding a donkey into Jerusalem.

The shafts, three to the front and rear, extended five men deep, although I could see at least two women. Welcome changes to what apparently used to be a strictly male preserve.

Sadly I had to leave before the procession got under way, and I was left with a question that occurred, unanswered. How do they compensate for the differing shoulder heights of the *Costaleros?* I still don't know.

In 2015, my walk into town was earlier, and the allotment gardens were deserted. I stood and admired the skyline I had remembered, a panorama of towers, spires, and cupulas silhouetted against the blue sky. I laid out my kit and rested my pad along the top of the river bank retaining wall.

I suppose I was there for about an hour in total. Perhaps because mostly I have my nose in a sketchbook, or I'm looking for a subject to draw; I can't say I'd previously noticed, a rather sad and disappointing trait, shared by many Pilgrims. In that hour, numerous pilgrims trudged by, behind me, heads down, trudge, trudge, up the flight of steps, and across the bridge. Not a glance back, or across the river. Their Camino is seemingly something of a race.

I had only walked the relatively short distance from Viana, those passing by me, were in the van of walkers from Los Arcos, or maybe further back. I imagined they were the chaps, and chapess's, who had left their albergue in the still pre-dawn gloom. No doubt entertaining those choosing to remain in their bunks, with minutes of plastic bag rustling, head torch flashing, and oft basso profundo commentary on their actions. They invariably seem to travel with deaf companions!

They crossed the bridge, focused, as for most of their walk, on but a few feet in front of them, headed for the next albergue where they will spend the afternoon recumbent on their bunks. They will be turning dorm lights out at nine-o-clock, and earlier; expecting, and usually getting courtesy and consideration from those retiring later, in the dark! A consideration not reciprocated in the early hours of the following morning, when the cycle is repeated, as no doubt it will be until they reach Santiago.

Perhaps it's unfair of me, retired, to be critical of those restricted to holiday periods. Nonetheless, I do feel they are somehow missing the point. A shorter, slower, section; savouring the history, ambiance, and comradeship of the Pilgrimage, and the glorious Spanish countryside and architecture, would in my view be more rewarding, and fulfilling, than walking the whole Way, in a blur.

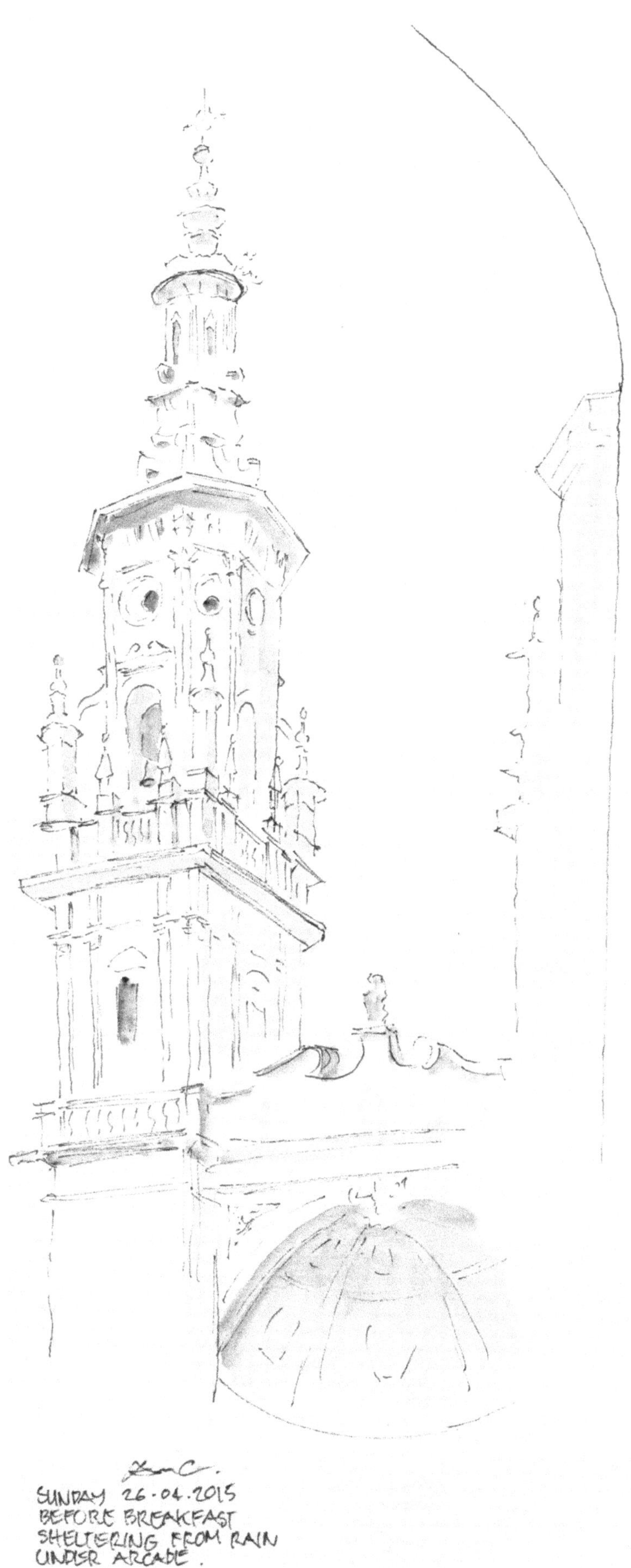

With more time available, I was able to explore Logroño. As I walked, stopping here and there, I eventually found myself back in the Plaza Mercado. I was intrigued by a group of attractive young girls, in their early twenties. All were dressed similarly, in red hot pants and top, carrying balloons, and making a lot of noise, singing, dancing, laughing, and generally having a good time. I sauntered across, hoping to find out what they were about. As I got close, a couple of the young ladies sprinted overt to me, and asked, in English, (how do they know?) if I would buy a balloon for one Euro.

Apparently, one of the party was to be wed later in the year, and she, and her friends were raising money, to help pay for it! Of course, I gave the euro, but declined the balloon. I also got a hug from the bride to be. How lovely. Looking back, I wish I'd had the wit to give more.

As the day wore on and into evening, I saw several such groups, which I assumed were doing likewise. I have no idea if this is a Regional, or indeed Spanish custom, or, one evolved out of necessity, following the financial crash, and consequent high youth unemployment in Spain.

Navarette

I felt I was due a rest day, and hit on the idea of two short daily walks, leaving afternoons free for drawing, So I just walked to Navarette, and on to Nájera the day following.

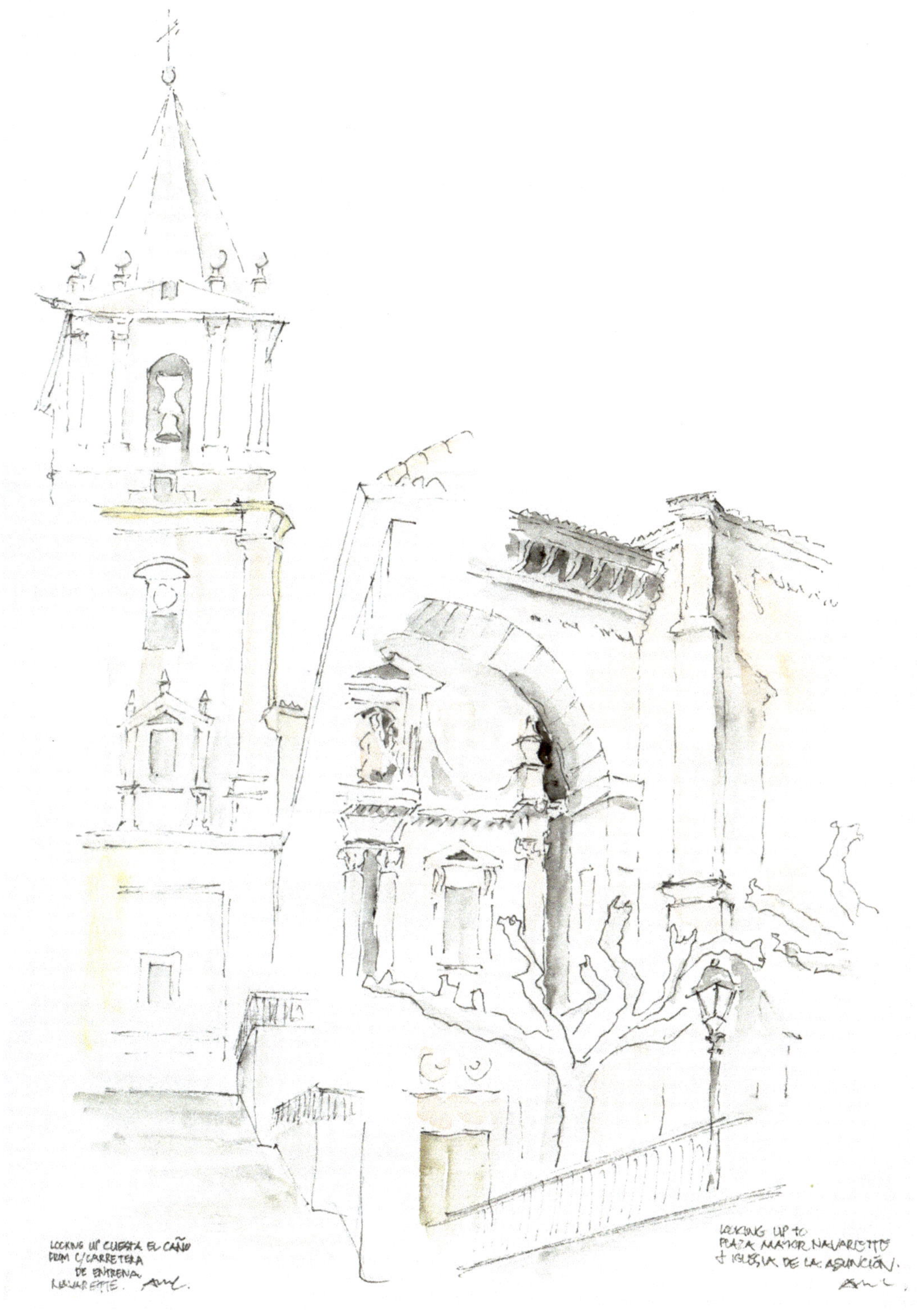

I spent a pleasant afternoon drawing, and saw Monty, the guy from Los Arcos, also drawing. It was a warm balmy evening, so after dinner I walked back to the low level Plaza. There at one of the bar tables sat Monty. He was talking with an urbane guy, who stood out from Pilgrims around him; elegantly dressed, not a hair out of place, carefully tanned.

Monty caught my eye, and gestured for me to join them. By way of an introduction to his companion he told me that this had been his first day on the Camino. He had speed walked over 40K with a sizeable back pack. Monty was evidently impressed, as indeed I was with the distance. He asked me how old I thought the guy was. Although I could see he was probably mid-forties, Monty had initially been seduced by careful grooming and sartorial elegance, and had thought him to be only around thirty. Assuming this was a sort of junior playground game, I hazarded somewhere around seventy!

Nicola joined us at the table, accompanied by a beautiful French lady.

She introduced us explaining that I drew along the way, and as group conversations often do, it fragmented, and I found myself talking with Caroline.

She had the most delightful French/English accent, listening made me weak at the knees, the kind of young woman that outside of the Camino, where age and gender barriers dissolve I would be unlikely to meet. We talked of drawing, and she told me of her interest in photography, playing with, photo shopping, the images.

Probably to my disappointment, no definitely to my disappointment, conversation again became inclusive. Apparently Monty's Superman, Olivier, was an Airline pilot. He was equally impressed with my drawing along the Way as I had been with the distance he had walked that day. He explained that, although he appreciated Art, and his wife liked to paint, he could not, and was intrigued as to how I understood perspective. He said his problem was that he couldn't judge angles! "Oh Lord!" I exploded, trying not to spill my *vino tinto,* and continued between waves of laughter, "An Airline pilot, who can't judge angles. Help!" He was hence referred to as the scary pilot!

Oddly enough, hazarding a tongue in cheek seventy, proved to be not that far wide of the mark. His 40k epic had been his first day, and the following morning walking towards Nájera, I came upon a crouched hobbling figure, just about achieving forward motion! As I passed, calling a cheery *"Buen Camino!"* I noticed it was Olivier, somewhat less impressive! Poor chap, he had a schedule to maintain to meet his elderly Father in Sarria. I hope he made it.

I stayed in Navarette again in 2015. I'd two sketches in mind, and failed to complete either! I climbed up beyond the Church to the peak where back in the middle ages there had been a castle. From that vantage point my intention was to draw from above the church and surrounding village roofscape. I tried valiantly, but the gale-force wind defeated me. I could not keep my pad still, nor even my pen hand.

I descended, seeking shelter in the church, with the idea of a sketch of the stunning Baroque Retablo, or more accurately a small part of it. Foiled again, as it was too dim, and I hadn't euro coins to activate the illumination.

I repaired to the bar, as much to avoid shadows of Pilgrims past on the terrace, as to take shelter from the wind.

Nájera

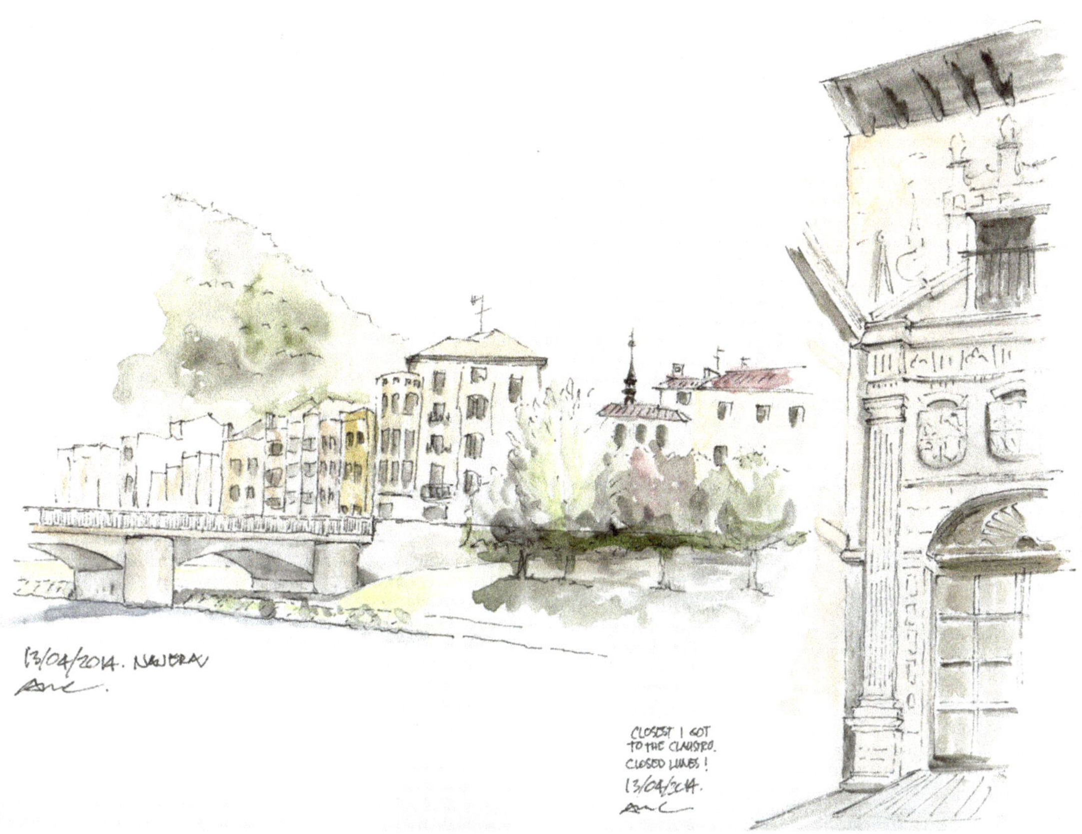

After spending time exploring, and sketching, I returned in the late afternoon to the alburgue, a little disappointed that, it being Monday, I had not been able to see the Monastery Cloisters. My spirits were soon lifted though, as there, just two bunks along from mine, I saw the captivating French lady I'd met the previous evening. We spoke and arranged to have dinner together.

We walked and talked our way along the river bank back into Town. It was a beautiful warm balmy evening as we left the albergue, behind us, steep sandstone cliffs rose from the river valley. The Monastery tower visible above rooftops to our left as we walked in the shade of trees passed the footbridge. Through the trees glimpses of the sparkling river coursing between the green banks, and soon into view, the elegant modern road bridge we had earlier walked across on entering the town. Just before reaching the bridge, there were a cluster of small restaurant bars, with tables set out on the grass river bank. Caroline chose a table and we sat admiring the view, wondering as the buildings were set well back from the grassed flood plain were we sat; if we would attract the waiters attention.

The clear blue sky held back dusk, *Menu* courses came and went, and as the evening wore on, the sky blue deepened through Cobalt to Prussian and finally Ultramarine as a huge luminous disc of a full moon rose above the rooftops on the opposite bank. Replete, I twirled the *vino tin*to in my glass, leaned back in the chair, listened to Caroline's enchanting English accent, and delighted in watching my beautiful companion. Her face moonlit, her expressions animated with an enthusiasm for her subject. Oh Lord. I thought; Caminos don't get any better than this!

Azofra

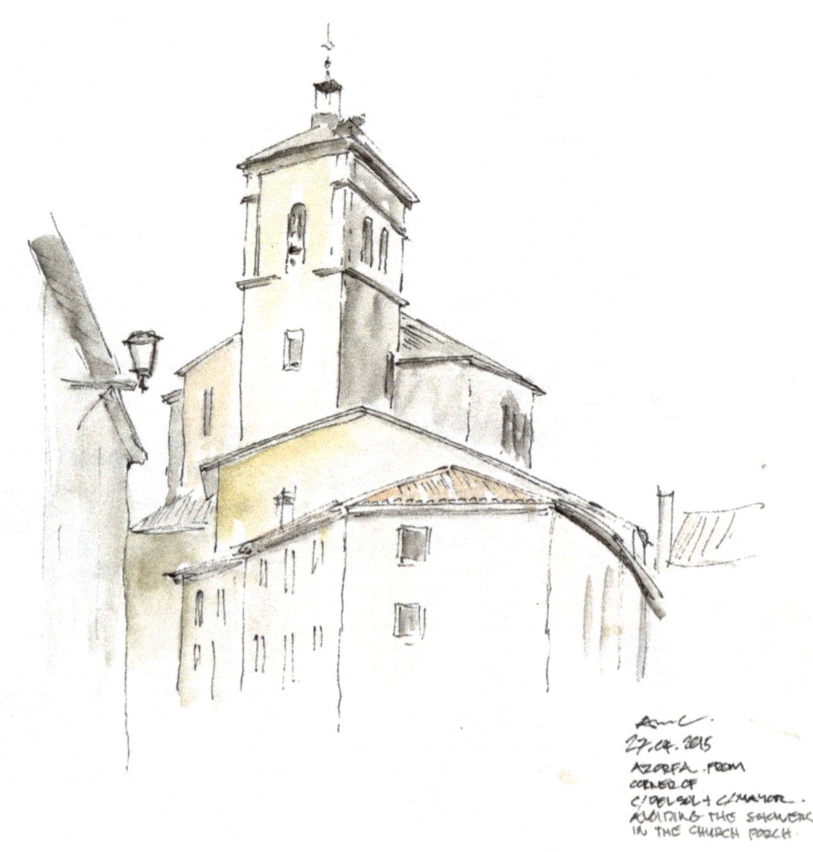

2015, I walked through Nájera, Sod's Law; it was Lunes, Monday, again! I am evidently destined not to explore the Monastery Cloisters! I stayed in the small village of Azofra. The Municipal albergue there was fantastic. Great facilities, and two low beds in each cell, not bunks. It was quite large too, and when full must have had double the population of the village.

I poked around in the late afternoon, and ended up in the church porch, just as it began to rain. It was only be a light shower, and fifteen minutes later, I ventured down the hill to the corner of Calle del Sol and Travesia Mayor, where I found a doorstep to sit on, and commenced sketching, *Parroquia de Nuestra Señora de los Ángeles de Azofra.*

No sooner had I started, it started to spit, spot. The doorway I was drawing from wasn't deep enough to take shelter, so I quickly gathered my things, and hoofed it back up the hill, to the sanctuary of the church porch. I should add that I'm not averse to a drop of rain, nor getting wet, but I don't use watercolour paper when travelling, just a reasonable weight cartridge paper; which would cockle in the rain, and the water colour wash would run.

After ten to fifteen minutes I was back on the step! And after another ten minutes or so, I was back under the church porch!

I was to and fro countless times, and what was, and looks on the face of it, a fifteen minute sketch, took over two hours! I cannot grumble, as by and large, I had glorious weather, over the two Caminos. This was the only occasion I recall having to take shelter whilst drawing. I was, and feel blessed.

Detour to Monasterio e Iglesia de Santa María de Cañas

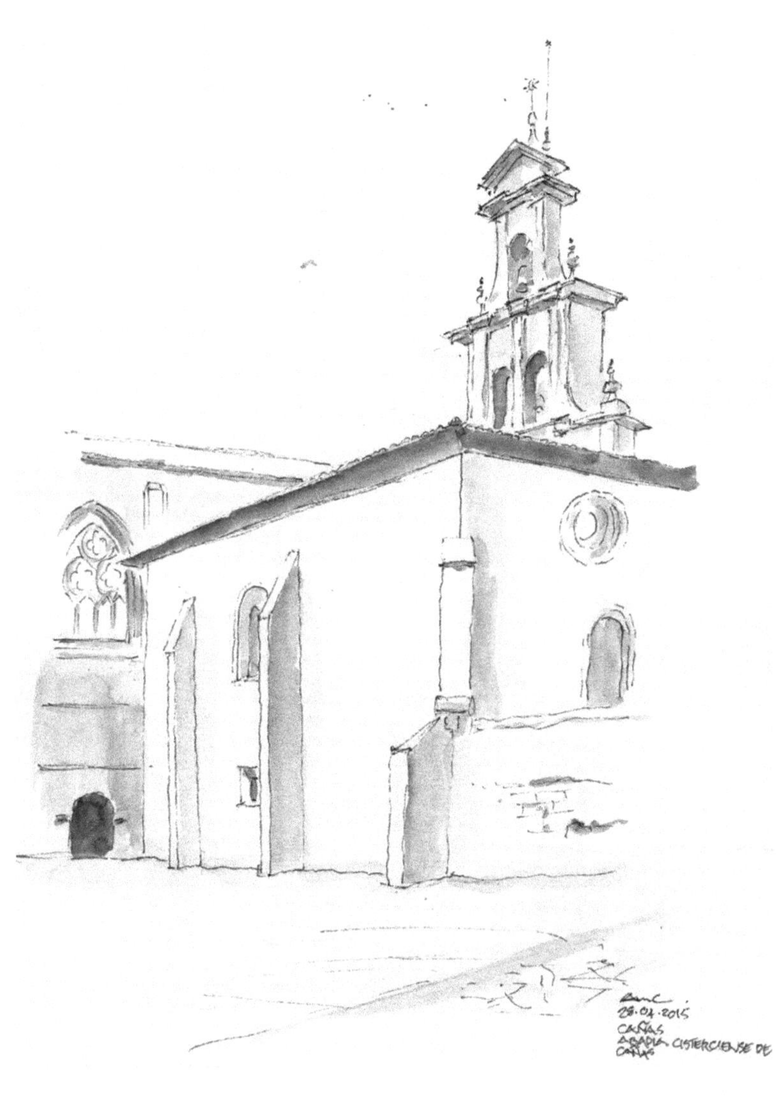

The following morning, I took the detour to the *Monasterio e Iglesia de Santa María de Cañas*. As I approached, what I thought was Cañas, the closer I came, I began to harbour doubts. From a distance, it appeared that the windows were boarded up! Then, oddly, blank white, set in the pinkish stone.

It was indeed what I'd come to see. I'd made notes from my Gitlitz&Davidson which mentions three semi-circular apses, lit by enormous windows. But as one approaches, the low apses to the side aisles, are hid by the hedge. The lofty choir terminates in semi-circular form, so the apse has the width and height of the main body of the Choir. Had I more closely consulted my Brierley guide, he mentions the windows are of alabaster, so my doubts would have been dispelled much sooner!

Having arrived relatively early, the only others I saw whilst drawing, were the delightful young lady receptionist, and a guy I took to be the caretaker. They came out together to see what I was doing. They had an obvious love, and pride the place, and seemed rather pleased I was sketching it. When I went in, I was still the only visitor; the lady took me into the church and gave a brief guided tour.

Once inside, I saw the alabaster lent a glorious pale ethereal light, which so suited the severe Cistercian 13thC architecture. Wonderful, the simplicity much to my taste.

The guy found me exploring the Cloister, and was keen that I did not miss his particular favourite, and lead me to the museum, opening up for me. When I returned to reception to collect my things, pleased to note folk were beginning to arrive.

Santo Domingo de Calzada

CATEDRAL SANTO DOMINGO DE LA CALZADA.
15/04/2014.
WITH SUN IN EYES + RUSHING TO AVOID THUNDER STORM!

I walked into Santo Domingo with Nicola. She had the bunk next to me in a pleasant dormitory with a resident alarm in the yard below, a cockerel in a rather splendid chicken coup. On the other side of me Caiã, a Brazilian guy and his wife.

Beyond them on the end wall of the dorm, the window looked out across the neighbouring roofs to the East side of the Cathedral and the elegant freestanding Baroque Tower. As I collected my drawing equipment together Nicola suggested I should stay and draw from the window. I declined, saying I preferred to scout around seeking out the best aspect.

I walked up the passageway, Calle Santo Domingo de Silos, hurrying past the masons cutting stone to repair the building opposite the Cathedral, and into the Plaza España, where I sat on the stepped plinth to the five lantern lamppost.

It was just far enough away from the stonecutting dust, but I had to cope with the glare of the afternoon sun in my eyes. Whilst drawing, I could see Cumulonimbus clouds building and bubbling up above the cathedral roof, to the West.

My drawing became looser as I strove to finish the sketch before the storm arrived. Dark glowering clouds rolled closer intermittently lit by the increasingly frequent lightening. The crack and rumble of nearing thunder reverberated around the Square. Fortunately the storm veered passed us to the North, and I finished the sketch in the dry! Although it does show signs of being hurried!

On returning to the albergue I found Nicola, told her I should have heeded her advice. She had met Caroline, and we all dined together in the evening. Caroline was suffering with a knee injury sustained on her first day over, or more likely, descending the Pyrenees, and was considering a rest day. She would then be behind, out of step with my schedule. I was saddened, as it dawned that I would be unlikely to see her again.

Occasionally walking together, sharing dorms, meals, coffee, a glass of wine, laughter, joys and pains; it's remarkable how quickly, across age, gender, and nationality, firm bonds of friendship are formed on the Camino. Walking Caroline back to her Hotel, I was forcibly

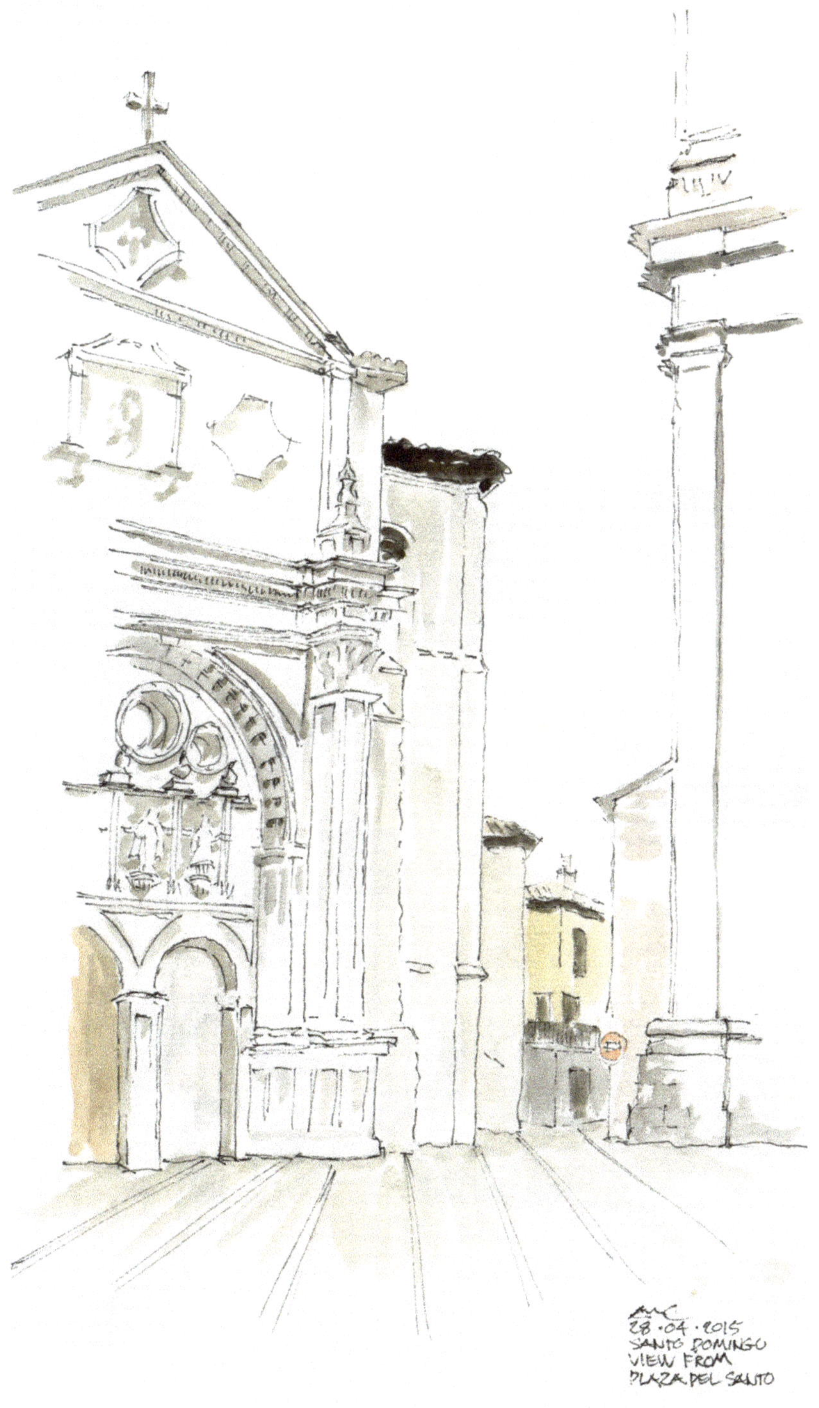

reminded of that. We stood saying goodbye, I held her hand, releasing it slowly, and watched as she entered and disappeared into the hotel. I stood motionless, gazing absently at the doorway; my emotions were that of having said a final goodbye to an old friend, rather than someone I'd known for an all to brief few days.

In 2015, I sat on the steps in the corner of Plaza del Santo, drawing the South face of the *Catedral de Santo Domingo de La Calzada*. I was about half way into the drawing when a delivery van drew up, completely blocking my view. I asked if they would move, there was plenty of room, and it would not have inconvenienced them. The driver smirked and shrugged, seemingly taking pleasure from his thoughtless actions.

I admit to having had a childish urge to let his tyres down! But in the end, common sense prevailed, and I waited it out. It was over an hour, and the shadows cast by the early evening sun, were totally different

I returned to the bar where I'd dined the previous year. It was not as busy, and there were tables free, but emboldened by the spirit of the Camino, I did something a typically reserved Englishman of my generation, would not normally dream of doing! I approached the table at which a sole Japanese lady sat, and asked if I could join her for dinner.

It was an interesting and fun evening with Mutsumi. Her English was really very good, so there were no awkward silences. I remember a lot of laughter too. She told me she lived in Tokyo. In 2014 she travelled from Pamplona to Logroño. When we met, she was walking her second Camino, from Logroño, headed for Burgos. She had plans for Stage Three, in the Spring of 2016.

By odd coincidence as I was editing this section a lady I met in 2015 sent me a link for a YouTube video. She told me that I was in it! Yes I am, and I confess ego dictated I watch the whole two hours. My moment of stardom comes about a third in, and lasts all of two seconds. She must have exceptionally sharp eyes as I would not have noticed myself, had I not been prompted.

It shows me looking like a lost soul walking from the dorm I'd been allocated trying to get my bearings and find the dorm window I'd remembered from the previous year. I gave up, ever the reserved Englishman, I couldn't bring myself to stray into other non-allocated dorms! So sadly I did not, as I had hoped capture the sketch Nicola had suggested.

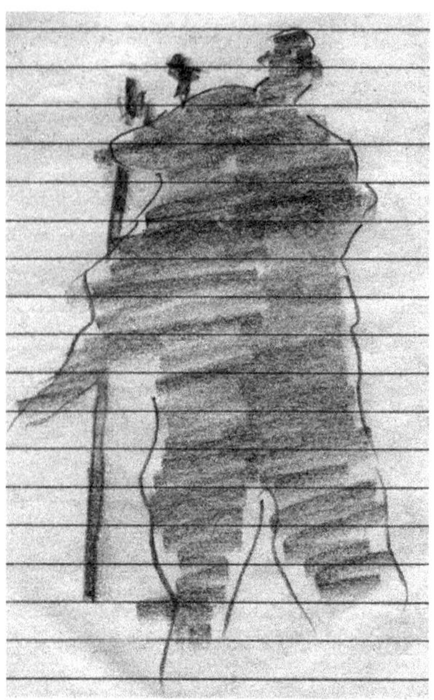

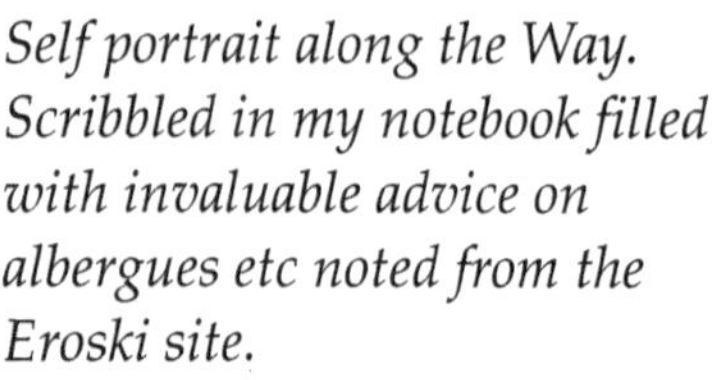

Self portrait along the Way. Scribbled in my notebook filled with invaluable advice on albergues etc noted from the Eroski site.

Walking to Belorado

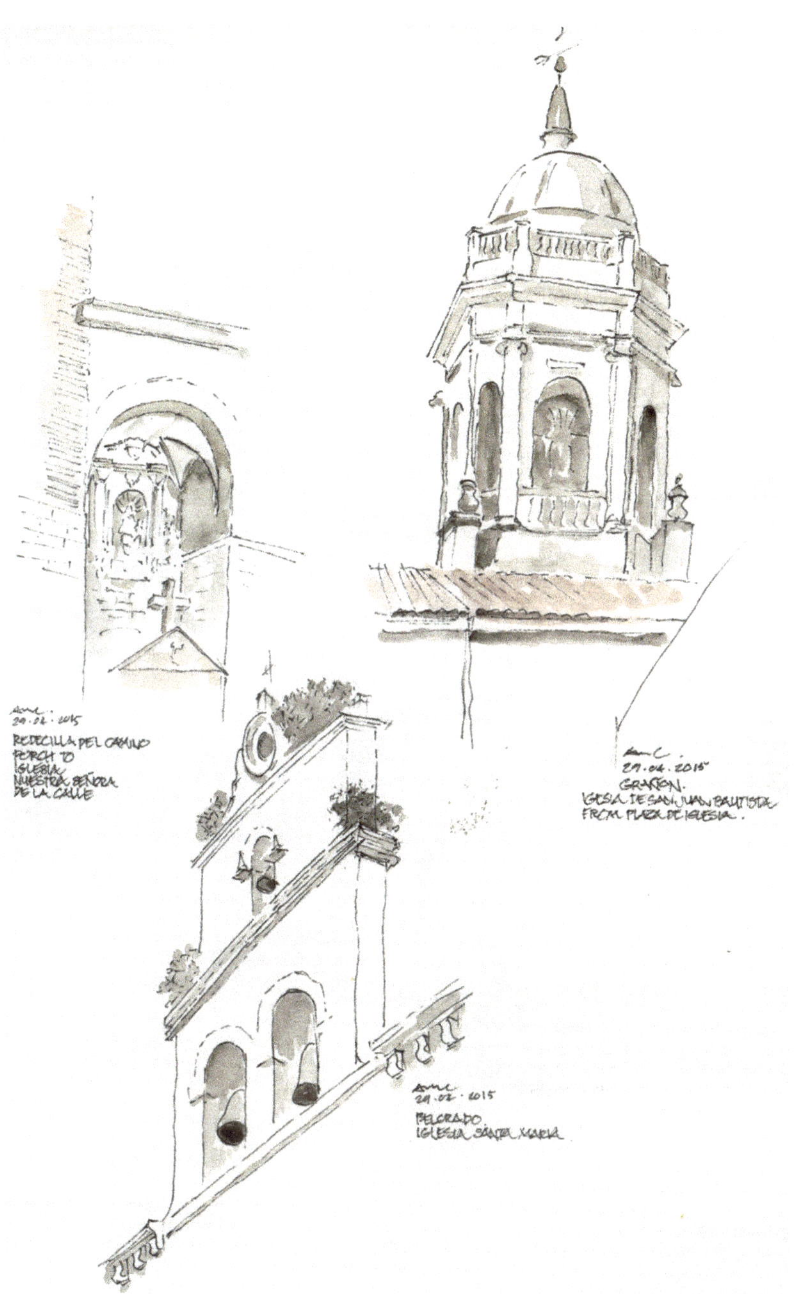

It was yet another pleasant day, as I left Santo Domingo and I took a leisurely pace, stopping briefly to make quick sketches a couple of villages along the way. In Redecilla I stopped for coffee opposite the *Iglesia Nuestra Señora de la Calle* and sat in one of the Bar's red plastic chairs.

As I drew a lady approached and asked if it was OK for her to take a photo. I probably gave her my stock reply about the danger of my face breaking her camera and continued drawing.

A little way out of the village, I came up to this lady and we got into conversation as we walked. To my astonishment she had come from Moscow, and looking back I didn't have the wit to ask if she was an Orthodox Christian.

Before setting off at my own pace and leaving her behind, we took further photos and exchanged details. I received copies of the photos she had taken almost before I'd completed my Camino, but sadly nothing since; so I don't know if she received emails and photo I sent. Maybe, I have thought, it is like trying to send emails to friends in Korea, I tried two networks before success with the third.

Anyway I am including a photo Natalia took of me on the Bar's red chair in Redecilla without permission. I'm sure she will not mind.

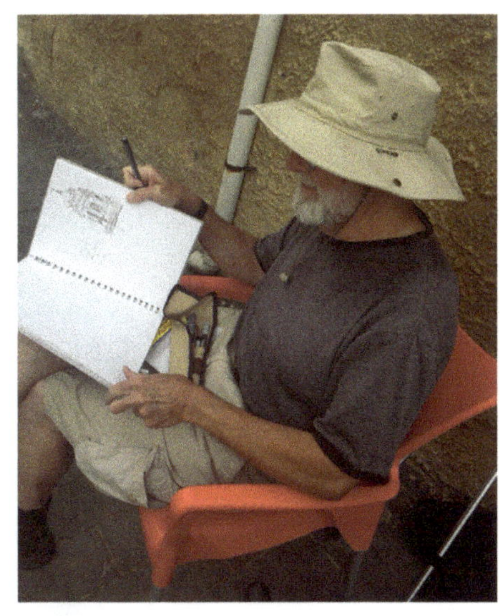

NATALIA FILEVA

When I reached Vilamayor del Rio; I turned a corner to see a small gravelled square. Benches shaded by the trees, children's swings, and a *fuente*, with a large circular pool.

Sitting at the edge of the pool were the Brazilian couple I met in Santo Domingo, Caiã and his wife Raquel, who was bathing his blistered feet. Very Biblical!

Enjoying a swing, and with her usual *Joie de vivre* and broad smile, Nicola, was just about to set off again, and said she'd decided to stay at the albergue with a swimming pool when she reached Belorado.

To my surprise and pleasure, recumbent on a stone bench, in the shade of the trees, was Caroline. She had changed her mind about taking a rest day, and set off from Santo Domingo very early. She was resting her painful knees. We spoke for a little while, but conscious that she would probably rather be resting, and not wishing to disturb her further, I said Goodbye, again wondering if we would meet again

On the edge of Belorado, I came upon the albergue that Nicola had referred to. I booked in with a young guy behind the bar. He consulted his chart, marked it with a cross, and gave me a dorm and bunk number. It was occupied, I returned and explained. The guy shuffled with his papers, and put a cross through another bunk number. Yes you've guessed; that too was taken. I went back again, and this time he called to a lady cleaning nearby to accompany me. Together we identified a vacant low bunk; she noted its number, and presumably returned to update his booking information.

As I was doing my laundry, two young German girls, I'd met along the Way spoke to me, they warned me not to eat there, as they had and it had been inedible!

Since the albergue was situated outside of the town, and I had no idea how far, and not much energy, or enthusiasm for more walking that evening, I ate at the bar, but chose carefully, *ensalada mixta,* and a plain omelette. I figured they couldn't do anything awful to that!

I didn't see Nicola, I found out later she had decided to press on.

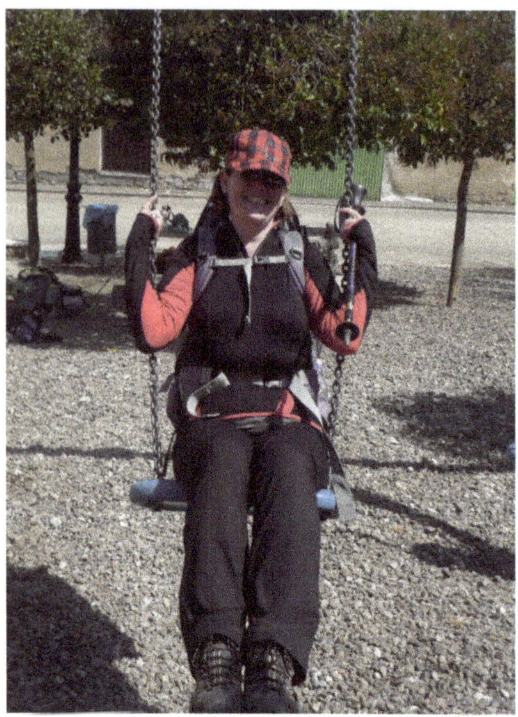

Nicola

Belorado

From my knowledge of the proximity of Belorado, from 2014, I passed by the Alburgue on the edge of town, and booked into one in the centre.

As I sat in the evening sunshine enjoying a drink in the Plaza Mayor, I met a guy who had been walking with two Irish ladies, whom I'd first met in Navarette, and here and there. He told me they were staying where I had stayed the previous year, and as they had only a few days, before their flight home, they had decided to hire bicycles, as they wanted to reach, and see León.

They were such lovely, funny ladies; I wanted to wish them Bon Voyage! So walked up to where they were staying, and found them in the bar!

We shared a bottle, and then another bottle, stories, laughs. I realised I would be unlikely to find a bar for dinner if I walked back, so joined them for dinner. Fortunately, it seemed that someone who knew what they were doing had taken this establishment by the scruff! It was excellent, a different place from the previous year.

I had noticed how the pleasant square becomes a cluttered car park, so in the morning I left the albergue early and made for the Plaza Mayor, sat on a bench under the still leafless pollarded Planes and drew the *Iglesia de San Pedro*. Vehicles were just beginning to obscure the view as I packed up and crossed the square for breakfast.

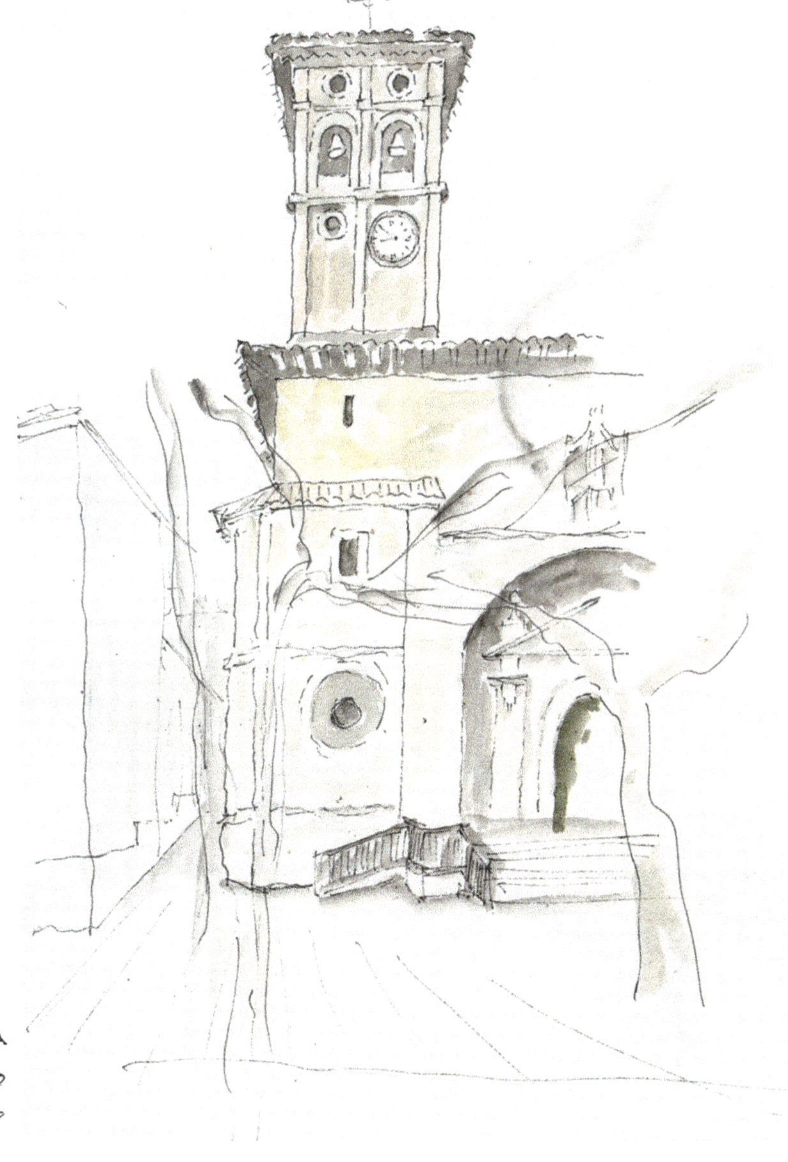

30 · 4 · 2015

BELORADO
VIEW ACROSS THE PLAZA BEFORE BREAKFAST.
IGLESIA DE SAN PEDRO SEEN THROUGH A MAZE OF POLLARDED PLANES.

St. Juan de Ortega

From Villafranca, it is a stiff up, and down climb, three times! So it was late afternoon as I reached St Juan. I recall I was feeling tired that day, and when booking in asked if I could have a bottom bunk, pointing to my grey beard!

He said he thought I would be ok, but if any problems, to come back to him. I could find no bottom bunks free, in either of the two, crowded dorms. I returned and followed whilst he retraced my steps, to satisfy himself there were none available. He then said, he would open up another dorm, but warned as it is North facing, it would be cold. The room had about a dozen single beds, six each side, such luxury.

Blankets solved any problem with cold, and the dorm remained quiet. Just the two German girls, who had warned me off the food in Belorado and the two young American guys I'd met with Nicola in Grañón. They had mentioned there that they had a friend who was taking a rest day, due to blistered feet. Sadly, they told me, he needed an operation on his foot, and had consequently been flown back to the States!

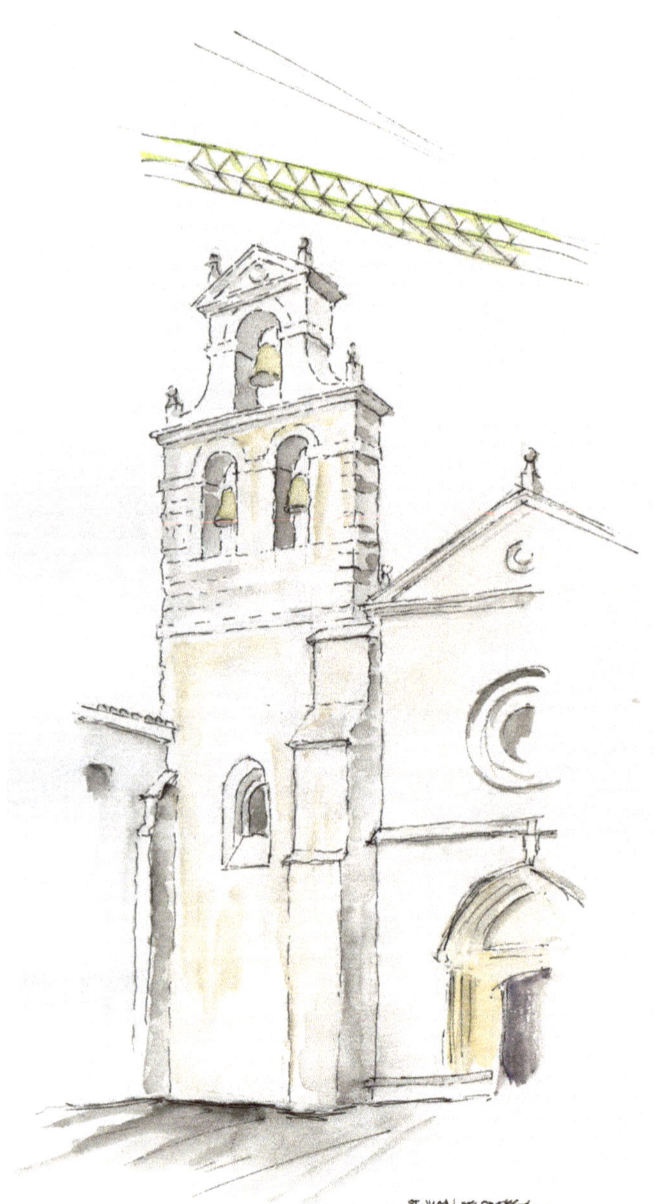

Feeling a little weary, I found a bench in the evening sunshine and sketched the church. Not the best view, but one constrained by where I could find to sit!

As I finished, and was packing away my kit, an American guy came and looked down on my pad. Hanging around his neck, he had an expensive looking camera with a lot of glass. He peered at the drawing, then turned to me, and said, "JEEESH! I've just spent an hour, trying to get a shot of that, without the crane jib, and you've DRAWN it!"

With my nose in my sketchpad, I hadn't realised that St Juan, was what I could see from my bench. The West face of the Church, the portico, doors (locked) to the remains of the Monastery, the albergue, a couple of cottages which seemed to be holiday lets ,the bar at the end or the terrace, and from there, the road out!

Consequently when I went to the bar and asked about food, the guy took my name, and said he would try to get me something, but it would be around nine-o-clock, and likely to be only a sandwich. I went back outside with a one euro tumbler of splendid rustic *vino tinto,* and read.

Luckily, folk who had reserved, had either got fed up, or at any rate failed to show, and the guy came and found me at about quarter past eight. I had a freshly cooked omelette and salad. Oh yes! And another tumbler of *vino tinto!* All for just over five Euros! Great bar, Great people!

In 2015 after sketching at Villafranca, I set forth upwards to the *Alto Mojopan,* I passed the *Monumento a los Caidos,* a Memorial to victims of the Civil War, and annoyingly I missed the Way, inexplicably, as I didn't have a problem the previous year! Maybe there were others to follow. I recalled coming to a junction in the path, not seeing any waymarks, and this time no one to follow, I took the path which appeared to me to continue straight on. In fact, it was a right, but incorrect turn!

I soon passed the first of, was it really close to a hundred, huge windmills. I wasn't perturbed, as I could remember, or I convinced myself I could remember, passing windmills last year. But they just continued, one after the other, a set distance apart, seemingly for ever! I recall thinking they had done an incredible job of installing so many in a year, or as I began to fear, I'd missed the Way!

When I'd left Villafranca, it was 12 Kms to St Juan. As I walk on average at 5Km per hour, dropping to 4 as the day wears on, so having walked for two and a half hours, I knew I should be close to St Juan.

I eventually left the windmills behind, and descended into a Mary Celeste of a hamlet, no bar, no sign of life, but it had a large signboard, and as luck would have it, a map of local walks in the area. I had apparently landed in Cerratón de Juarros, and I was 13Kms from St Juan! Further away than when I'd left Villafranca.

It was 13 Kms measured in Scottish Miles, or my pace had seriously dropped. So my hopes of an improved sketch at St Juan were dashed. Fortunately, it was less busy than the previous year, but I was still the last customer in the bar.

Although no time for drawing in St Juan, I did manage to sketch

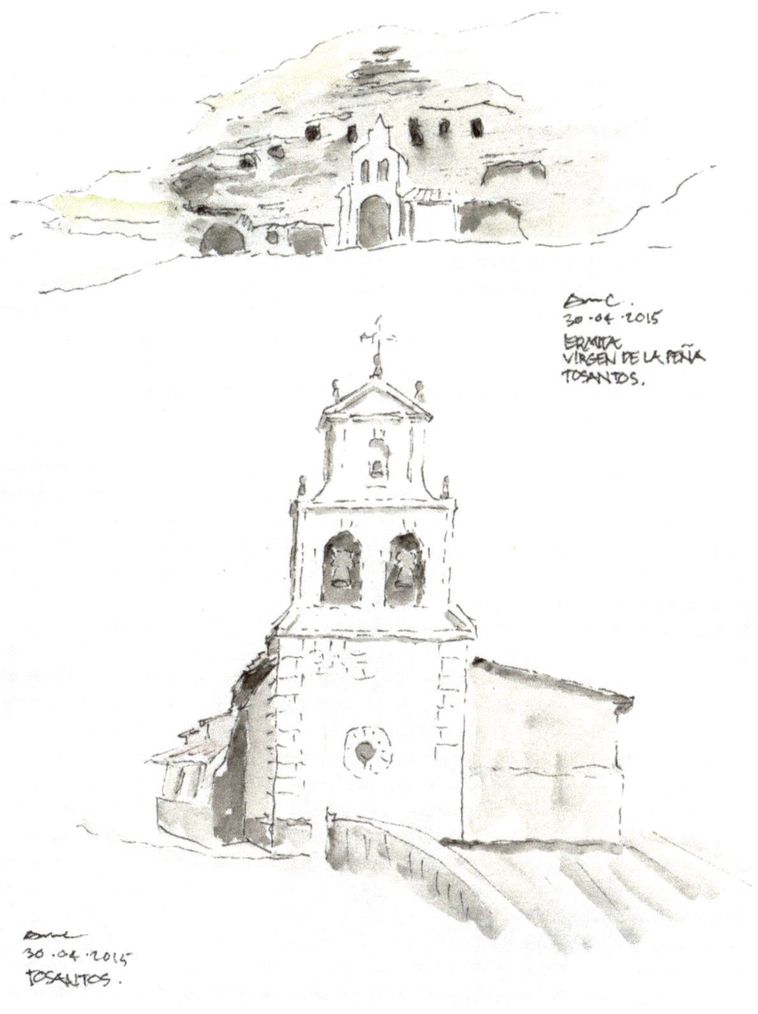

on the Way, with Mutsumi in mind, the lady; I'd dined with in Santo Domingo, who had been looking forward to visiting the *Emita de la Peňa.* Also as I approached the village of Espinosa del Camino I saw tantalising glimpses of the church across the fields. It was too distant to draw, and seemingly with no access to get closer. When I reached the village, I walked off the Way and backtracked through the deserted streets to find the church. Sod's Law I could only access the view of the South side I'd seen walking in, but this time I was too close. So in an attempt to lessen the severity of the upward looking angle, I climbed a slide in the children's play area adjacent, and stood teetering on the top platform.

My final drawing, made whilst taking a rest in Villafranca Montes de Oca, before the steep climb, and getting lost!

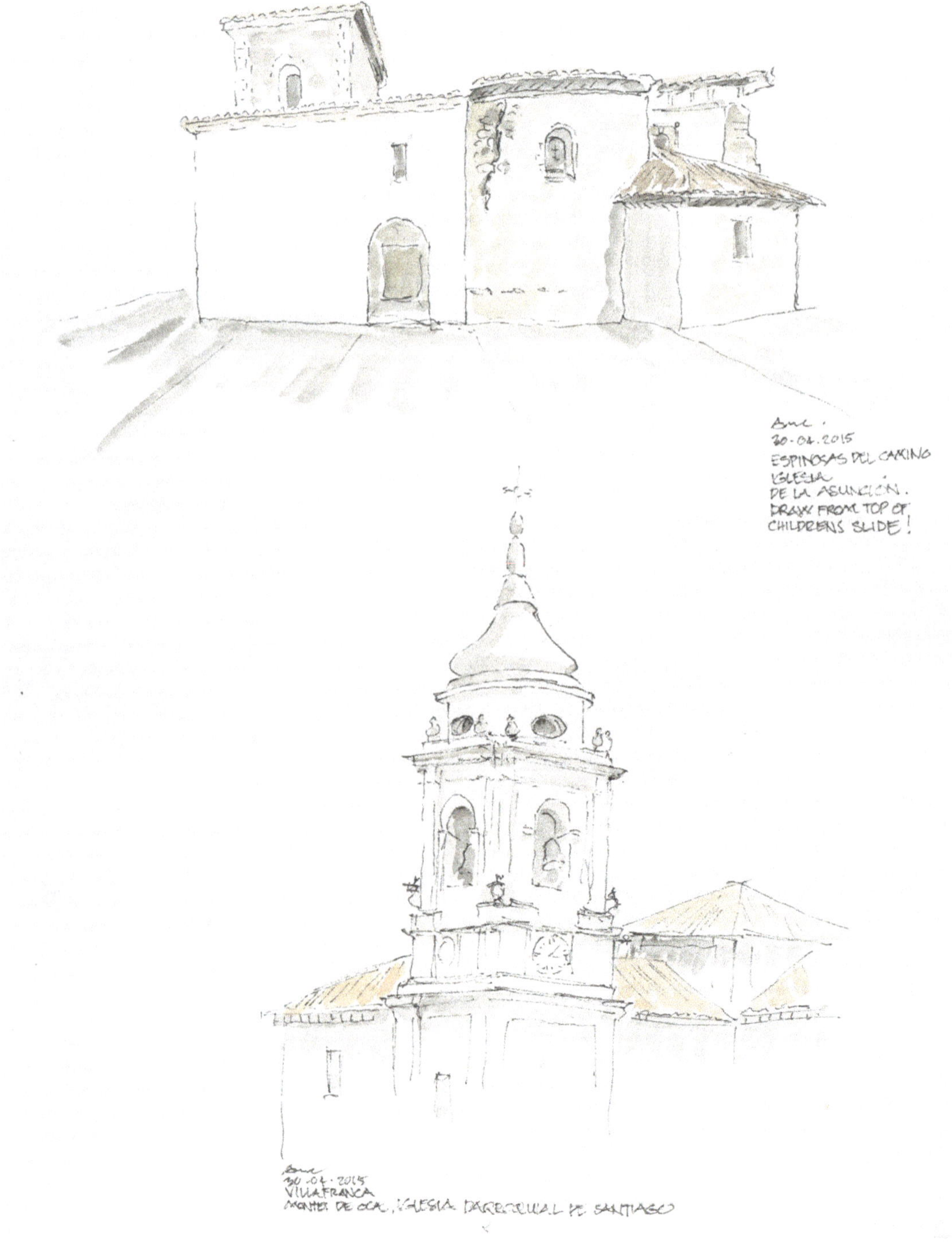

Arriving in Villafría

I missed the more pleasant River walk into Burgos, and consequently walked into Villafria around the seemingly interminable perimeter fence of the Airport. Relieved, finally I crested the bridge over the railway line, with tantalizing views of the church below. It had an interesting looking square belfry tower, with a South facing gable pediment extending above.

I crossed the road for a better view, but I could see no way down, and the way forward along the pavement took me further away from the church.

I realized from my Guide, that I was now faced with an 8Km walk through dreary and oft depressing ribbon development suburbia into the centre of Burgos. Personally, I find such environments unpleasant, and certainly they have but the merest tenuous link with the historic Way' so if I found a bus service I determined to use it.

The newly developed housing gave way to a small playground and landscaped area. Benches were set at intervals along the pavement edge, and sitting on one of them an elderly couple, well Ok then, younger than me! I asked in my basic Spanish, if there was a bus service into the centre. Amazingly, they understood, and showing his watch, at 12.50, the guy indicated I could catch a bus in ten minutes, from the bar I could see, across the traffic island.

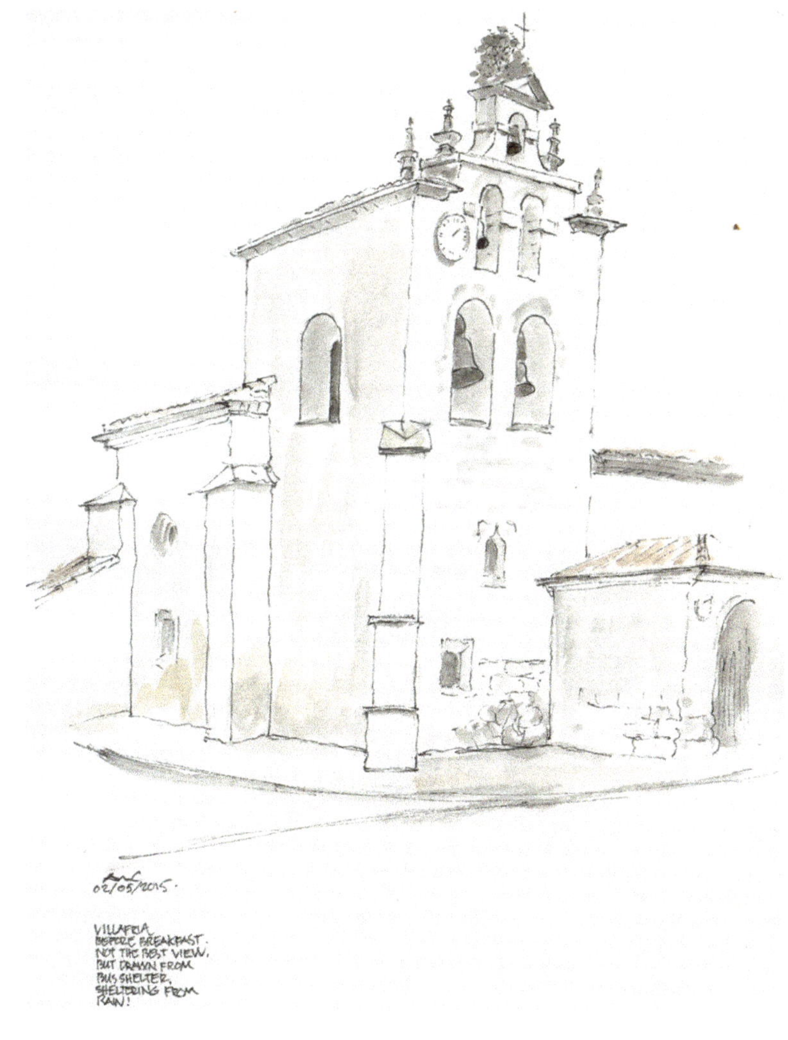

Disappointing that I would not have the time to explore, and maybe sketch the church, but a One Euro, twentyfive minute bus ride, instead of a two hour dreary slog, allowed me time to draw on arrival in Burgos.

Already on the bus, was a small French lady Pilgrim, not much younger than me. She gestured for me to sit opposite her. She wore a perpetual smile, and chatted merrily away to me, although I'd explained I could not understand. I saw her further along the Way, several times. Still smiling, and chattering, unless I happened to be drawing, when if I looked up, I would invariably see her, a little distance off, with an acknowledging nod, and of course a smile.

The bus terminated within sight of the Cathedral. I could see the pinnacles of the Crossing Lantern visible above the rooftops across Plaza Santa Domingo de Guzman.

It was the afternoon of Good Friday, *Viernes Santo.* I wandered around getting my bearings, and eventually arrived back at the Cathedral, at the top of the steps, leading up from the Plaza Santa Maria.

Looking down, the Plaza was packed with people watching the Marching Wind Band that I'd heard as I approached. I must have just caught the end of the Good Friday Parade, as soon the band ceased playing, and they, and the crowd dispersed.

Later, as I sat on the doorstep of an apartment in the Plaza Sta. Maria sketching the North tower of the West Front, Chris and Geraldine, a couple whom I'd met earlier along the Way, came and asked for my email address as they had taken a photo whilst I sketched. This was the end of their Camino, and they promised to send on when they reached home. It was the only photo of me at work, in 2014 and one of which I'm extremely fond as it illustrates what I often sought but was not always able to find; a step to sit on and shade from the heat of the Spanish sunshine.

BURGOS CATEDRAL.
WEST FRONT, NORTH TOWER.
18/04/2014

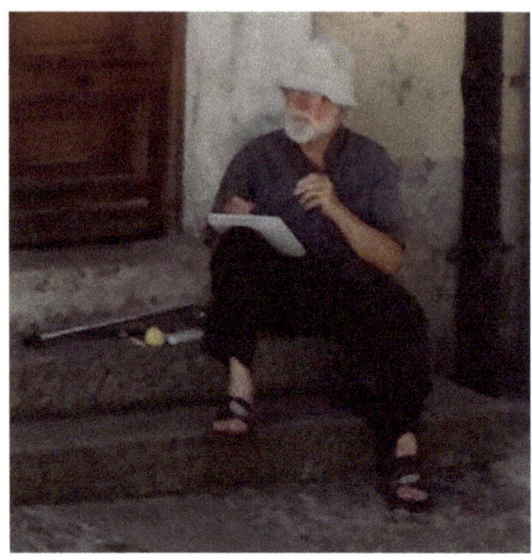

CHRIS & GERALDINE FUSSEY-DARVER

Burgos

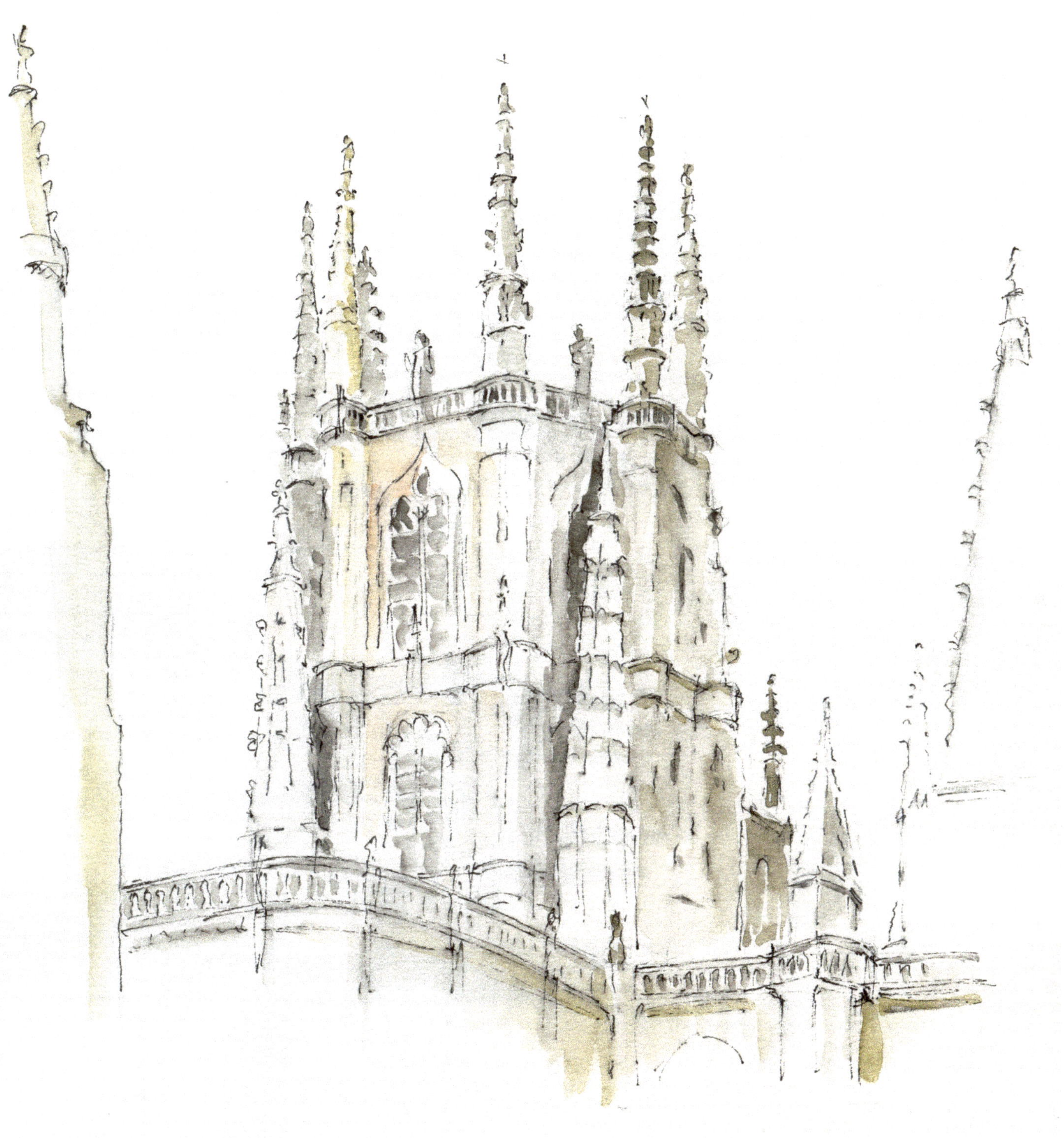

BURGOS CATEDRAL.
19/04/2014.

I started to draw early morning, in the little square, just uphill from the municipal albergue. No one else about, save for a middle aged lady leant against the wall adjacent to a doorway of what I took to be an apartment. After a while, up the hill near the *Puerte de la Coroneria,* I could see the morning light reflected on the gleaming wet road, and a guy diligently hosing down the street from a wheeled water cart. I Kept one eye on the drawing, and one on him, as he worked his way closer, and closer down the street. When he was within hailing distance, I asked if the little square was his next target, it was, and I speedily gathered together things I'd spread out along the bench that had afforded a rare luxury of sitting and space for my kit. I made a hasty retreat from the square, rucksack slung over one shoulder, sketchpad tucked under my arm, and hands full of other bits and bobs, as I had the distinct impression that I would have been included in the street ablutions, free of charge.

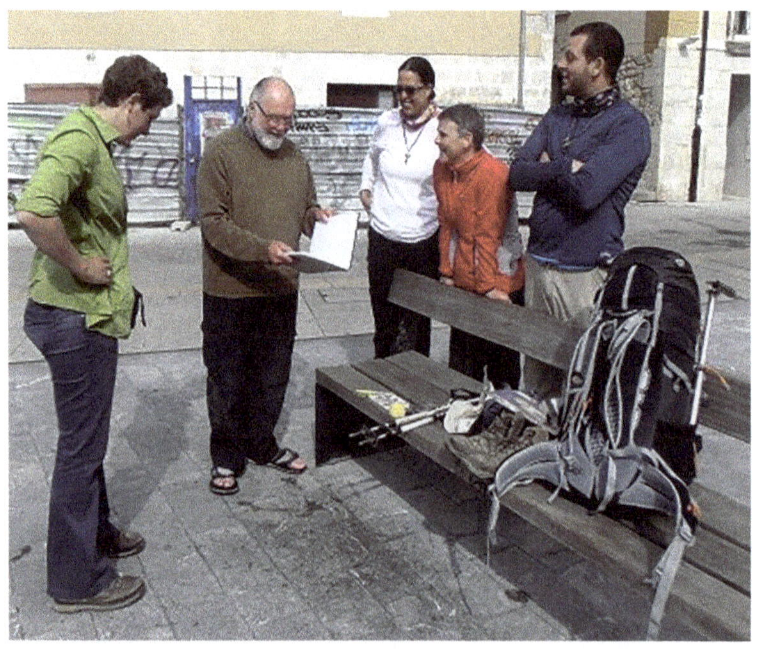

PIAHAUTOP

It was fortuitous as, downhill, in the Breakfast bar, by chance I was able to bid farewell to two friends, who were headed back home to Germany. Breakfast over, I watched the street cleaner bearing down towards the Bar, and judged it safe to walk back up the hill, carefully avoiding his hosing, as I skipped quickly by him.

The square, benches, everywhere, was still wet, and steaming in the morning sun. Whilst waiting for the bench to dry, I noticed that the lady waiting at the door had been joined by four others forming a small and curious queue. Soon my bench was dry and I continued drawing. Out of the corner of my eye, I caught sight of the little smiley French lady, watching me from a discreet distance. I looked up, waved, called to her in my non-understood English, and she babbled back merrily in equally non-understood French. A lovely moment of shared companionship!

The moment was gone, as I heard a familiar voice. It is the Brazilian guy and his wife. The Biblical scene I witnessed earlier as she bathed his blistered feet, seemed to have performed the desired miracle; and he walked without a limp, or trace of pain!

Concentrating on the drawing, I had missed the disappearance of the queue, and out of curiosity I wandered across to inspect the doorway to see if it held any clues. There, grey against the background of grey masonry, a small plaque*, 'Peluequeria Clari'* Of course, it was Easter Saturday morning; the ladies were having their hair done for the weekend.

After my first night in Burgos, staying in the Albergue Municipal, I had a Hotel room booked; as I had planned to meet up later that day with my Nephew and his Son, but sadly, his Father had died the day before he was due to fly out. My reservation information stated I couldn't book into my room until after three-o-clock, but, hoping to leave my rucksack in

Reception, I made my way to the Hotel. As I arrived, a couple stepped out, closing the door behind them, and walked from under the arcade, stopping in the pleasant morning air, obviously deciding in which direction to explore. As they turned they saw me reading the notice adjacent to the door, and trying to figure out how to get in. They told me it was not just booking in, the Hotel Reception located on the first floor, was not manned until after three. Access too, was via a code for the entry system given only to guests on arrival.

Before setting out, they gave me the code number. I went in, and climbed the stair to the First Floor Reception. There was no one about, no lights on, with the only light source, borrowed light from the adjacent Office, making the area very gloomy.

I could not find a safe place to leave my rucksack. It was disappointing that I would have to lug it around, as I was unlikely to find conveniently free bench space as I had done earlier. I headed back towards the Cathedral and stopped at a Bar for a coffee in the little street that runs alongside the Chapels, *Capillas* that flank the East side of the Cloister, *Claustro*

By now, the breakfast rush was over, and lunchtime trade had yet to start; so I was more or less the only customer. The barman bustled back and forth between the adjacent Kitchen, and the counter; busily setting out the Lunch time *pincho* fayre in the glazed counter display cabinets. After a while, the counter seemingly heaving with food, he paused, and looked up and down the display; admiring his handiwork, and making the odd minor adjustment. He looked across to where I sat and asked if I was a Pilgrim. A pretty superfluous question I thought, given my anorak, rucksack, and poles, would make it pretty obvious. However, this was just by way of a preamble to him telling me he had walked the Camino, four times.

He had a large amiable red face behind heavy spectacles, a bright red, white, and blue check shirt. He swivelled round and took something from the backfitting shelves, then came through the access gap at the end of the counter. As he did so he turned sideways, raising his hands from the elbows, in the fashion of Stick em up! to squeeze through the gap.

I could now see he stood about five feet tall, and was not much less in width, or depth. He waddled briskly across to me, and showed his Camino photos. Many were of him on various parts of the Way in snow. I supposed having a Bar to run; wintertime was the only time he could get away.

We chatted amiably in Spanglish, and having been shown his photos, I returned the compliment and showed my sketches. When he saw I'd drawn his beloved Cathedral, he called excitedly to the lady in the Kitchen. Safe to say, I was now a friend for Life! Taking advantage of that status, I asked if I could leave my rucksack till my Hotel opened. Before I could move, he swooped down picking up my poles with one hand, my 15Kg rucksack with t'other, and before I'd got on my feet, was half way down the bar at a pace I found difficult to match.

Late afternoon, sticky and tired, I made my way back to the hotel, collecting my rucksack on the way. By happy chance I met Nicola, who told me she had had a message from Caroline, they both had smart phones. She was catching up and hoped to be with us for dinner. Nicola was worried, as she had heard that being Easter Saturday; Pilgrim numbers were swollen with Spanish tourists. All the alburgues were reportedly *completo,* and hotels were virtually fully booked. We arranged to meet outside her Albergue in the evening, and I continued to my Hotel with rejuvenated step, at the prospect of seeing Caroline again!

When I reached the Hotel, I remembered the entrance code, and let myself in. I followed the sign to the First Floor Reception. The guy behind the desk was checking two other guests in. Finally he turned to me, abruptly asking where had I come from, was I starting my Camino here, or somewhere before?

Having established that this was a stop along the Way, a black sack was thrust across the counter, Boots! He said, shaking the sack. As I grabbed the sack, he thrust another at me, rucksack!

It was not the warmest welcome I'd experienced along the Way! Maybe, I reasoned, this was to protect a fastidious cleaning regime. I was wrong! At this point a lady carrying cleaning equipment came down the stair and into the Reception Area. She and the guy, ignoring me, embarked on a lengthy conversation, obviously in Spanish, so I could only catch bits here and there. Their conversation was occasionally punctuated by a long stare in my direction. After several minutes, the guy turned to me and asked how I had got in.

I explained, he seemed put out, muttered, *"Momento!"* and disappeared, several minutes later he reappeared. He had changed the entry code number! The checking in formalities were then completed and he gave me a key card for the door, and lights, plus the new entry code number!

On entering my room, the card reader for the lights was in pieces. Since the guy on the desk had been so helpful, I decided against troubling him further, and reassembled it myself. Praying that such devices were on a low voltage circuit! Success, Let there be Light! I had to go through the same performance, each time I entered the room.

The shower required a pilot's licence to operate! Stunningly contemporary, knobs and jets everywhere! A problem I found later, as I was on the First Floor, the waste from rooms above syphoned the shower trap, and the room tended to stink of drains!

Maybe the guy on the desk was not the sharpest knife in the drawer! as later that evening I met guests who were locked out, having left their room earlier in the day with the old code!

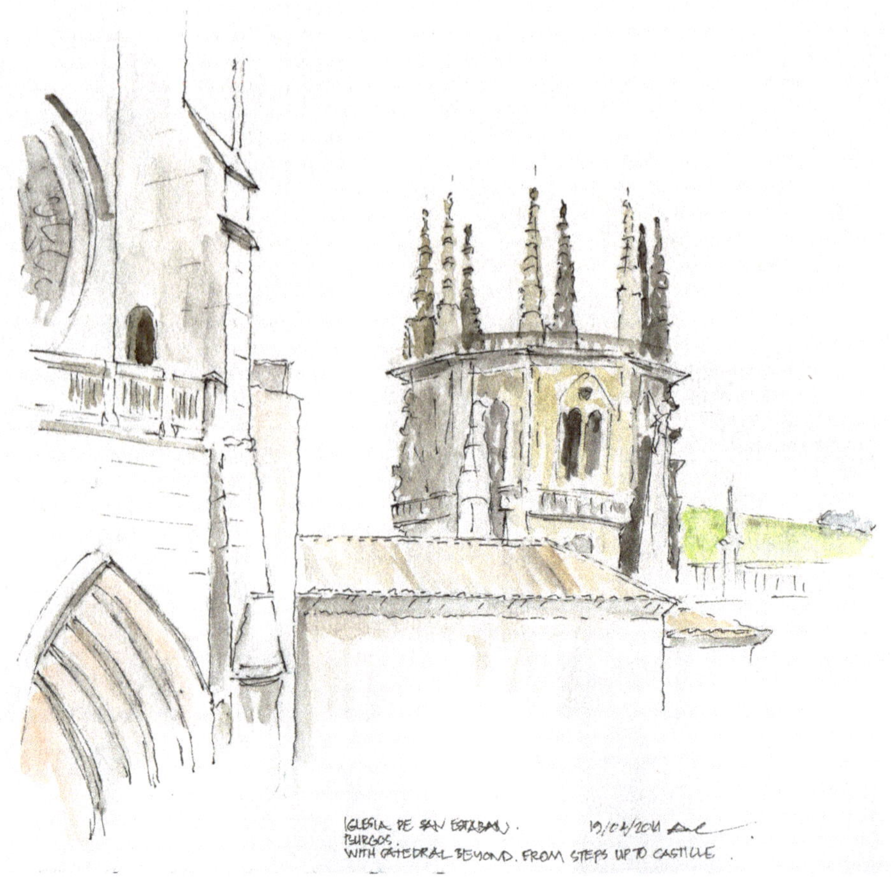

They had been trying in vain to raise the Guy on the phone. I let them in and gave them the new entry code. I hoped that the couple, who had given me the code in the morning, didn't suffer a similar fate.

After showering I left the room, and headed for the Plaza Mayor. It is very pleasant and popular places to sit, stroll, shop, meet! Ever the optimist I calculated that most if not all Pilgrim arrivals to the City pass through it, as indeed I had. Since meeting with Nicola, I worried about Caroline and the difficulty she may have in finding accommodation. I hoped to meet her as she arrived as I had formed in my mind what seemed at the time a perfectly logical solution, but in hindsight was, well, just crackpot! Maybe I'd been in the sun for too long.

I suppose I stood there for 30 minutes or so, a forlorn hope I suppose, akin to finding a needle in a haystack, it was so busy. I did not see her, but she did me! She smiled radiantly as she approached, had I not been so besotted I might have noticed she had no backpack, and it would have avoided an embarrassing situation. But smitten I was, and I began stutteringly my suggestion. I mentioned my conversation with Nicola, who had expressed concern that she may experience difficulty in obtaining accommodation arriving so late.

I explained my Nephew regrettably had had to cancel his trip, and consequently I was left with a Hotel room with three beds. It would, I began, be like.... But with head cocked to one side, and in her knee weakening English accent she interjected "You want to go to bed with me!"

Suddenly all the beetroots within a fifty mile radius were drained of their pigment and it all flooded into me. My skin prickled, I could feel the hairs on my neck raised. I stuttered in embarrassment, repeating and trying to explain. In retrospect I can see that my embarrassment was partly due, to the realisation that it had been a madcap idea, and also I suspect, by guilt, as a part of me probably wanted to scream very loudly.....YES YES!

I struggled on, explaining and re-explaining the en-suite three bed hotel room, would be as a mini albergue. I was so flustered, I do not now recall what I said, and I wasn't sure she'd understood, but she explained she had arrived much earlier, and had already booked into an albergue. I was still flushed and prickled, but relieved, as she left me, amicably agreeing to meet together with Nicola, for dinner.

I meandered through the narrow streets, probably still flushed, and certainly still prickling, as I dwelt on my recent encounter. I'm not sure which I felt most embarrassed by, my absurd idea of offering my room to share, or that Caroline had apparently thought I was soliciting!

In the late afternoon I stood a little while near the *Iglesia de San Lorenzo el Real,* watching as a Parish Fraternity arrived in their Easter regalia ready for what I guessed would be an imminent Procession. I could hear distant drums, and so wandered back along C/San Juan to the junction where C/La Concordia meets it, and it opens into a pleasant little Plaza, with space to afford views of any passing procession. I could hear the drum beats getting louder, so felt confident I was in the right place.

Soon the first group appeared from the C/ San Juan. White robed and purple cloaked, some with the pointy hats *Capirotes.* The Standard bearer marked time, beating his staff on the ground. The drums from the left got louder and louder, until, like a scene from Monty Python, Nobody expects the Spanish inquisition! The Fraternity from the left arrived, men in vivid crimson, robes, *Tunicas.* Pointy hats with menacing eye-holes, *Capirotes* with a *Capuz* over. I found it quite disturbing, frightening in fact, one can't help visually associating, the

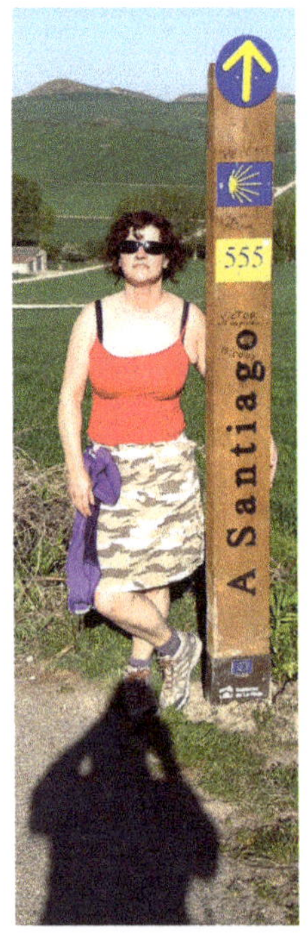

CHRIS FUSSEY-DARVER

hooded pointy hats with the horrors of the KKK, although I should add the symbolism is quite different. They took the lead down towards the Cathedral, with groups from their left feeding in at the appropriate point so that the various Parish fraternity Tableaux, depicting the *Via Crucis* Stations process in correct order.

The Tableaux were life size, and unlike other town and City parades were pushed along on draped wheeled platforms, and not the stout upholstered poles, shouldered by the faithful.

We met as arranged outside of Nicola's albergue. Over dinner we chatted and caught up with each other's news. A main topic of course, much to Nicola's amusement, was my encounter earlier with Caroline, She went over what I'd said, or tried to say, clarifying for Caroline why and how I'd come to have a room with three beds. Until then, I had rather selfishly been focusing on my own embarrassment, without realising it must have been just as, if not more so for Caroline.

I asked rhetorically, "Had Caroline really thought I'd asked her to sleep with me?" A pregnant pause ensued, then Nicola cut in, and enunciating in an exaggerated Scottish accent said "That you will never know!"

Whilst in the restaurant it had started raining, the first heavy rain I'd encountered along the Way. The two girls had a rest day planned for Sunday, but I was moving on. Caroline said she wanted to treat us to a posh breakfast. So we agreed to meet at eight the following morning.

Caroline was keen to see the late evening procession, that I'd watched earlier, and given the weather Nicola went back to her albergue, and I to what turned out to be a rather smelly room! Perhaps just as well Caroline did not share the room.

Sadly for Caroline, the parade was cancelled due to the weather.

We met outside the albergue and walked through to the Plaza Mayor, where I'd met Caroline the previous afternoon, and where as it happened, she had envisaged buying posh breakfasts. Steady light rain fell, and heavy cloud held back the morning light. The rain polished paving reflected the dark shadowy images of the buildings across the Square. There were no lights showing; everywhere was closed.

We followed Nicola to a places she thought may be open, but it was Easter Sunday, and there were no signs of life. I suggested to the girls that they take shelter whilst I checked out my new found Camino Amigo's bar. Fortunately it was open, and I jogged back to the girls. Not posh! but a memorable breakfast none the less. I never knew what a posh breakfast was, but hope to find out one day!

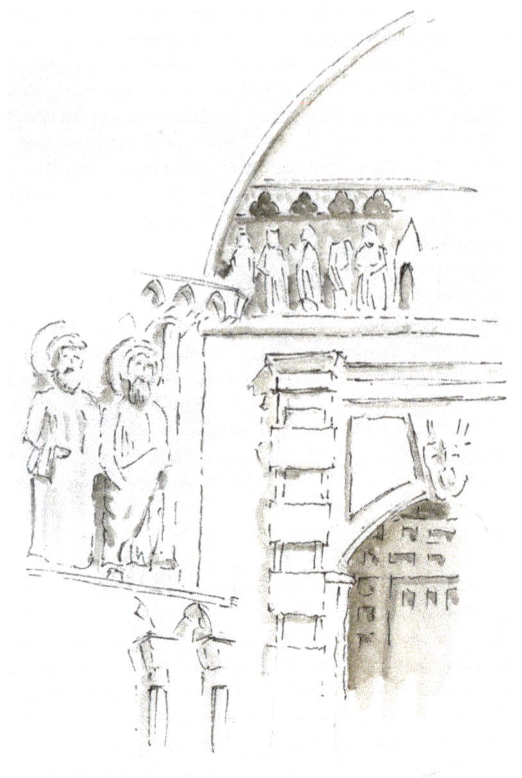

Burgos, 2015

I managed to miss the sign for the pleasanter River path into the centre, again! So found myself encircling the interminable Airport Perimeter Fence, which if anything seemed longer, and more boring, than before.

Villafría though, was just as I remembered, although this time I'd just missed a bus, and passed time with lunch in the Bar. I'd arrived on the Friday 1st May, *Fiesta del Trabajo*, a Public Holiday in Spain. Additionally Sunday was *Dia de la Madre*, or Mother's Day; so another busy weekend ahead. It explained the longer interval between buses than previously. When I arrived in Burgos, it was as I'd feared, busy with tourists and Pilgrims, and I spent a fruitless afternoon searching for somewhere to stay.

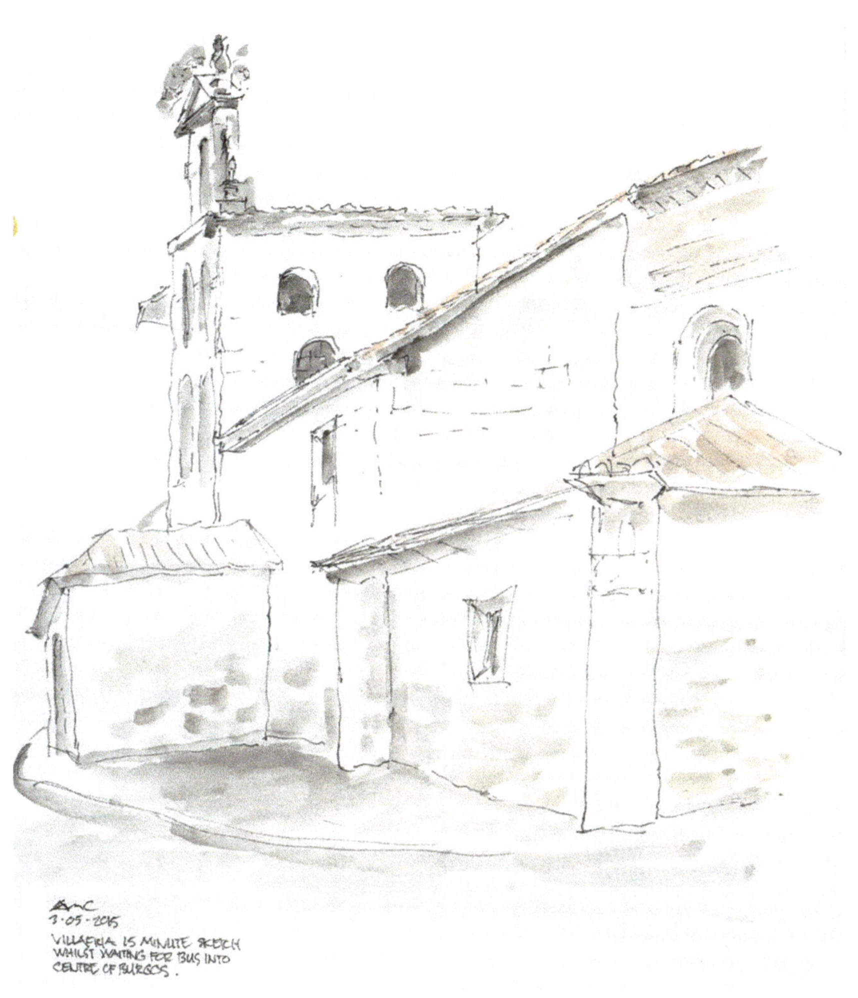

By late afternoon, I gave up, and caught the bus back to Villafría, I was not aware of an albergue there, but I'd noted a number of *Pensións* close to the bus stop, and where I rightly suspected, it would be less pressured.

Light rain fell the following morning, as I walked before breakfast to the church I had had tantalising glimpses of on my Way the previous year. The church, *Iglesia Parroquia de San Esteban Protomártir*, was interesting, It was the first of a number I would see further along the Way, where the Belfry Tower opened on three sides. According to a local Newspaper article, the church in its present form dated back to 1914-17. Apparently Basque influence is reflected in some of the interior detailing, as the architect originated from that region, although as usual, the church was closed, so I never gained access.

Opposite the church, conveniently situated for my purpose was a bus shelter, complete with bench, and after a brief walk around the church, I settled down, seated and in the dry. Fortunately, I had almost finished, when, as the shelter formed the Terminus, for the service into the Centre; a bus drew into the layby, completely obscuring my view. So the sketch was completed by a series of dashes out of the shelter, and along the pavement to where I could see, memorising the part of the sketch I was working on; and dashing back to record it on my pad in the dry.

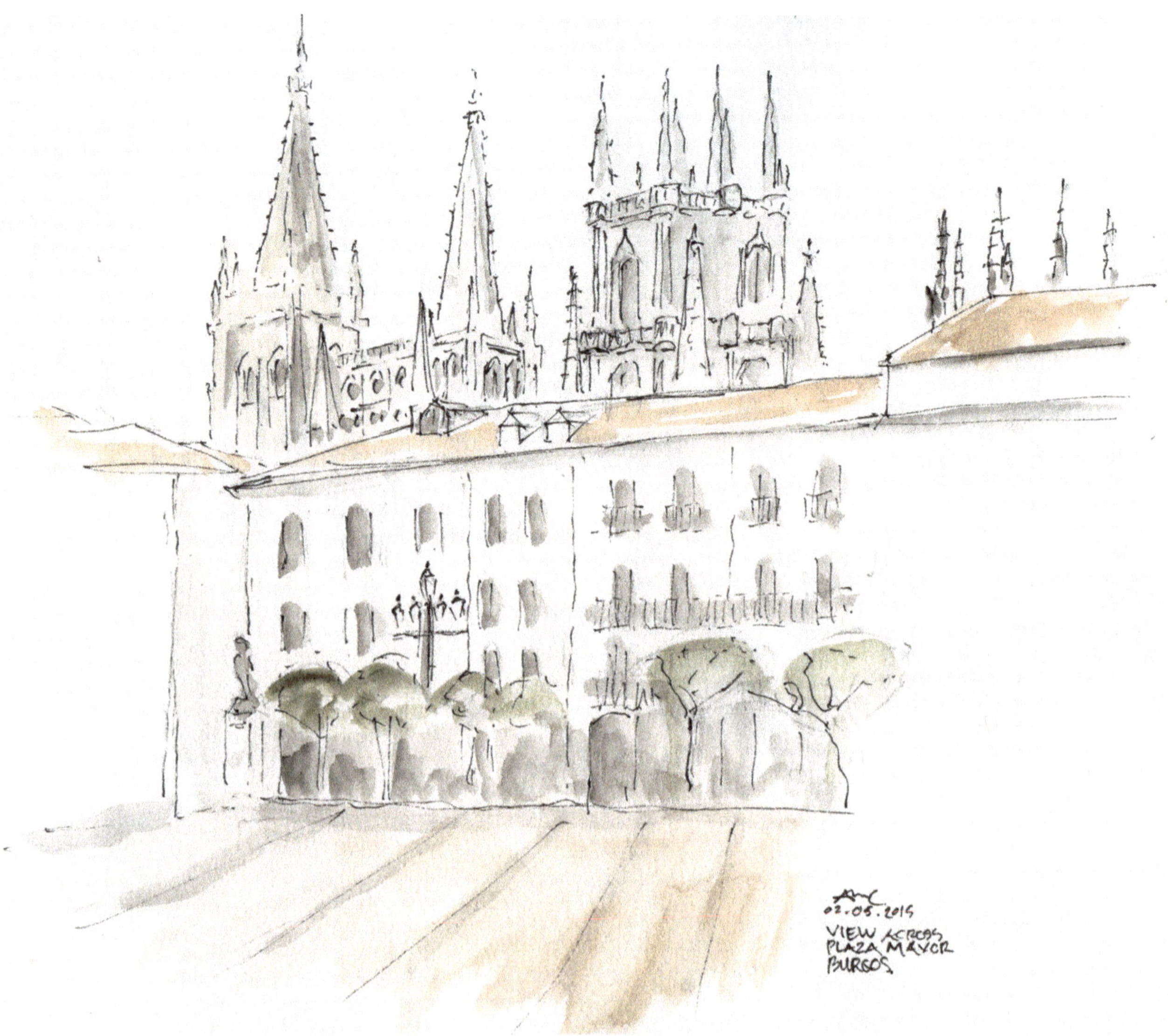

I did this several times, to the amusement of the Bus driver, until I'd done. I found the times of the buses, and had just over an hour to head back for breakfast, and catch the bus to the centre from outside the bar.

By the time I caught the bus the weather had cleared up, and I spent a pleasant half hour, or so, watching the world go by, on the journey through the suburbs.

I'm afraid, little things please little minds, as they say; and I was tickled by a huge storey height sign, on the first floor of an apartment block, above the Street level shops. The "T" shaped sign read, horizontally, "ABAD" and below vertically "DENTISTA" I chuckled and struggled to get to my camera, but the bus, and the moment, had passed.

I made a number of bus trips along that route, subsequently, always with my camera at the ready, but alas, I never managed to see it again. For those with like minds though, I found on my return, by Googling, it displayed a wonderful street view, complete with the said sign. So I hadn't been dreaming, as I was beginning to suspect!

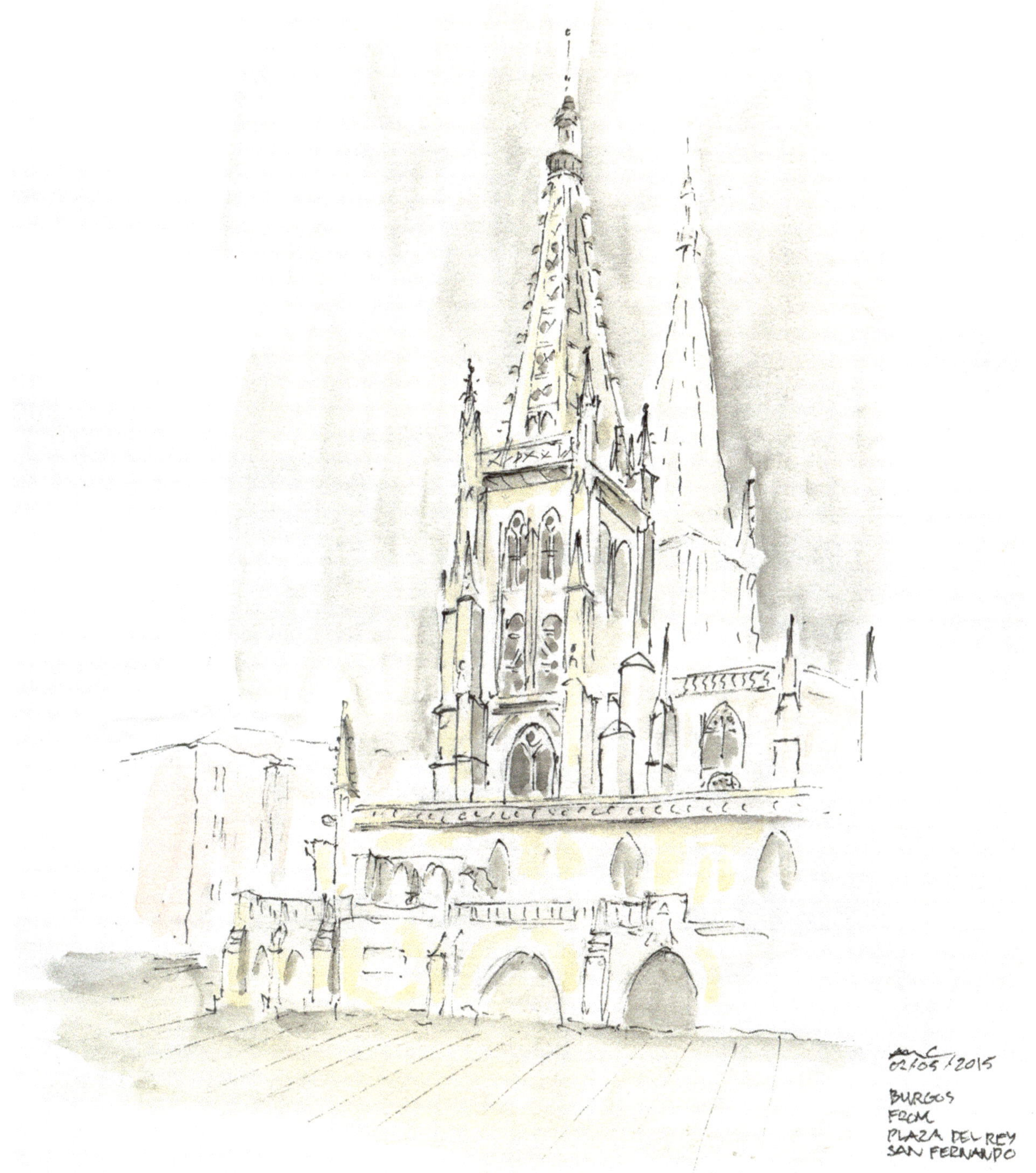

This year I had more time to wander around Burgos, and enjoy. In the afternoon I decided to look around the Cathedral interior. I was fascinated with the two storey cloister. It was the first I'd become aware of along the Way. Back home, Norwich, I believe is unique among English Cathedrals in having a two-storey cloister; but it's some years now since I visited, and I have no recollection of it. Having previously drawn the exterior of the octagonal Crossing Tower, I was keen to see the interior, and was not disappointed. Soaring high above the lantern windows, a wonderfully intricate *Mudéjar* openwork 8-Point Star dome, lends light, and airiness. The star is Christian symbolism for regeneration. The octagonal structure below the lantern, is skilfully reduced to the rectangular by four squinches, decorated with a scallop motif; transferring the weight to four massively stout circular piers.

The pier mass disguised and lightened with engaged columns. I think you may have gathered, I enjoyed!

I moved on to the equally, some would say more, stunning *Capilla del Condestable,* sited at the extreme East end, and forming a rather grand Apse. The plain walls are covered with armorials, but the real interest for me was again the Lantern above, an 8-Point Star whose nerves transfer the weight to engaged columns at the East end, with just two sqinches, again decorated with the scallop motif, and carrying the weight onto the wall separating the *Capilla* from the aisle *Trassagrario.*

My skills, such as they are, were not up to capturing sketches in the time I had, so I chose to sit on a stone bench in the North transept and drew the *Escalera Dorada.* My Gitlitz and Davidson Guide compares it favourably to Michelangelo's stair in the Laurentine Palace. I lack their erudition, nor have I seen it, but from illustrations I've looked at, there is a similarity; it has a balustrade, treads, risers; but then don't all staircases!

On Sunday morning, the weather was kinder, and allowed a quick scribble at the bus stop, without the need to take shelter. I spent a leisurely day drawing in Burgos. My Nephew and his lad were arriving late afternoon, joining me for a few days, as they had hoped to do, but sadly had to cancel in 2014. I had had my two nights in the comfort of a small Pension in Villafria, and needed to find an albergue for the three of us for Sunday night.

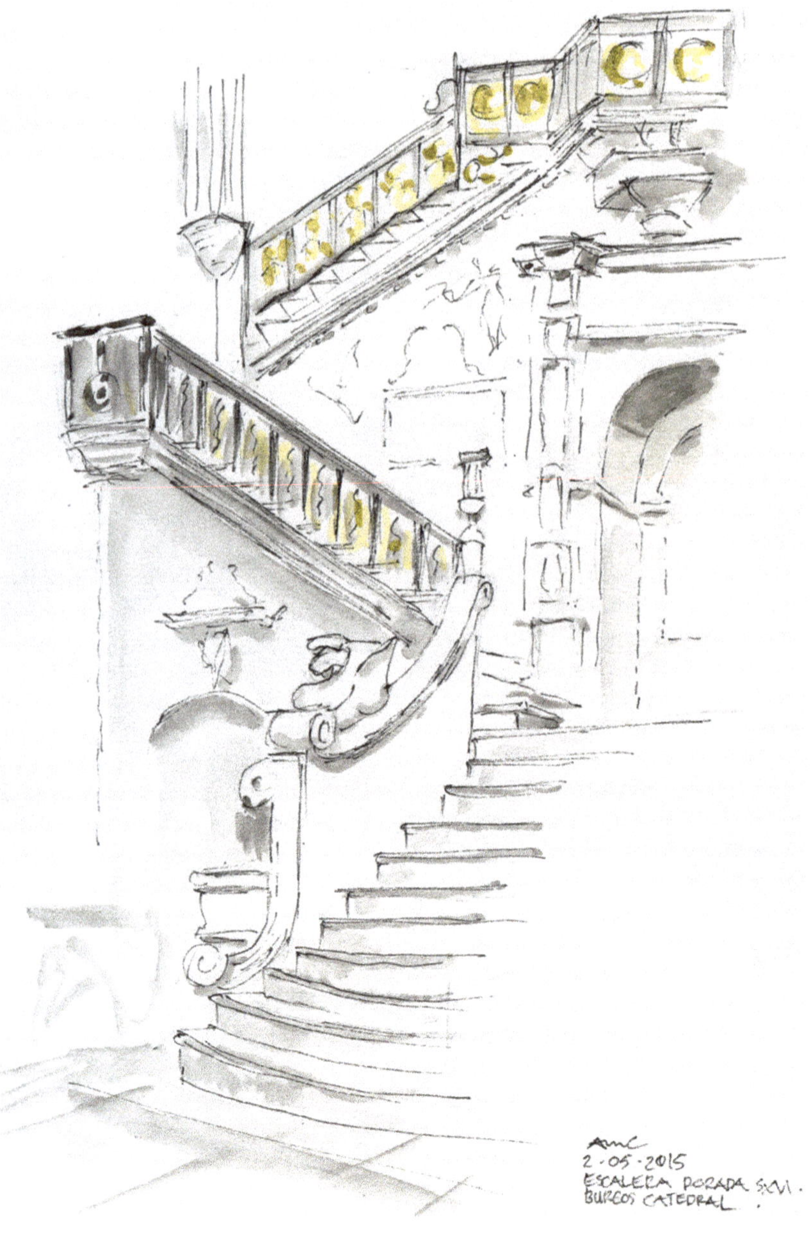

I tried the Municipal, where I'd stayed last year, explained my Nephew wouldn't arrive till five in the afternoon, and asked the hospitalero if as reservations were not accepted, was it likely there would still be room at that hour. He checked his logs from the previous few days, and showed me it had been *completo* before that time.

Next on to where Nicola had stayed, Divina Pastora, the lovely hospitalera kindly booked us in, reserving three adjacent bunks.

Cheered, I walked back towards the bus station, deciding to find something to draw, close by. I stopped on the bridge, Puente de Santa Maria, and whilst drawing had a long and interesting chat with a local lady artist.

Shortly afterwards I got a call from Richard, and went off to meet them. This would be their first experience of an albergue, so I was glad that it was small, with limited but adequate facilities The Hospitalera too was lovely, an over used word I know, but she was! In the morning she sat at the bottom of the stair, leading from the dorm to her private space and we were gently awakened by her sweet singing to her guitar accompaniment, such a splendid way to start a day.

Richard, nor Jack, are regular walkers, so it gave me great pleasure and pride that they should choose to join me. We did though think it prudent to arrange bag transport, for the first day, at least.

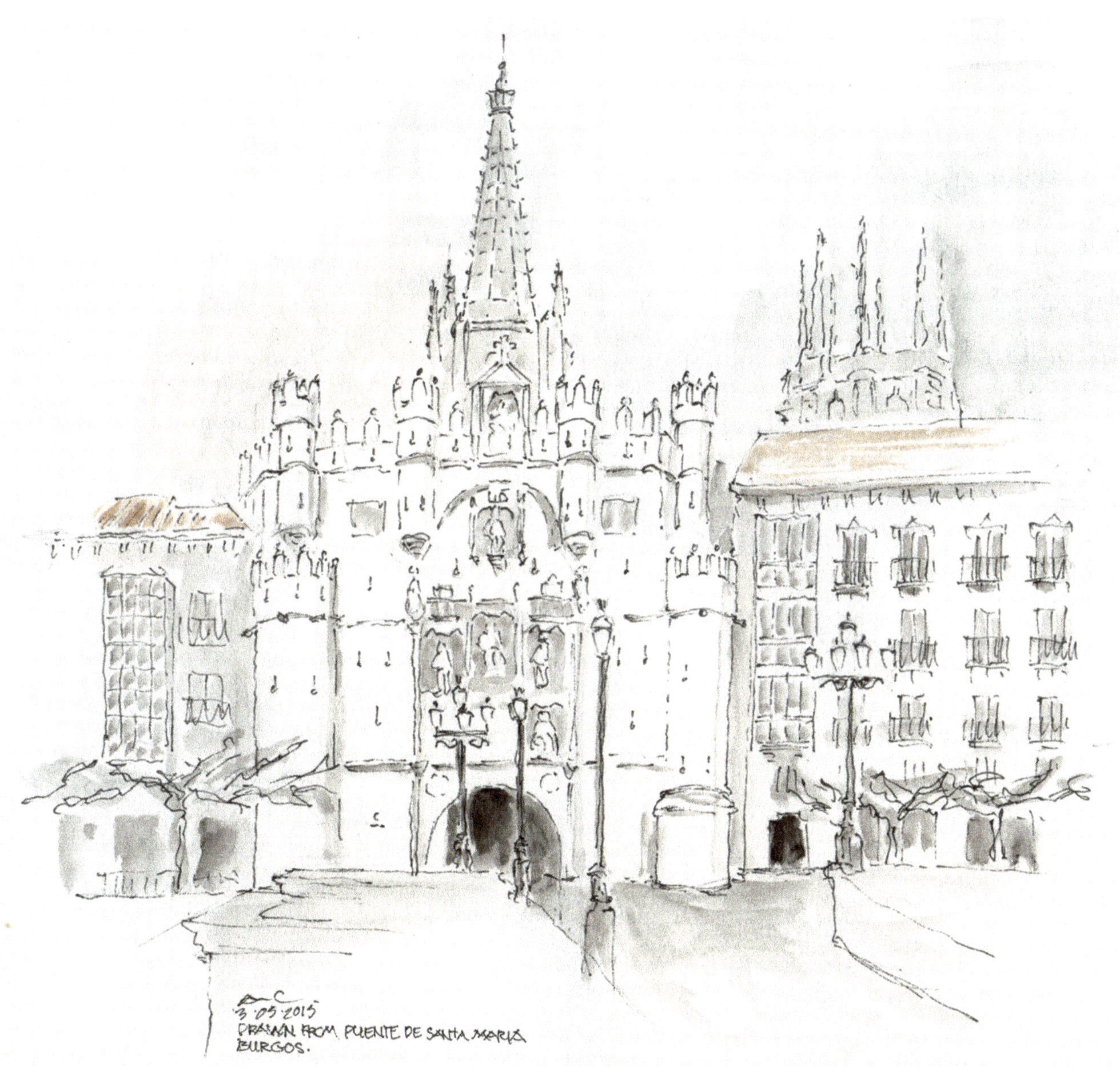

Leaving Burgos

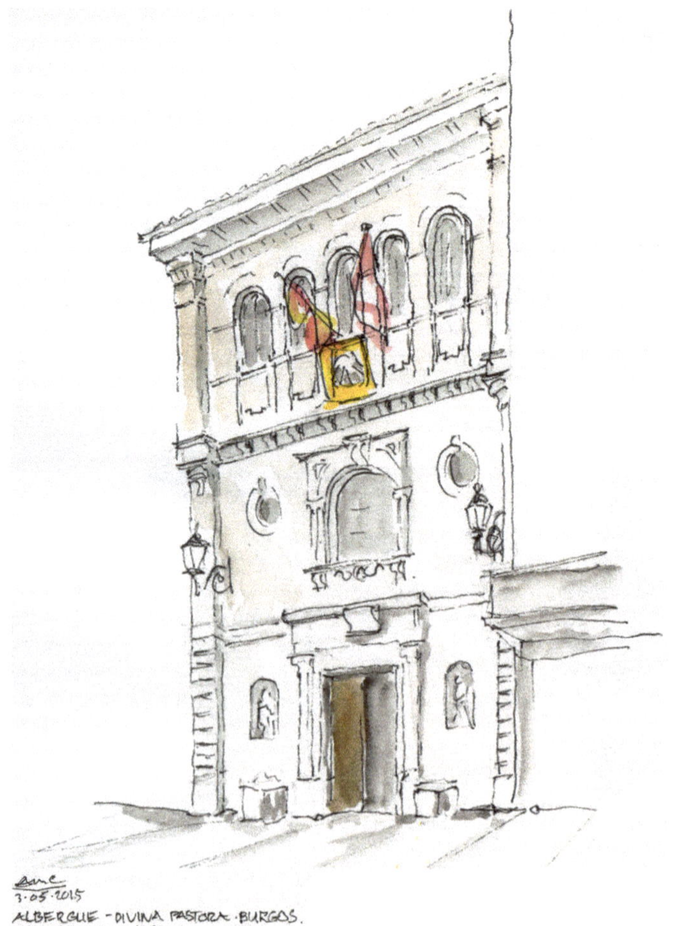

After our 'Posh' breakfast, we said our goodbyes. Nicola was meeting a friend, and Caroline was hoping to get some rest, and then watch the Easter Morning parade. Sadly, I heard that this too was cancelled, due to rain.

I went back to the Hotel, collected my things, and left. The light rain had stopped as I reached the outer suburbs. On the edge of Villabilla I stopped, checking the waymark. Just as I spotted it, and made to make off in the direction indicated, I was virtually kidnapped by a local man on his morning walk. "No NO" he said, taking my arm. I just about caught the gist of his Spanish, vehemently maintaining his way was better, shorter.

I noticed, glancing back over my shoulder, that a guy I'd recently walked by calling cheerily *"Buen Camino"* and eliciting no response, had followed the waymark. I'm not certain if it was shorter, but at one stage our path looked down along a lengthy stretch of the Way, and I could see Pilgrims squelching through ankle deep mud. The guy wished me well, and left me as we reached Tardajos.

The albergue at Hornillos was complete. The village is virtually just one street, along the Way, and I had not passed any other accommodation. There was just one bar, and that was closed. According to my guide book, which admittedly is a few years old, the next albergue was possibly 11Km further on in Hontanos, so having walked nearly 19 Km the unexpected extension was met with less than enthusiasm.

In 2015, with my Nephew and his Son, we were more fortunate. There were bunks available, and although we had to await the second sitting for dinner at the bar across the street, we had a fine meal. We shared a table with an eighty year old American guy, a sometime Catholic Priest who at retirement decided to walk the Camino. This was his twelfth consecutive Camino. Fantastic!

He told a rather poignant story. Three or four Caminos back, he had come across a guy along the Way, and walked briefly with him. As they came to a *fuente*, he turned to fill his water bottle, and as he did so heard a thud. He looked around to see the guy had collapsed, and sadly died.

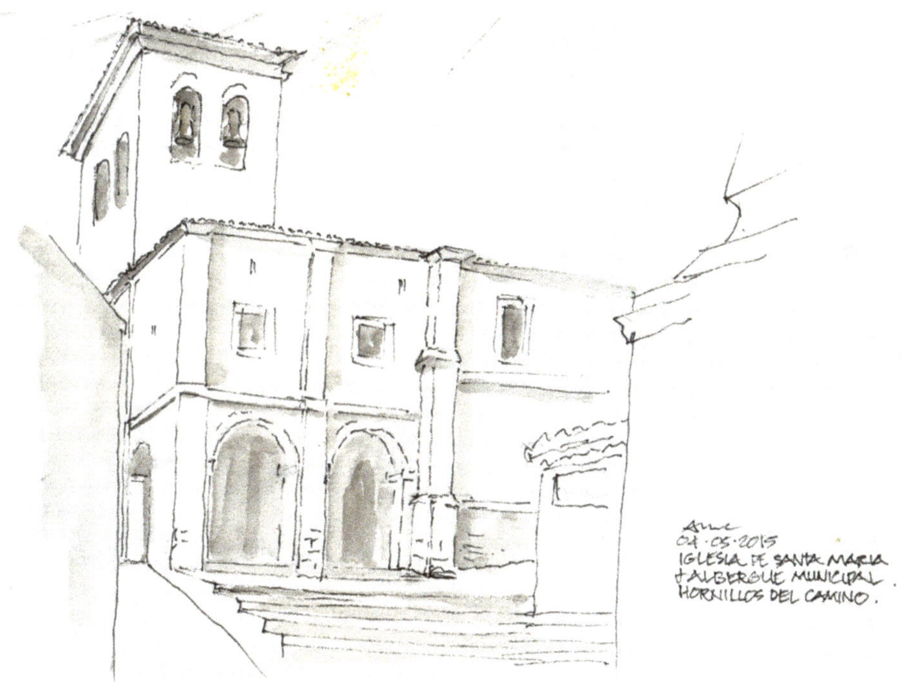

He had only known of the guy's first name, so this year was pleased to have found a recently erected memorial at the spot where he had died, so now had his full details.

With my usual doubtful taste, I commented that if one is to keel over along the Way, who better to be with, than a Catholic Priest! He smiled, "No" he said, he no longer held a Licence.

With no accommodation to be had I walked out of Hornillos without a spring in my step, and felt grateful for any distance the Tardajos guy had saved me. I was then overjoyed, when on reaching San Bol, contrary to my out of date Guide, to find a fully functioning albergue in a pleasant peaceful setting.

It only has twelve beds, and I was the eleventh. The only available bunk was an upper, and since the bunks had no ladder attached I was doubtful that I could manage. I explained to the lady hospitalera and she disappeared onto the Terrace, returning with a French lady of about forty, who volunteered to switch bunks, assuring me it was no problem and demonstrated fine athleticism by hoisting herself onto the top bunk, as if gravity did not exist.

Sharing a splendid communal dinner in the evening, by chance I sat next to her at huge

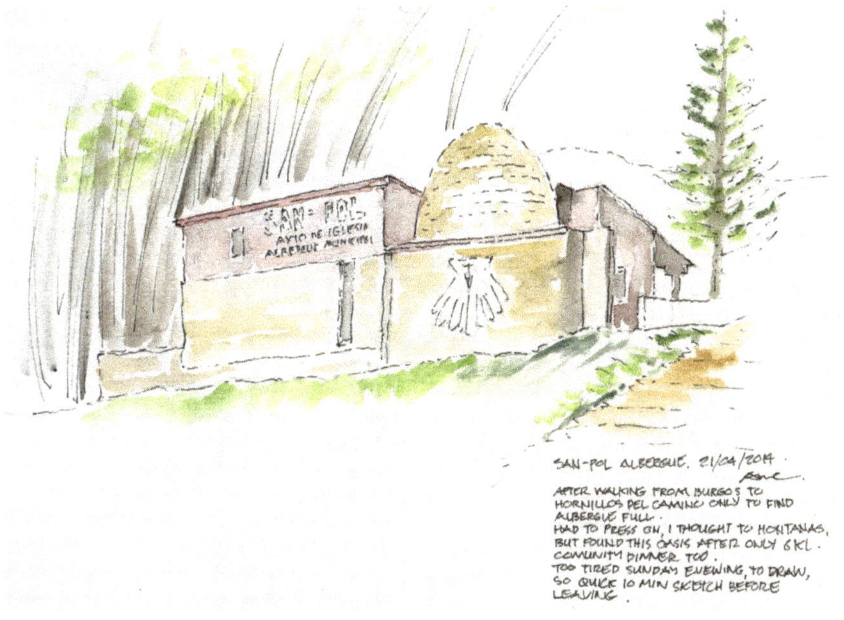

round table set under the dome. I greeted her with the words "My hero!" she shrugged cocking her head to one side replied in English, "No! Just a woman"

On my other hand, sat the guy I had passed, just before being kidnapped, not uttering a word, to me, or anyone else. To compound my embarrassment at taking the French ladies' bed, I noticed the silent Pilgrim across the dorm, he had taken the last available top bunk. He was about my age, although stiffer, and slower, but obviously much brighter than me, as I noticed him descending from his bunk, via a chair he had strategically placed below!

I was last to leave after breakfast. The hospitalera was taking the laundry to Hontanas, and probably recalling our conversation of last evening, offered me a lift. I declined, with thanks, and did a ten minute scribble before setting out.

I recall that section of the Way, from San Bol, to Hontanas, it was memorable in that it had extremely claggy ankle deep mud. I pitied a cyclist I passed, it was impossible to ride, so was carrying his bike. He had though attempted riding, as wheels, chain, and gear mech, were well and truly gunged up.

A little further on I came upon an elderly American lady, precariously balancing on one leg, with the assistance of a pole, and attempting to knock mud of her boot. She commented that her boots had become just too heavy to walk with the thick coating of clinging claggy mud.

Hontanas takes one by surprise, a pleasant surprise. As the path starts to descend, suddenly the whole village comes into view, nestled in the little river valley, a view that stayed with me and was able to capture in 2015.

As I sat enjoying coffee, outside the village albergue, I saw the American lady approaching. I looked, and looked again incredulously. Her boots were pristine! Shiny, not a trace of mud, nor speck of dust "had she met a shoeshine boy" I asked. I sang with the Alaskan guy and Justin his Son *"Come with me follow, down the Camino, and there we will wallow in glorious mud!*

In the same bar, my Nephew and his lad, rested whilst I made a quick scribble up the hill. The church tower, *Iglesia de Hontanas,* scaffolded and netted; a foretaste of Santiago, although yellow netting here and not blue. Perhaps as in medieval painting when Lapis lazuli was the pigment, blue remains for the very special.

We didn't have mud this time, but we all struggled against a strong headwind, as we crossed the open *Mesita.*

Castrojeriz

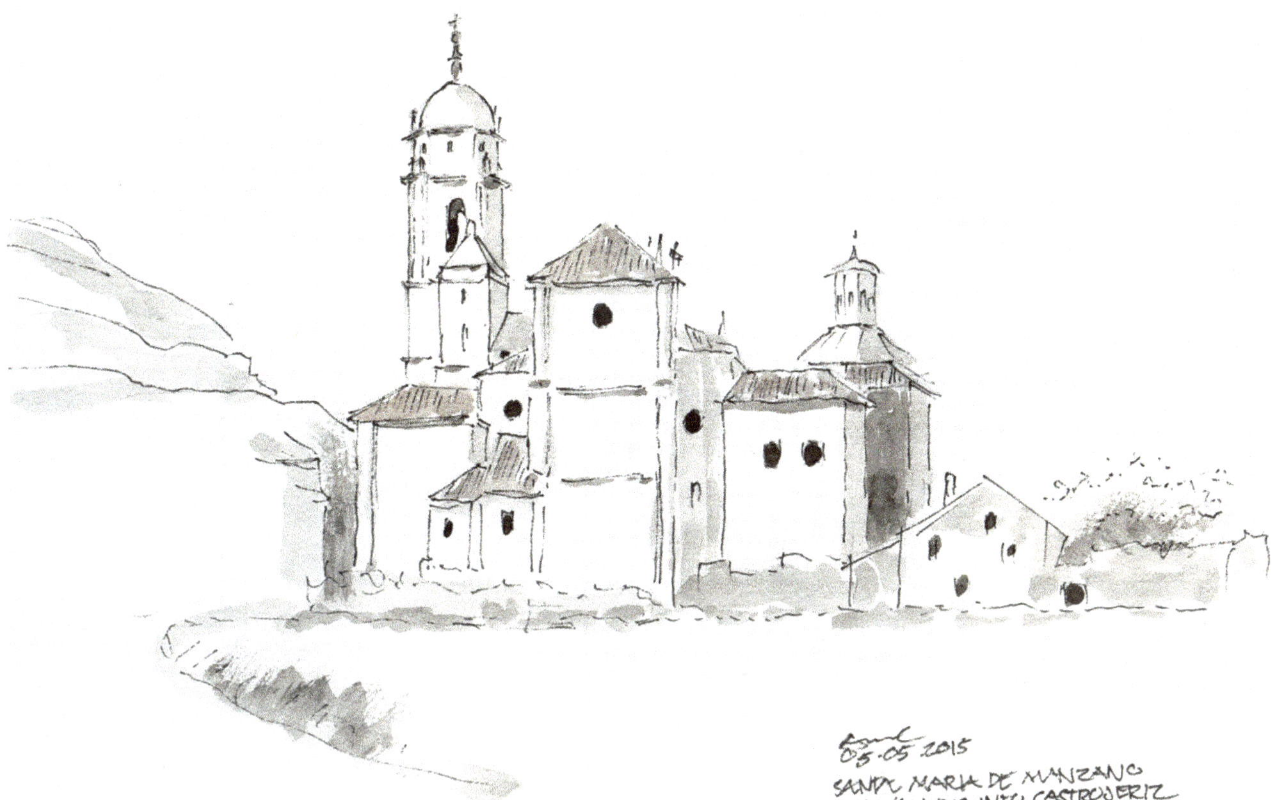

As one passes through the ruined arches of the *Monasterio de San Antón*, clears the old farm buildings adjacent to the road, Castrojeriz comes into view. Or rather the hill on which the remains of the castle sit. Soon a bend in the road to the right, reveals a long straight road, with the silhouette of the *Iglesia de Santa Maria del Manzano*, at the end of it. I believe anyone who has walked the Camino, will recall this view; as one walks, and minutes pass, but the church, obstinately refuses to get any closer!

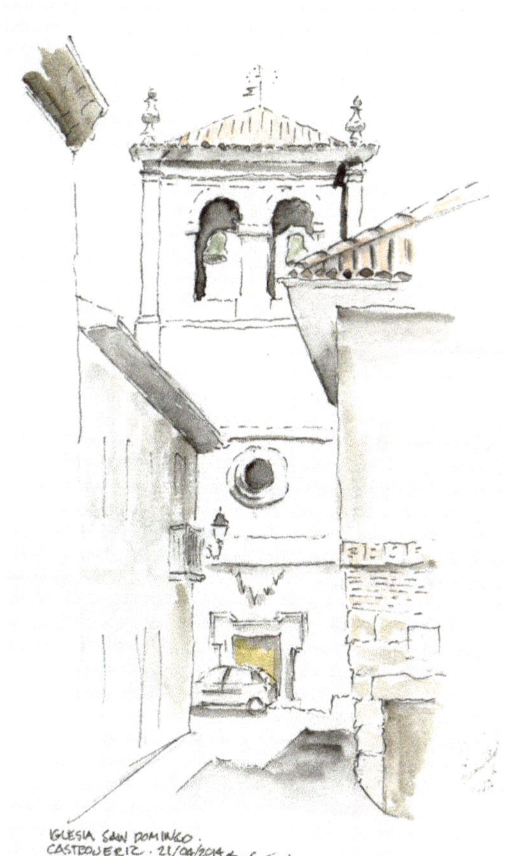

I knew from my guide book, the plan of Castrojeriz describes contoured arcs, beneath the castle ruins on the hill. The two Church buildings of interest are situated at either end of the arc. I had planned to sketch one or the other, and consequently booked into an albergue more or less in the centre, opposite the redundant church of *San Domingo.*

I ventured out of the alburgue to explore, and had not gone more than 10m when, aaagh! I was hit with an excruciating pain in my left shin. I was to find out later, it was tendonitis, or shin splints. Very painful, I stood with the weight on my right, for a while,

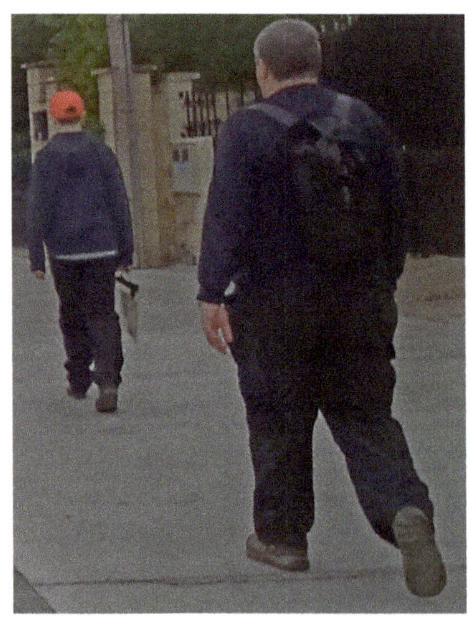
Jack leads the Way!

before limping a few metres to a little Square. There I sat on a chair outside the closed bar, and drew, probably the most boring drawing in my pad; as I had no chance of reaching either end of the Village.

I had the luxury of a single bed, in a spacious airy dorm, shared with just one couple. Never having experienced tendonitis before, I didn't know if I would need to rest, or if I could continue. I lay awake worrying that this might be the end of my Camino.

In the morning I limped up to the little Square where I'd sat drawing the day before. The bar was now open, a wonderfully scruffy no-nonsense Spanish bar. The morning sun had driven out my nightmares. I thought, well if Caroline can do it, then so can I. She was my inspiration, as I limped through the day, checking at the entry of each village, for a *Farmacia* symbol on the sign board. I found none, until I'd painfully limped the 25Km to Fromista.

In 2015 we had again sent the bags on, which was just as well as we struggled against energy sapping headwind as we crossed the open *mesita*. My younger companions were particularly affected; their lack of walking experience began to show. When we reached Castrojeriz our bags had been delivered to the Municipal albergue, but it was *completo.*

The hospitalero mentioned another albergue that didn't open until three-o-clock. I left the lads resting, whilst I looked for it, meeting and helping three German ladies who were also trying to locate it. A simply splendid albergue, I am not sure whether permanent house rules, or just a quirk of the volunteer hospitaleros resident for that period; but they controlled and imposed lights out at ten, and not before. And really sensibly from my view, they controlled, and did not allow any rising, or disturbance until seven in the morning. Glad to say, no one demurred.

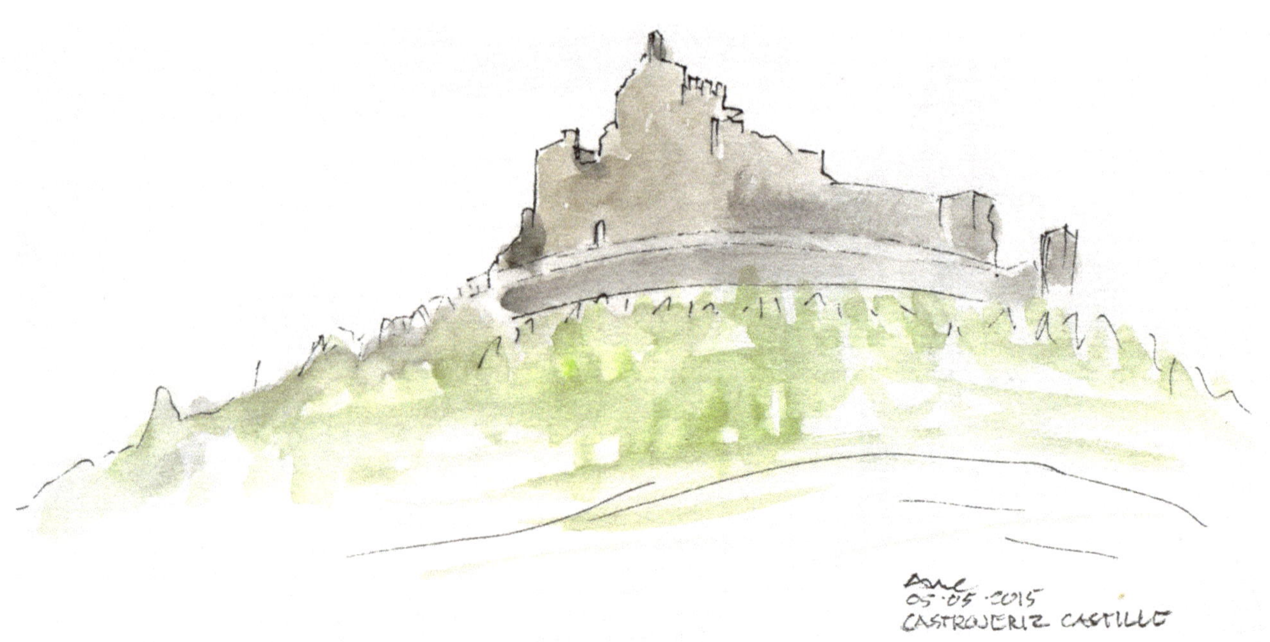

Itero de la Vega

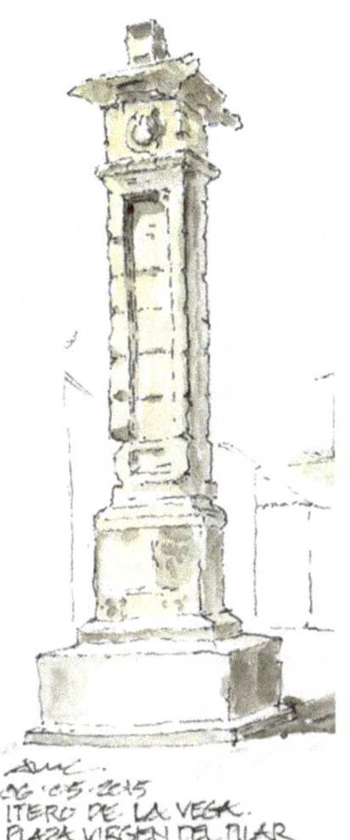

After what had been a hard day's walk into Castrojeriz, we determined on a shorter section as we left. We arrived relatively early to a pleasant sunny Itero de la Vega after just 11Km. Although it did include the breath catching stiff climb up the *Alto Mostelares* with glorious views, over the plane and to the ever reducing Castrojeriz beyond. We stayed at the Hostal Fitero, privately run, but the family were very kind and helpful.

Richard and Jack enjoyed a leisurely afternoon in the sunshine, on the albergue's garden terrace, where I guess Richard lubricated his painful knees with the odd beer, or two! And I mooched about the village and managed the odd scribble.

In the morning, they had both concluded that sadly, it was time for them to quit. Richard was concerned not to inflict permanent damage, by continuing. My basic Spanish helped to arrange a taxi to take them to the Railway Station in Fromista, from where they could travel on to Bilbao and a flight home.

It was sad that they had left earlier than we had hoped, but I enjoyed their company for the three days, and felt, and still feel privileged that they chose to walk with me.

I waved their taxi off at the cross-roads, and continued the relatively short walk into Fromista, which gave me the time to draw, unlike previously.

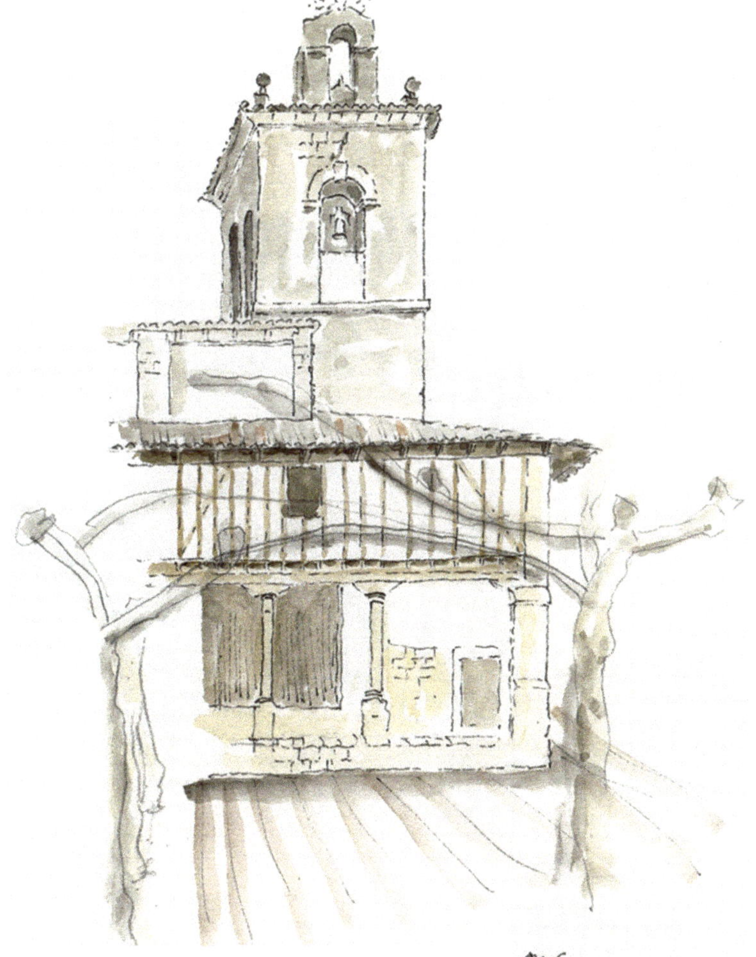

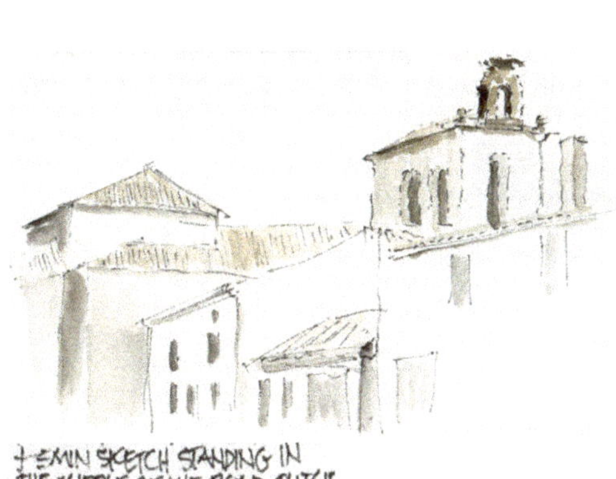

To Frómista

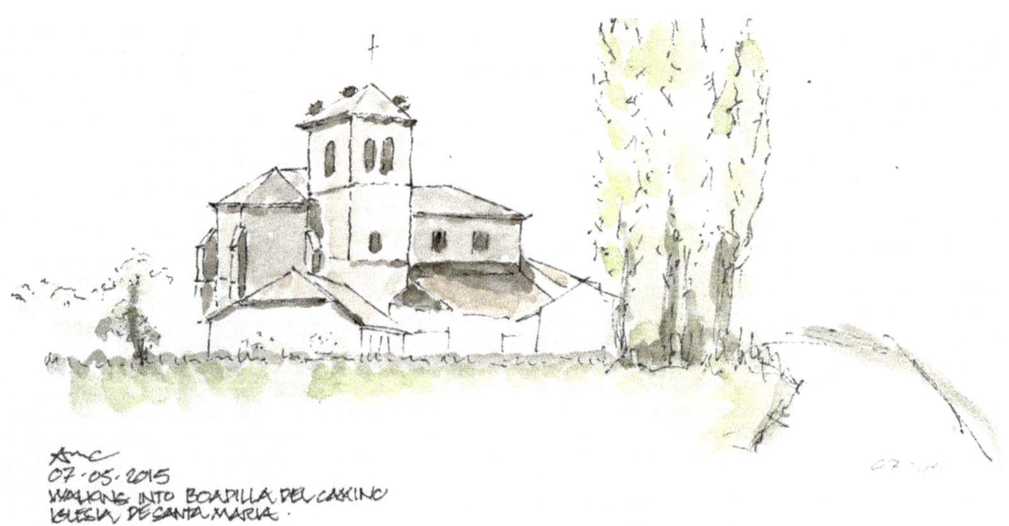

I rested in the albergue bar, sympathizing with a young lad, who was enduring an unwanted private arithmetic lesson. The young woman teacher patiently and persistently repeated non-understood explanations. From my vantage point, I could see the teacher, her concentration on the page, unaware that for most of the time, the lad's attention was elsewhere.

This little diversion, helped me forget for the moment the pain, and so I slowly limped into the Town Centre, looking for a Pharmacy. I reached the crossroads; I could only see one guy to ask for directions. He was diagonally opposite, and appeared to be coming my way, but on the other side of the road. The lights were against me, but hoping any traffic would take pity my hobbling gait, I crossed, attempting to cut him off. I just failed, but called out to him, and he kindly turned and walked back to me. I made an effort to meet him half way, so I think he was almost anticipating the question. He took me back to the junction, and pointed down the street. There, roughly 100m away was a flashing green *Farmacia* sign. I thanked him, feeling like a desert traveller who had stumbled on an oasis.

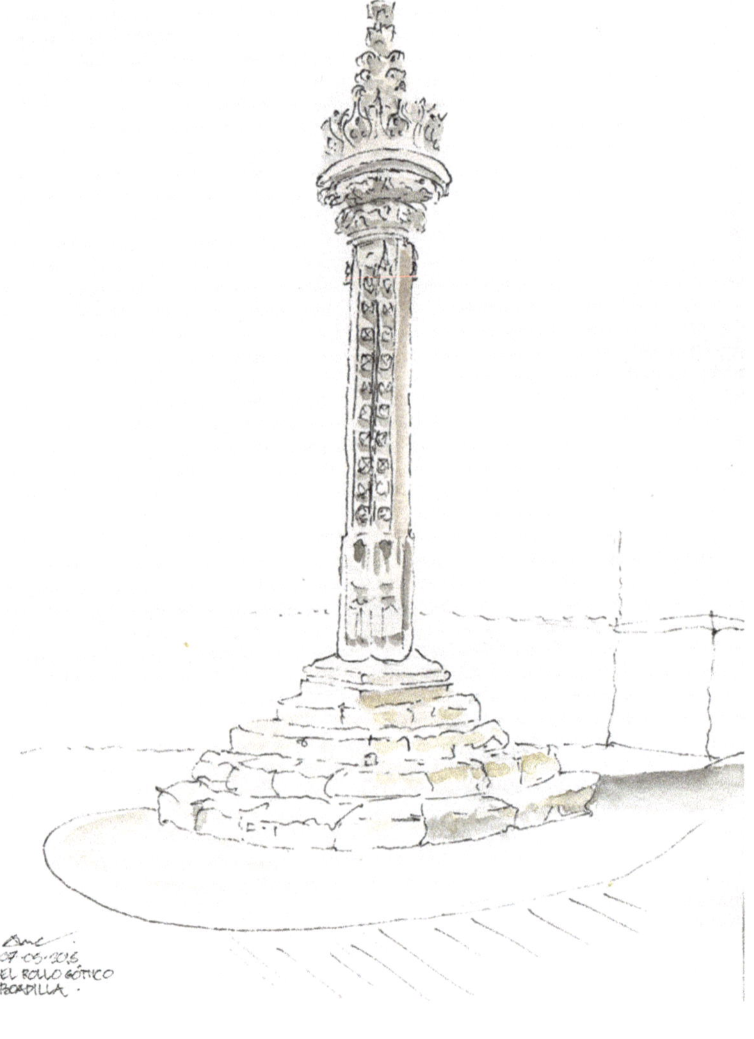

If it's possible to have a spring in ones limp, I had it. I waited for the pharmacist as he served a couple ladies. My turn, and in tortured

Spanish I set about seeking advice. He simply replied that his partner had English, and continued to attend to others who had entered.

In between each customer he went outside, looking up and down. Finally he disappeared for two to three minutes, muttering something I didn't catch as he returned. At last, another few minutes passed and his partner appeared.

He quickly diagnosed tendonitis, recommended and sold an elasticated tube, and an organic ointment, which he proudly explained he made up himself.

I neither had time nor energy to explore and draw, but did so in 2015, the wonderful Romanesque *Iglesia San Martin* on a balmy sunny evening, and *Iglesia San Pedro* leant on a support column of the arcade building opposite, before breakfast on a cold blustery morning.

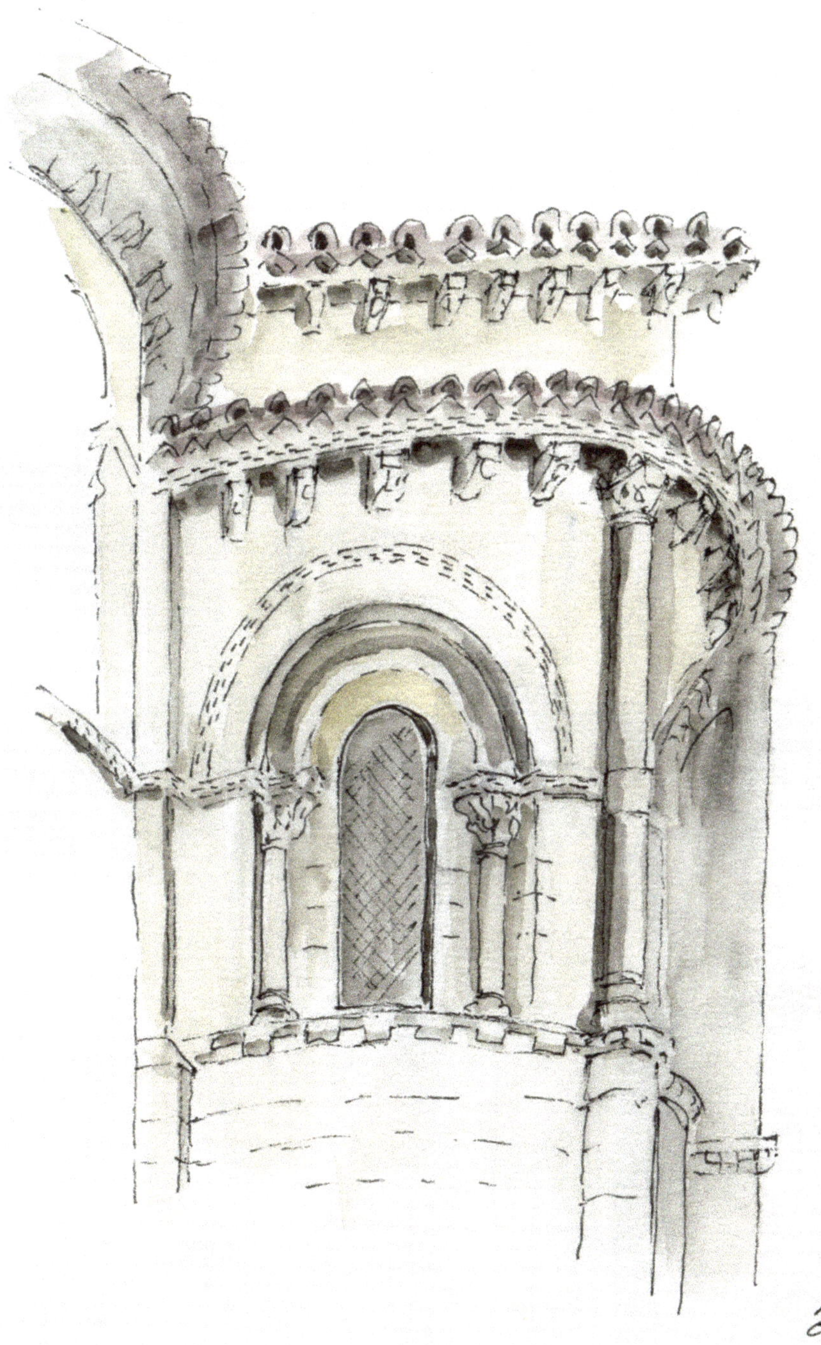

Leaving Frómista

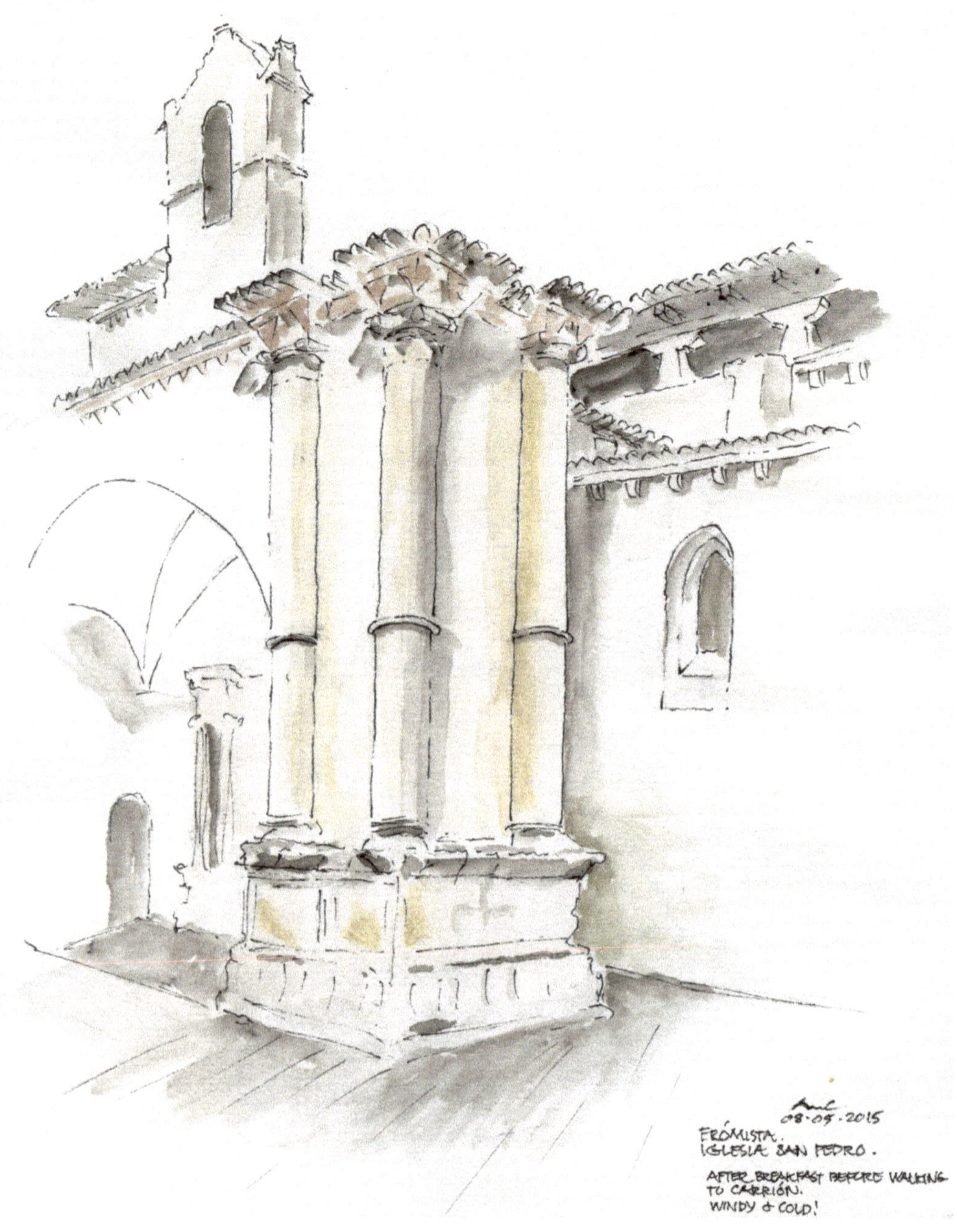

Smelling of wintergreen, my leg supported by my new elasticated tube, I walked tentatively from the alburgue. I planned just to walk as far as I felt able. After 7 or 8 Km I rested in the little square adjacent to the church in Revenga de Campos. The church, closed! but brought a smile, the tower had an asymmetrically sited clock, fixed I suspect for the convenience of the fitter, with scant heed for aesthetics. He had done a similar fine job earlier along the Way at Población de Campos. Additionally, like a stopped clock, which is correct twice a day, the Tower is Seasonal once a year, over the Christmas period! Fixed below one belfry window a forlorn Christmas tree decoration, and straddling the two belfry windows a shooting star with Feliz Festiva slung beneath. I imagine they are illuminated at Christmas, although, which one?

Villasirga (Villacázar de Sirga)

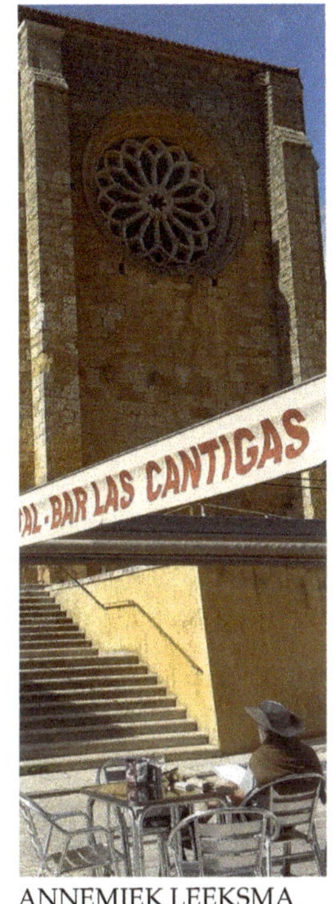

ANNEMIEK LEEKSMA

In 2014 I walked from Frómista towards Carrión de los Condes and because I was nursing raw shin splints I opted for the more straight forward and slightly shorter if soulless path, or *senda* that runs for most of the distance alongside the straight main road.

At Villasirga, I lunched on the bar terrace with my eyes glued on the *Iglesia Santa Maria la Blanca.* It's a wonderful church and a favourite of mine. I was torn, should I stop and draw or press on, and at least maintain my schedule whilst able. I chose the latter, but this was high on my wish list in 2015.

I did just that, sat at one of the same bar tables. Whilst I was drawing a lady spoke to me, interested in the drawing; she came back a little later as I'd almost finished, and remarked at the progress in so short a time. I jokingly responded that it was easy when not interrupted. Oh dear, I hope she did not think I was serious, as it was said and meant purely jokingly. We did dine together later though, as she was at the same albergue. She had unbeknownst to me, taken photos, and sent me copies on her return.

I next saw Ann Marie in El Burgo Ranero, not feeling too well.

With two working legs in 2015 on reaching Población after leaving Frómista I followed the more pleasant river route stopping briefly to sketch the *Ermita Virgen del Rio* before entering Villasirga.

Sitting on the bar terrace looking up into the enormous porch at the two tiered frieze. It is simply awesome and one of my favourites of the Camino.

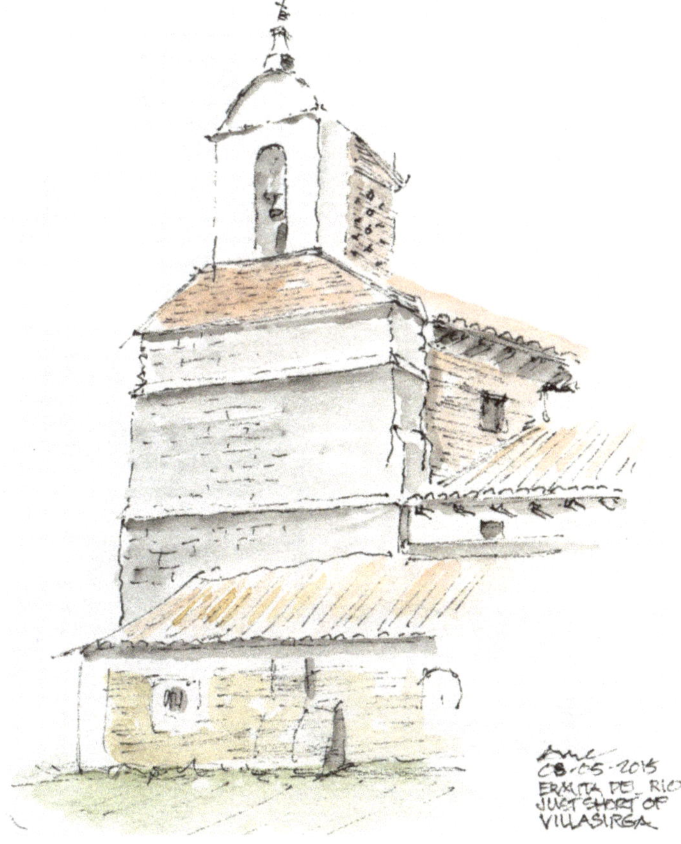

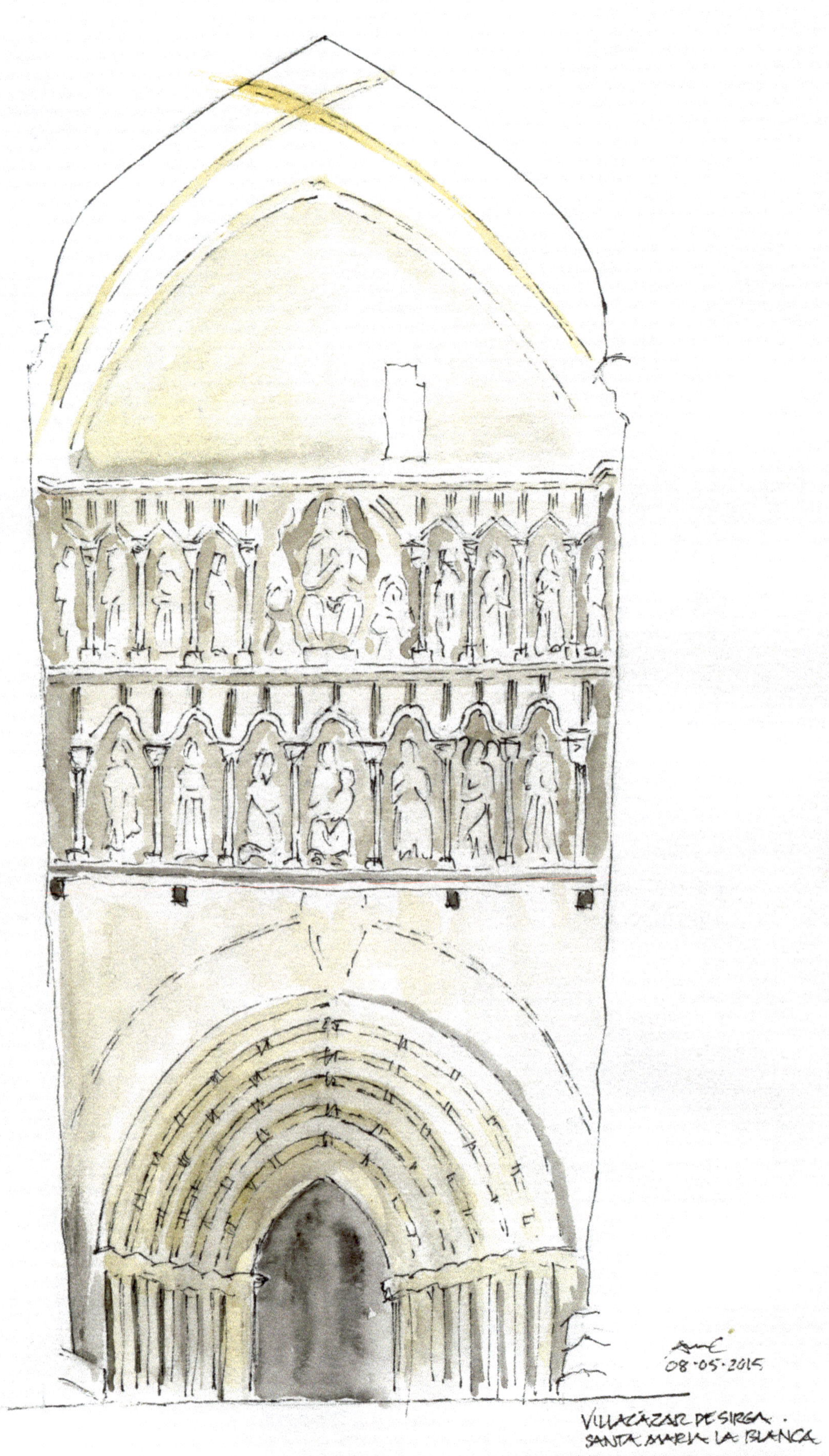
08·05·2015
VILLACÁZAR DE SIRGA ·
SANTA MARIA LA BLANCA

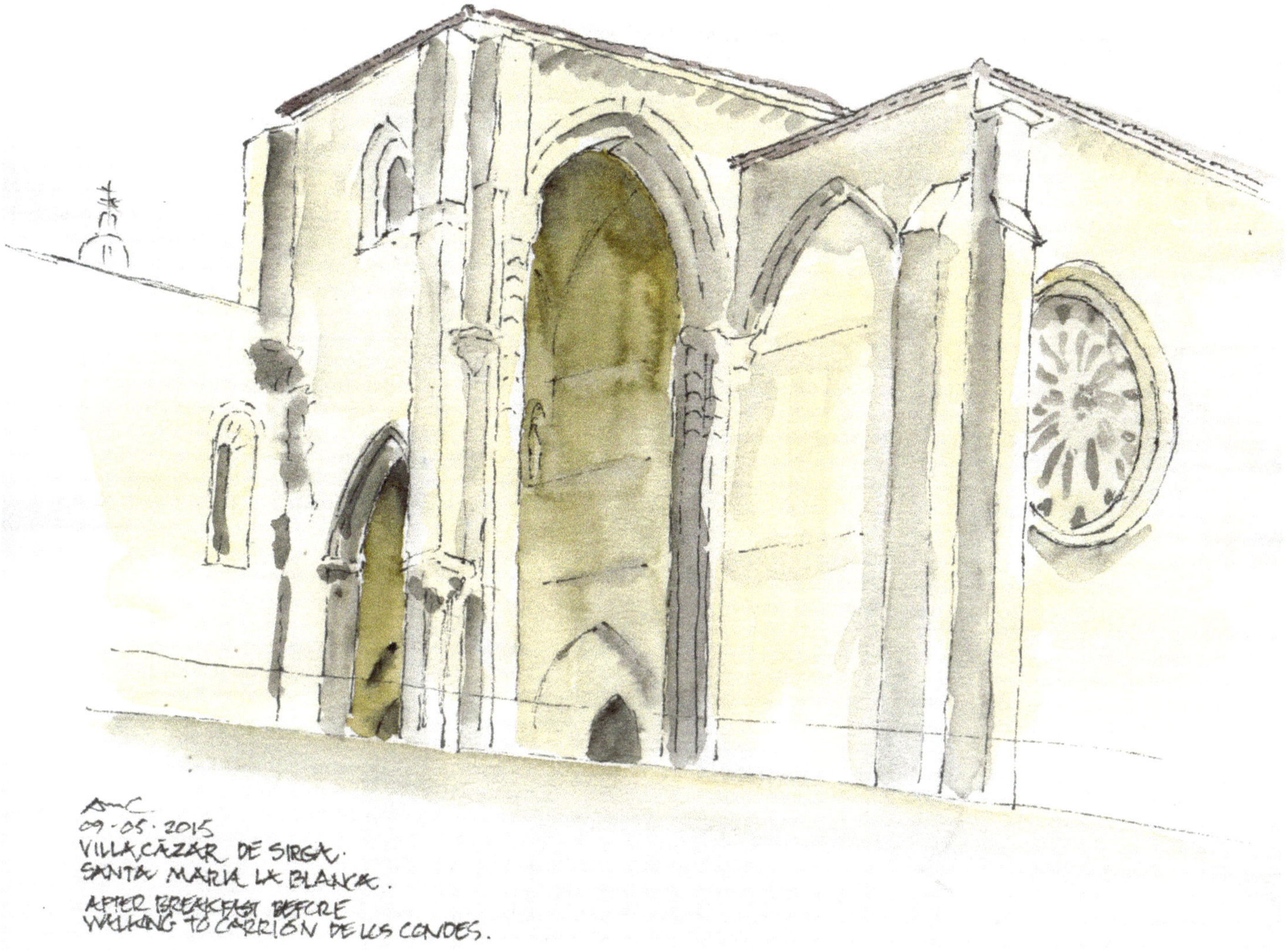

AMC.
09-05-2015
VILLACÁZAR DE SIRGA.
SANTA MARIA LA BLANCA.
AFTER BREAKFAST BEFORE
WALKING TO CARRIÓN DE LOS CONDES.

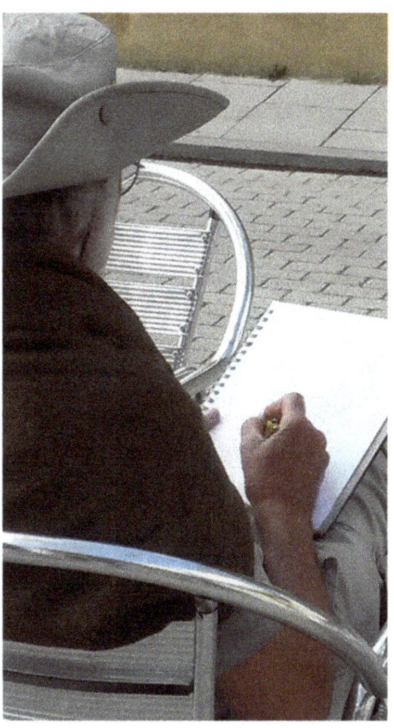

ANNEMIEK LEEKSMA

Carrión de los Condes

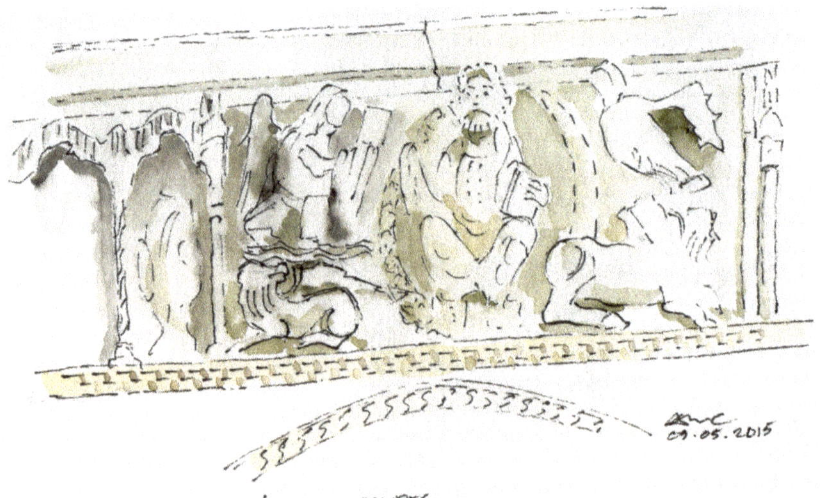

CARRIÓN DE LOS CONDES
PART FACADE OF THE CHURCH OF SANTIAGO

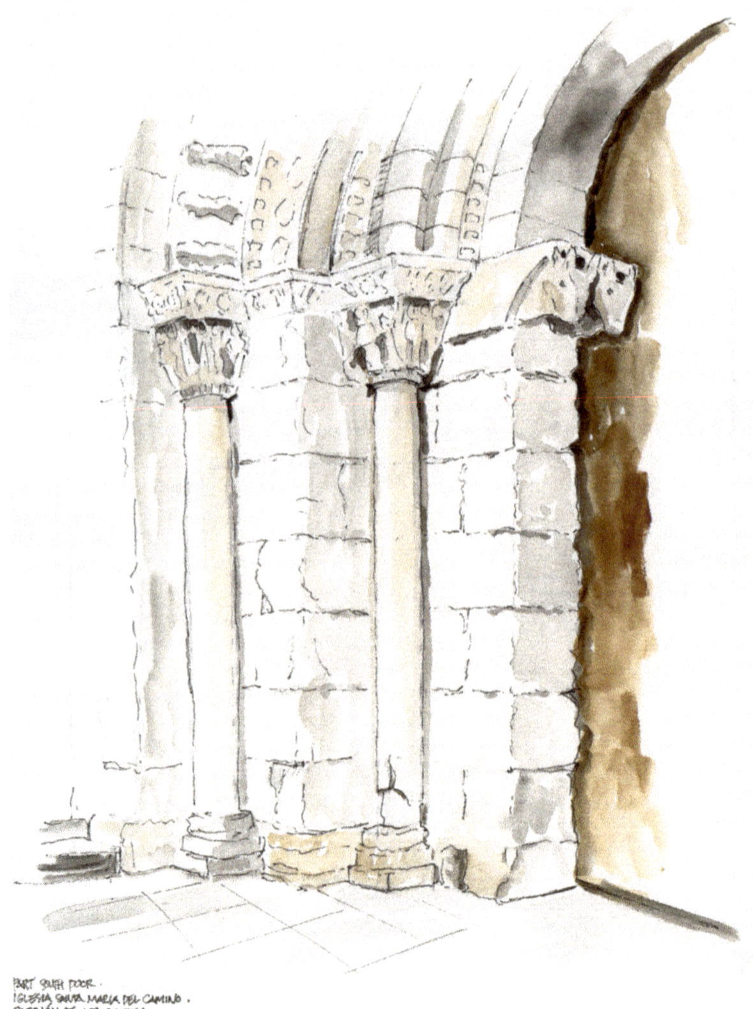

PART SOUTH DOOR.
IGLESIA SANTA MARIA DEL CAMINO.
CARRIÓN DE LOS CONDES.
28/04/2014.

I was met at the crossroads by two competing ladies selling rooms in small Pensions. I declined as I'd an albergue, 'Espiritu Santo' in mind, from notes off the Eroski site. I initially found some directions, but then I must have missed them. Looking around for clues, it must have been obvious I was lost, and an old gentleman called, and waved his walking stick in the direction he was walking. I walked with him a little way, he, still on the opposite side of the road, and then he pointed to neat two storey building, set back behind railings on a brick plinth. He then gestured at the gate, where I hesitated, as it didn't look much like an albergue to me; causing him to repeatedly point toward the imposing entrance door.

I thanked him, still not convinced, waited, plucked up courage and rang the bell. Moments later the door opened, and I was ushered into the beautifully polished Hallway, by a Sister. She was short, not many years my junior, pleasant and welcoming, although she had minimal English.

I was shown into an office, where she booked me in. Afterwards she stood and beckoned me to follow, whilst picking up some of my kit. We crossed a yard, and climbed a metal fire escape stair to a spacious first floor corridor, off which lead on one side the facilities and dorms on the other. All single beds, luxury

Whilst drawing, a French family paused as they exited the church. (Yes, it was open!) The Mother asked politely if the children could have a look, a girl about twelve, who liked to draw, and her young brother, who said I was a good drawer.

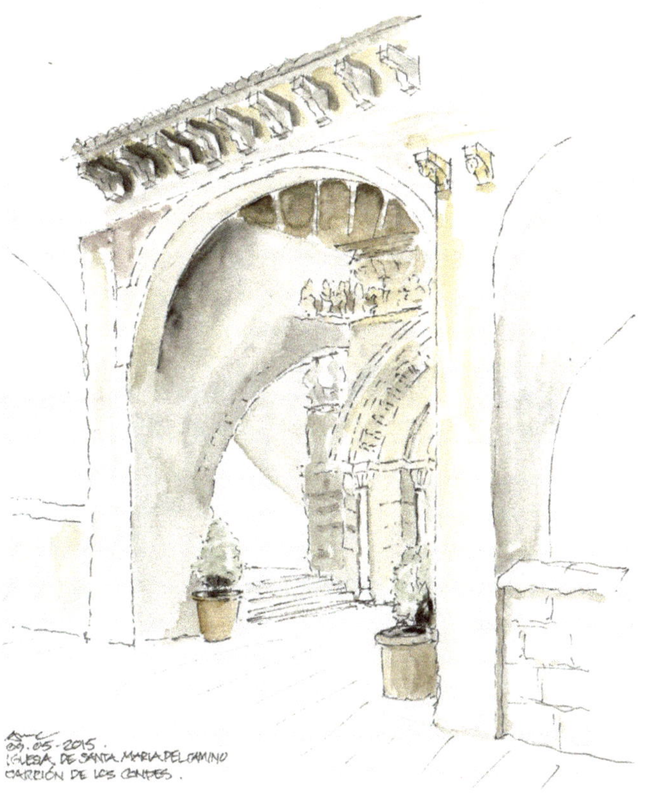

I returned to the albergue to drop off my kit, and set out again in search of dinner. As I crossed the yard, Nicola called to me. A pleasant surprise, I waited for her to finish her laundry, and then we dined together. The French family were dining in the same restaurant, and as we left I called to the young girl to keep on enjoying drawing.

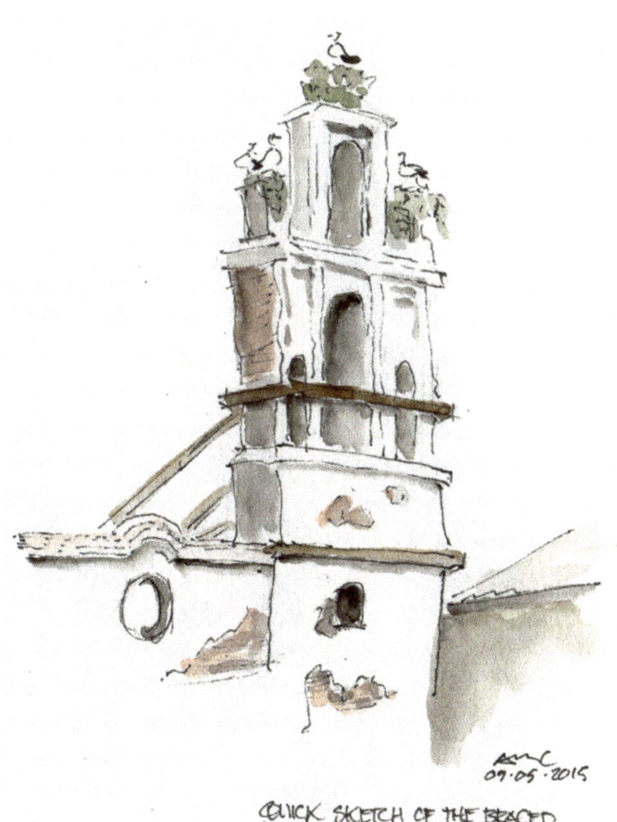

In the morning, sat on the boot bench tying my laces, the little French lady who had befriended me on the bus into Burgos, came tripping down the corridor toward me. She presented a somewhat comical figure, dressed in winter weight long johns, wrinkled a la Nora Batty, topped with a floral patterned flannelette nighty, a knitted bed jacket, and a frilly night cap. Her normally smiley face had instead a hint of sadness, and for the first time, she acknowledged I didn't understand French and spoke to me slowly in English, dredged up I suspect from years past, as had been my German. She had come to say good bye! How she knew I was there, and leaving, is a mystery.

With a gesture to her wrinkled long john clad shins, she said tendonitis. The Sisters had advised her to stay there and rest for three days. She thought her Camino over. Oh, I really hoped not, but sadly I will never know.

Terradillos de los Templarios to Sahagún

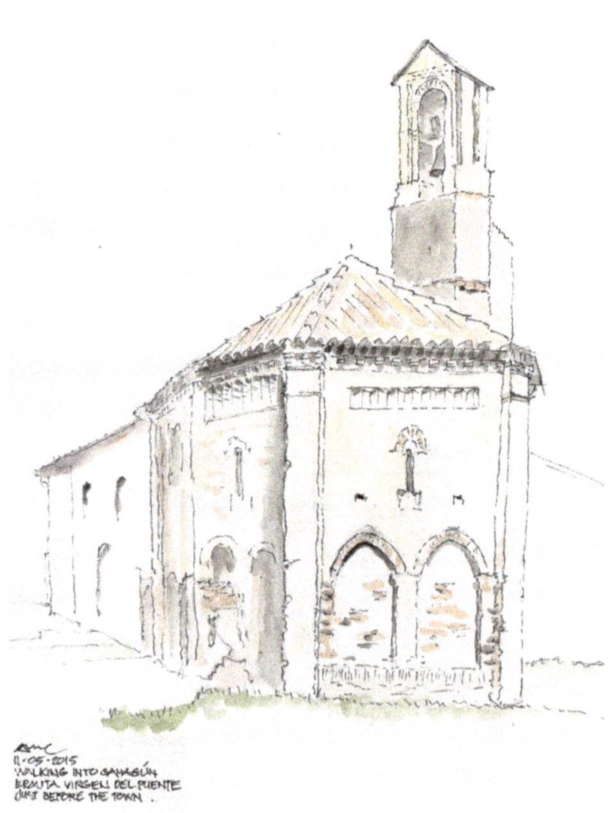

Leaving Carrión Nicola and I took breakfast together at a bar close to the *Iglesia Santiago*. I made a mental note to draw if ever I passed that way again. We walked a little way together, before she set off at her pace, somewhat quicker than mine. We leapfrogged one another several times throughout the day, until as I was approaching Terradillos de los Templarios, and in sight of the albergue, I heard quickening footsteps behind me and a familiar voice "Guess who?"

The lady booking us in, looked at us sternly, and enquired, were we together. As we were not, Nicola was shown to a 4 bed dorm, shared with three other ladies. I on the other hand was given a 4 bed ensuite dorm, which for that moment, I had to myself; much to Nicola's pretended chagrin. We laughed and said we should have said we were together.

After dinner we sat around in the bar with other pilgrims. I rang my wife, and on cue we sang, *Feliz Cumpleaños a ti,* as it was Ann's Birthday. At ten-o'clock I returned to my dorm and was pleasantly surprised that I was still the sole occupant.

Sometime after eleven, I was awakened as the dorm door opened. Two men stood silhouetted against the lighted corridor. They stood talking quietly for some time, before disappearing, leaving the door ajar. I had no idea who they were. One hears stories of theft in albergues, usually in Cities, but this one was very isolated, a little distance from the small village. None the less, I was a guy in his seventies, alone. I waited awhile, straining to hear any sound, then I got up closed the door, and propped a chair up against it.

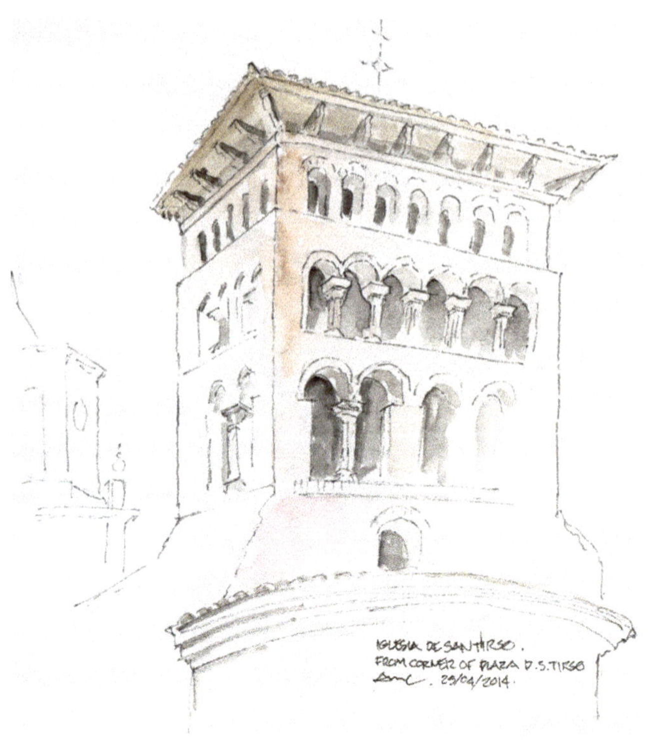

Some time passed, and sleep still eluded

me, suddenly I was startled by the scraping and clatter of the chair crashing to the hard surface of the floor. Two silhouetted men again stood in the doorway, probably equally startled, as they appeared to take a step backwards.

I sat up, and shouted "Bugger off!" I heard indistinct mutterings so I repeated at the top of my voice, "Bugger off, bugger off!"

They appeared to get the message, or at least they disappeared. I replaced the chair alarm, and settled back in my bunk. I lay awake for some time, but eventually drifted off. The chair was still in place in the morning when I awoke.

As I left the dorm, a member of the Birthday choir was coming from the dorm on the opposite side of the corridor. I apologised for the disturbance, however he had slept through it all. Later chatting with Nicola, outside her room, we were approached by an American guy, who explained there had been confusion over his party's booking. There were five of them, and only four beds!

He extended his apologies, and said on reflection he understood how I might have felt. I was pleased and relieved to have an explanation. I added had I known, I was not certain that I would have had the grace to approach and apologise. I thanked him and we shook hands.

Nicola and I felt it odd that he, nor any of his party, hadn't noticed the number of beds, until turned eleven-o-clock. Or to paraphrase a colloquial idiom, he was one bed short of a dorm!

She mentioned she had met him somewhere along the way, and he was a friend of a lady we had known at the very beginning of the Camino. She was I remembered, beautiful, tall and athletic; a seasoned walker, and was well ahead of us. He was hoping to meet up with her in Santiago. Old romantic that I am, if that was her wish too I hope he made it!

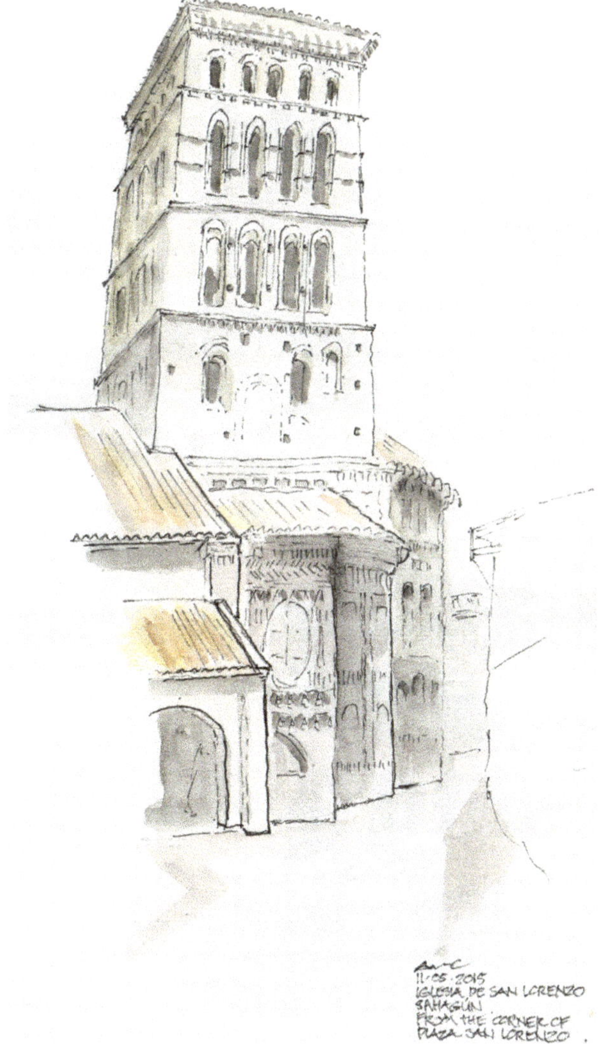

In 2015, I called for a cool drink at the bar as one exits Ledigos. Afterwards, along the Way towards Terradillos I was caught by a guy who slowed and adjusted his pace to mine as we exchanged pleasantries. He spoke with an Irish accent, fortyish, give or take. We spoke of this and that, and as was often the case, my grey beard seemed to substitute for a confessional. He was struggling with having separated from a violent alcoholic wife. Although friends and family were supportive of his actions, he obviously still felt a responsibility. I don't think I contributed much, if anything, to the conversation, save for an ear; an anonymous ear.

As we approached the edge of Terradillos, the albergue where I had stayed the previous year, was *complto.* We walked on with two disappointed American ladies, to the Municipal albergue in the village. We turned into the garden entrance, to find Pilgrims everywhere, on the grass, lounging on chairs, drinking at a few tables, all enjoying rest in the afternoon sun. We picked our way through this maze to and through a doorway and found Reception. There was just one bunk available, so no good for the ladies who wished to stay together. My new found Irish friend said I should take it, but I declined, saying, if he had maintained his pace, instead of slowing to mine, he would have been booked in already. So he stayed, the hospitalera said the next albergue was about three Km, so off we set.

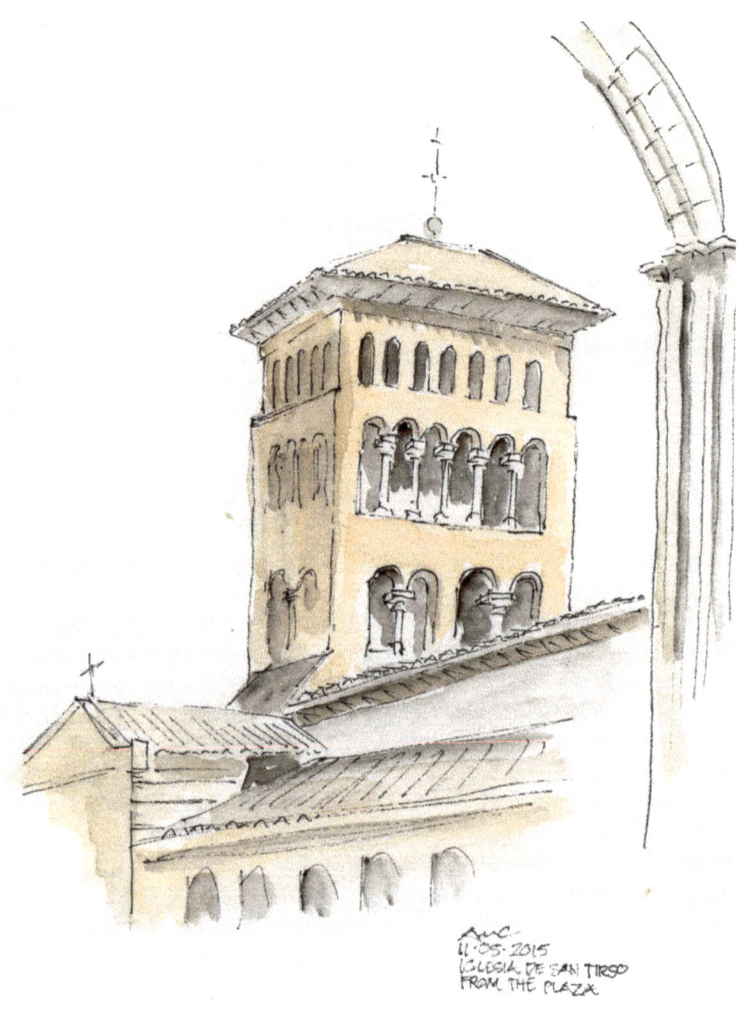

Moratinos

The dormitories looked pretty crowded, but I was shown up a metal fire escape stair to a spacious, airy dorm, with about a dozen mattresses *(colchones)* in neat rows along each side. I had the choice, apart from two adjacent to the door which had been reserved.

When booking in, I was pleased to find he offered a communal dinner, and said he was preparing a wonderful traditional Italian dish. As those things go, it was at the top end money wise, of what I had met previously. He had though a captive market.

As the appointed time drew near we all gathered, and a series of trestle tables were joined together in long refectory style along the terrace, so we could dine enjoying the balmy evening air.

The eagerly anticipated first course arrived, a lettuce leaf with a slice of unidentifiable tinned meat. It certainly broke the ice, as pilgrims within, and I guess, out of earshot, queried its origins.

Whilst awaiting the arrival of the main course, I noticed as I looked along the table, the two American ladies, siting towards the head. They must have arrived after me, and probably because they wanted to be together, had a bunk between them in the Ground Floor dorm. I went to speak with them, and I must have been showing obvious signs of Hay Fever, as the one lady insisted on giving me pills for the next few days until I could buy some at a *Farmacia.*

The wine was placed sparingly along the table. One bottle strategically placed to serve eight. I sat next to a particularly thirsty Korean guy, so when the main course arrived, there was little left for anyone else. The main course, spaghetti Bolognese, I think! It was a generous serving of spaghetti, and the most that could be said for it, was the entertainment value in spotting the very few, and well hidden, specs of Bolognese.

I met a lady further down the Way who had shared this banquet, sitting some distance from me down the lengthy table. She told me with amusement that she had asked for a vegetarian dish, and had had the spaghetti, without the joy of seeking out the bits of Bolognese.

It was a most memorable meal, if not for the right reasons.

Somewhere along the Way out of Moratinos I passed a heavily burdened lady. I had an urge to tell her to adjust the straps on her rucksack as it hung loose from the shoulders, but I must have left my 'know it all' hat off that morning, as I just wished her a cheery *Buen Camino.*

Further along I stopped on the grass beside the path for a mid-morning break. I had just opened a packet of my favourite Spanish biscuits, the ones with a thick chocolate coating on the one side, as the sagging rucksack lady approached. "Would you like a biscuit?" I asked, and she replied "Oh yes I'd love a cookie thank you" Taking one, and walking happily on.

From her reply, I guessed she was from the U.S. I didn't overtake her on the short walk into Sahagún, I guess as I stopped off to draw at the *Ermita Virgen del Puente,* but I did bump into her further down the Way, pleased to say, looking fit and with straps properly adjusted.

I had only the briefest of time to sketch as I passed through Sahagun in 2014, sat on the doorstep of a house in the corner of the square. But as I love *Mudéjar* architecture, I made sure I found the time in 2015.

I joined three French ladies at dinner, communication was pretty minimal as only one of them had any English, and my French is pretty well non-existent. I met them several times further along the way, and they seemed to share an in joke, as when we met there was always friendly greetings, but one lady always made a guttural sound , curled her lip, and said *"Il est naturel "*

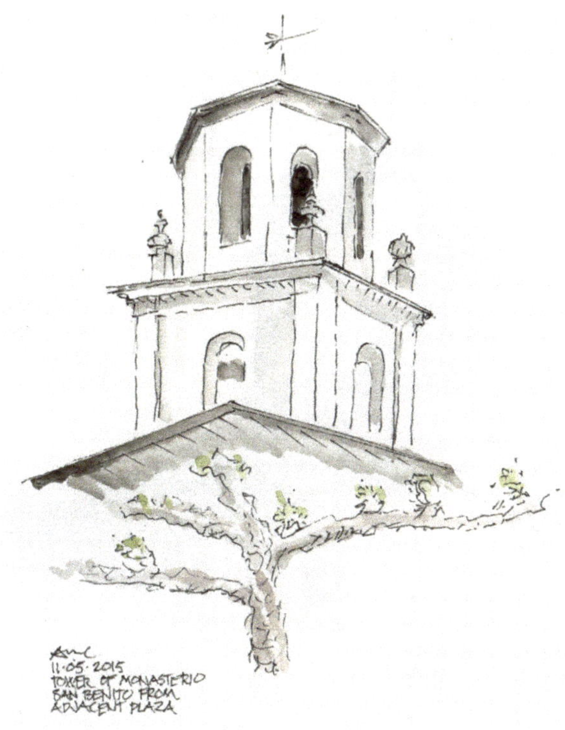

El Burgo Ranero

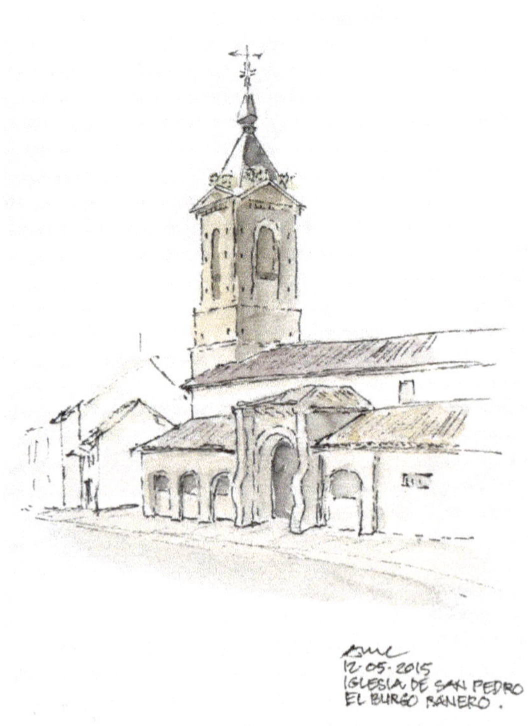

In 2015 I stayed in El Burgo Ranero. Not that it has much to offer, it was just that I'd lingered in Sahagun, with its splendid *Mudéjar* architecture till quite late, before setting out; hence the short walk.

As I was packing my rucksack, in preparation for leaving, last as usual, or so I thought till I noticed the lady I'd dined with in Villacázar, sitting on her bunk. I ambled across and spoke, she had eaten something which disagreed with her, looked very pale and wan, and had arranged with the alburgue to stay and rest. Her Sister had volunteered to join her, but she told me quite vehemently it was her Camino, and she wished to do it her way. She came outside with me as I left, we exchanged a perfunctory hug and away I went, although not without a tinge of guilt, feeling that I should have stayed, if only to fetch and carry fresh water. I salved my conscience at the thought that I would have come a poor second to her Sister.

She must have recovered with just the one day's rest, as our paths crossed a few times further on, no doubt due to my habit of staying two nights in Cities. She was a delightful person, and I was amused to find she was Dutch, as she spoke very good English with that distinctive rhythm and accent, of the French. She had she said, been taught English for nine years of her schooling by a French lady teacher!

I last saw her by chance, at the Ministry of Funny walks, or as some call it, the Pilgrims Office, in Santiago. We were in the same queue for our *Compostela*, I photographed her, smiling radiantly as she exited, holding her *Compostela* aloft in one hand, a protective tube tucked under t'other arm.

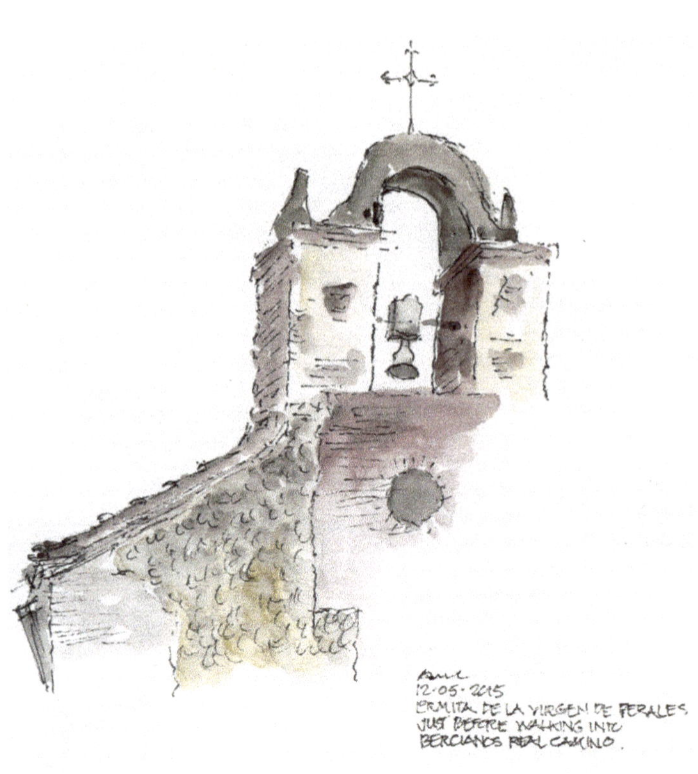

Mansilla de las Mulas

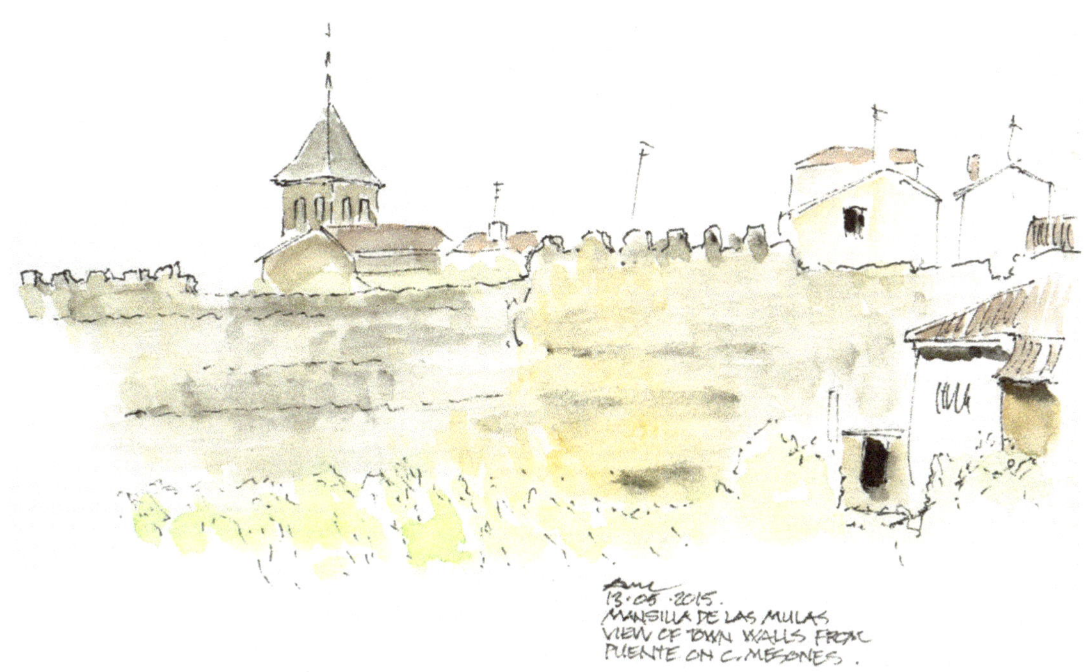

As I prepared to leave the albergue in the morning, I met the German couple with whom I'd shared a dorm in Castrojeriz. They were looking for people to share a taxi into León to offset the expense. I succumbed to the temptation, seduced by the prospect of more time to draw in the City.

Back in Mansilla again in 2015 I called at a pharmacy, for some Anti Histamine pills to curb my Hay Fever. The lady pharmacist told me she had seen me earlier, from from a window in her home. She evidently had a pride in the town, and particularly the medieval town walls, and was pleased I was interested, in drawing the *Arco de la Conception*.

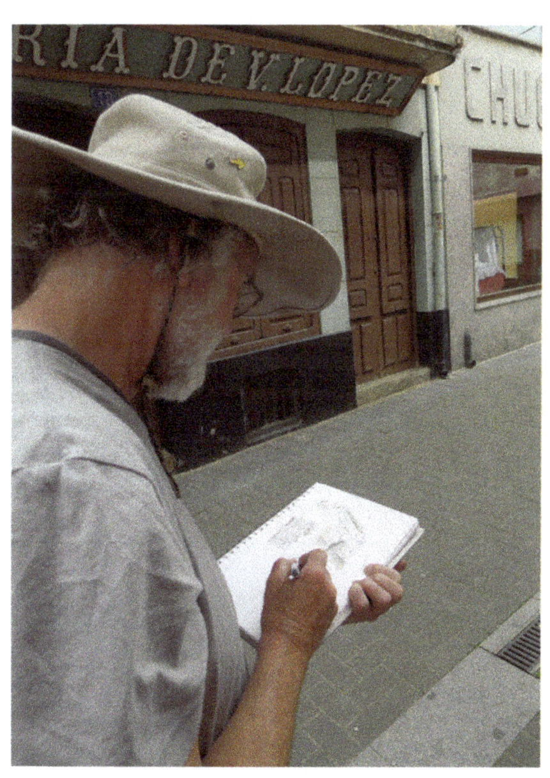

TRACEY EDSTEIN

Later whilst drawing, a lady I'd nodded to whilst booking in at the alburgue took a photo of me. I was neither aware of her presence nor the photo, but by chance we met further down the Way over a communal dinner were we exchanged details and Tracey sent the photos on her return home.

Close to where I'm standing in the photo I had noted a small hotel advertising a *Menu* and afterwards made my way back to it and enjoyed interesting company over dinner.

In the morning, no tempting taxis on offer, but I enjoyed the walk, new ground for me, into León

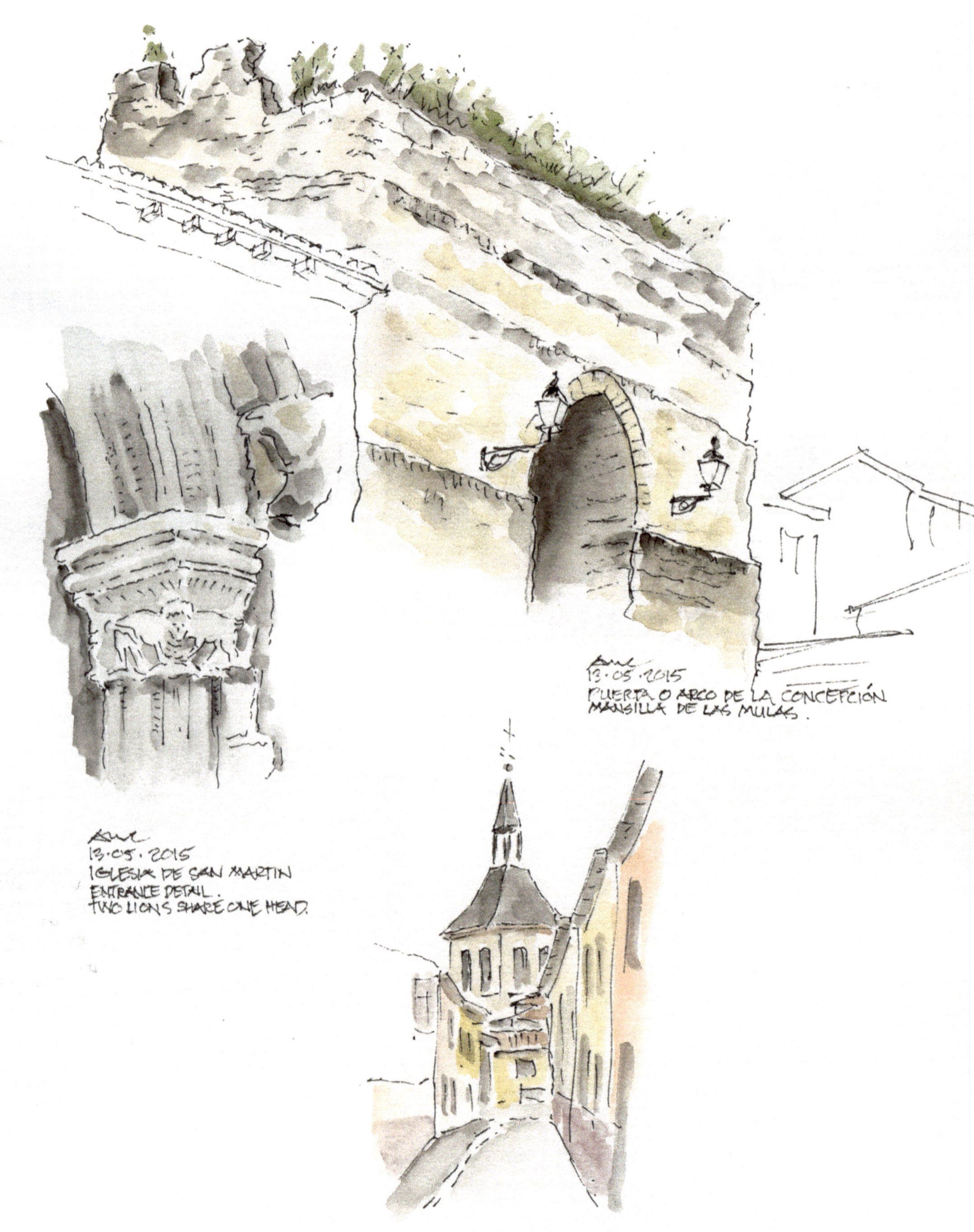

13·05·2015
LOOKING UP C/. JOSE ALVAREZ
TOWARDS IGLESIA DE SANTA MARIA

León

As was my custom in 2014 as I passed through a City, I had prebooked two nights in a small hotel/*hostal.* Arriving early, thanks to a shared taxi from Mansilla, I couldn't book into my room until the afternoon, so I wandered the streets in early morning sunshine, with an eye out for somewhere to draw

Gaudi's building from the Roman walls seemed an idea and I mounted the Corten steel steps in the corner of *Parque Del Cid Campeador,* which lead to a perfect viewing platform atop the Roman City walls overlooking the rear of Gaudi's *Casa de Botines.* I had just finished my sketch, and fortunately had packed my kit safely away, as I spotted two very attractive girls, around twenty I would guess, coming towards me. They were both giggly, and loudly proclaiming they were *Leónese.* One girl came very close, talking in my face, and when I could take my eyes off her hypnotically low neckline, yes I admit it! I noticed a slightly glazed expression in her eyes. She, they, were evidently high on something, and it wasn't the open, but miraculously unspilt beer bottle she swung carelessly about, as I tried to dodge what seemed an inevitable spillage.

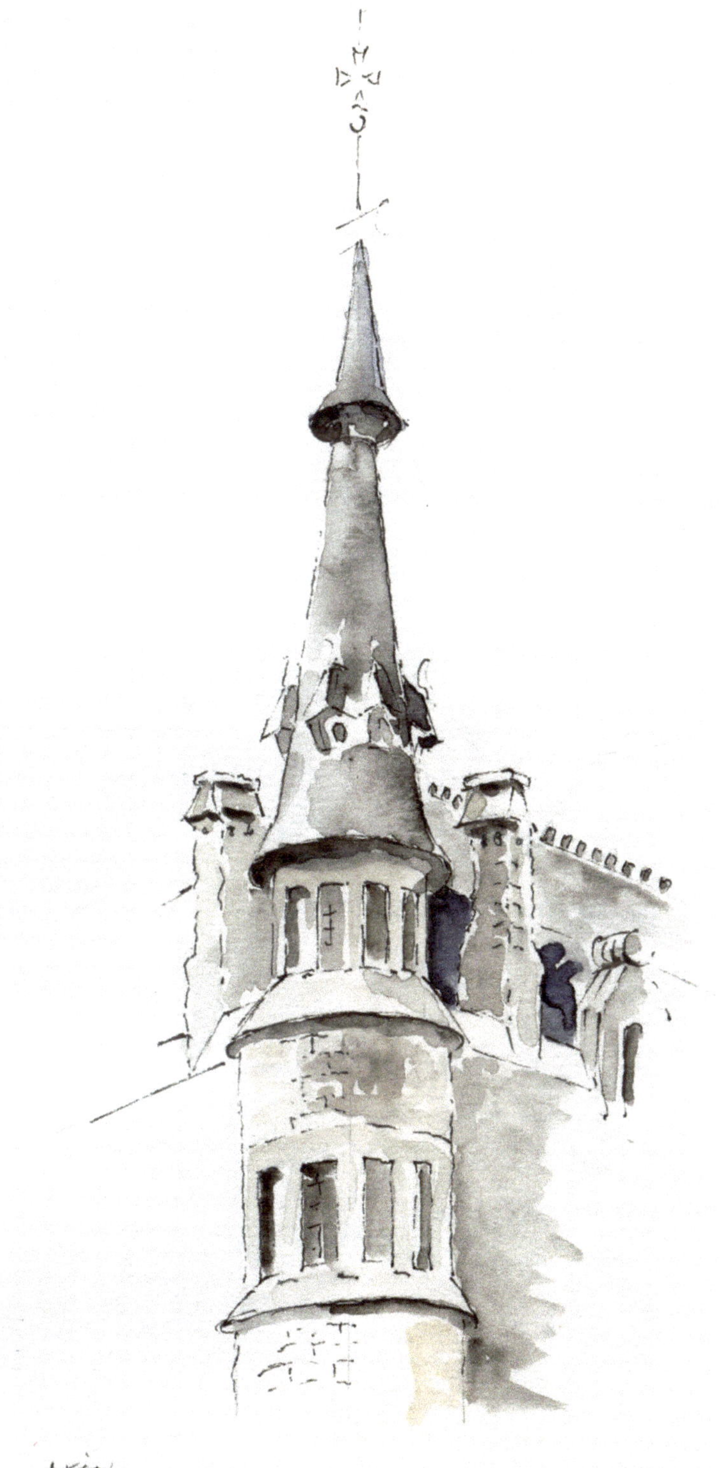

The girl, still with the bottle in one hand, had conjured from I know not where, a smart phone, which was thrust in my direction with a request to take their photo. She fiddled with it, I think trying to switch it on, either too high, or as I later suspected she had never used that phone before.

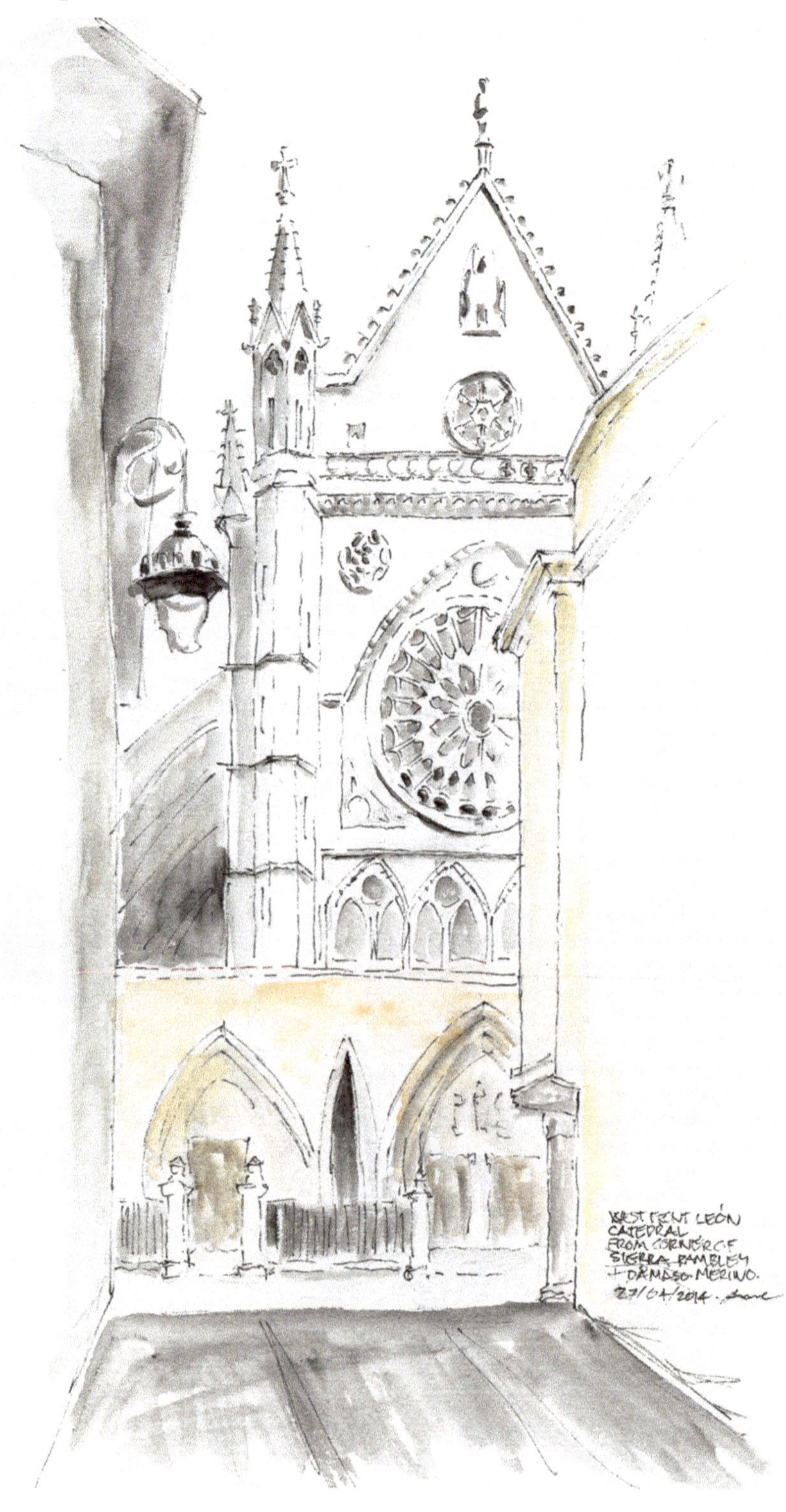

Slightly embarrassed I looked around to escape, when I noticed a fair haired guy, around forty, East European features, and a permanent half smile, observing the proceedings. At this point the girl noticed my rucksack and walking poles leant against the parapet, the drugged veil seemed to lift from her eyes, her face more naturally animated as she cried out *"Peregrino!"*

The phone was given up on, I wasn't crowded, as the girls chatted merrily, telling me their Grandparents were *Peregrinos.*

Soon, interest in me was lost, they drifted away with the Guy, who gave a wry shrug, half smile still intact as he walked away.

I checked pockets, and made certain nothing had been taken, as I had concluded they were being trained, as dippers, (pick pockets) maybe forced, certainly exploited. The lead girl's neckline was a distraction, well it certainly distracted me. I felt sad though, as I had briefly glimpsed the true nature of two lovely young girls.

I gathered my things together, and headed for the steel steps, sadly as I looked down and across the park, the whole process was being repeated with another guy.

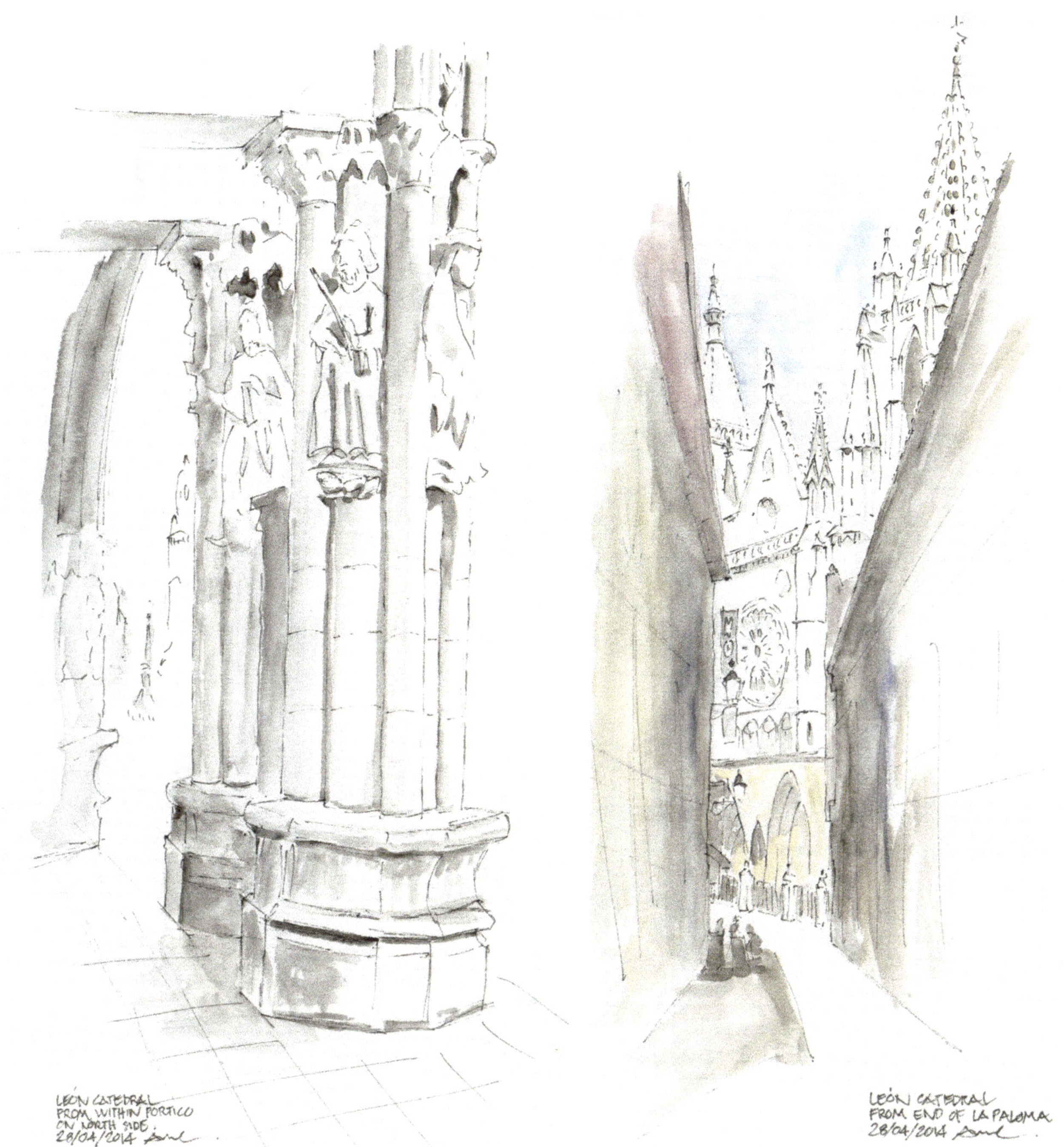

Whilst drawing the following day, by chance and to my delight, Nicola came and chatted, and to my further delight, apparently Caroline too was in León. We arranged to all meet up in the evening and dine together.

I had certainly been blessed with fine weather virtually for the whole of my Camino so far, and it was another clear, warm, balmy evening, as we met in the Plaza Regla, the sun bathed, West front of the Cathedral a glorious back drop. We had a drink in a bar, catching up on our news, and then found a table in the C/ Paloma, which by coincidence I scribbled shadowy figures sitting earlier that afternoon. The *Menu*, was a few Euro more than the norm, but then it was in a City. The food was excellent and we had a magnificent view of the Cathedral. The evening sun sank lower, and the shadows on the West Face crept higher and higher, until during the desert course, the floodlights came on and the whole facade shone a bright creamy grey again.

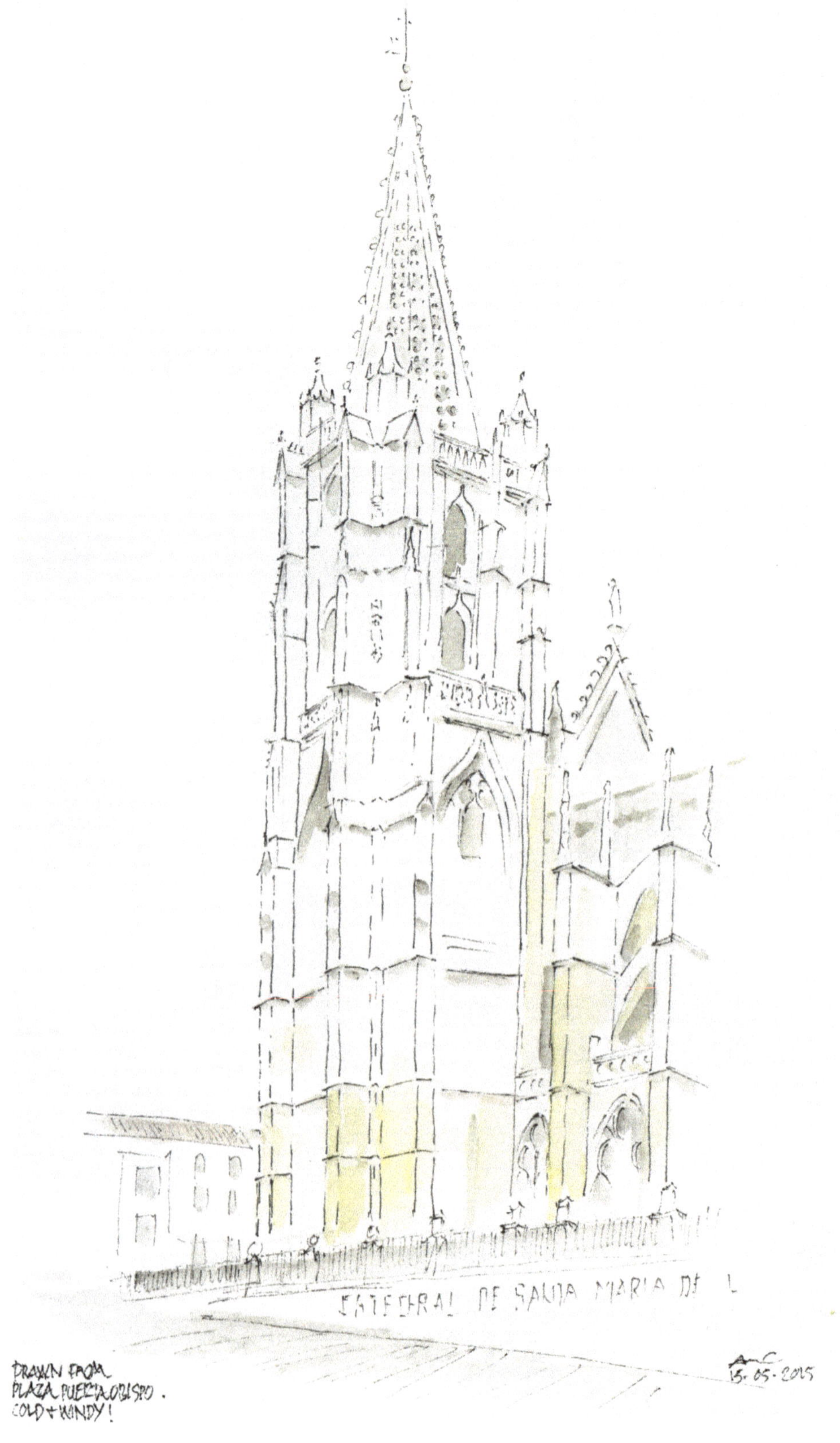

At some point during the meal, a guy pushing a bike, stopped, leant it against the wall opposite, took off his backpack and squatted with shoulders propped, knees bent up. He fumbled in his bag, took out a recorder, opened up a handwritten sheet of music, and began to play what I think was meant to be a tune, but put me in mind of chalk squeaking on the school blackboard.

As we were the only ones seated outside, his serenade was evidently directed at us. Ever generously spirited, Caroline suggested that I give the guy something, so he would move on and others might benefit from his skills. I got up and gave him a few euros, he left us in peace. Money well spent!

It was only after I had returned home, and looking through my photos, I noticed the guy in Puente Reina who I had originally thought was begging, probably was. It was the same guy.

I walked Caroline back to her hotel, it was yet another good bye. Surely I thought, rather sadly, this is goodbye!

In 2015 I'd enjoyed walking the section from Mansilla into León that I'd missed by opting for a shared taxi previously. On arrival I was anxious to use the time productively, but I'd no plan as to where I was to stay. Consequently I ambled around aimlessly, a Korean lady rightly assumed I was lost, and directed me to an albergue. I followed her instructions, but must have gone wrong at some point as I failed to find it.

Aware that valuable scribbling time was slipping away, the more anxious I became, and the more I missed the obvious. Finally I decided to try the hotel that Caroline had used last year. I knew it would be much more expensive than an albergue, but it was in the centre, and very convenient. The receptionist quoted me €90 for the Thursday night, or at the then current exchange, about £55. I decided to go for it. I then queried for the Friday night too, and she quoted €150 . Oh well I thought, a little comfort, and luxury, so booked the two nights.

And here is the moral of this story. A little knowledge can be dangerous, or in my case, a little understanding of the Spanish language. When I came to check out, the bill was €90 for Thursday, and €150 for the Friday ! Not €150 for the two nights, as I'd thought! .... *Note to myself, improve my Spanish language skills!*

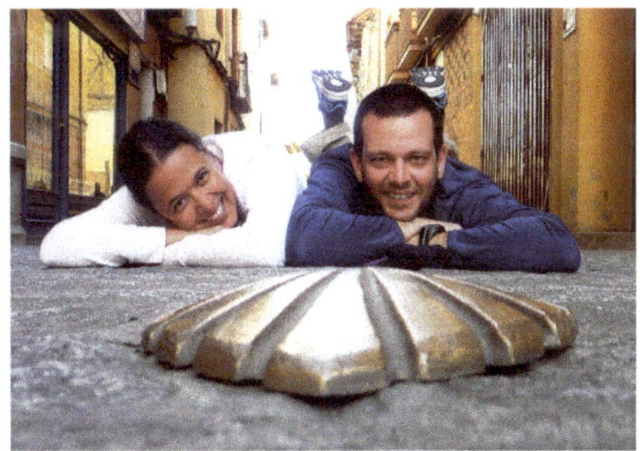

CAIÃ MESSINA

Caiã and Raquel outside their albergue

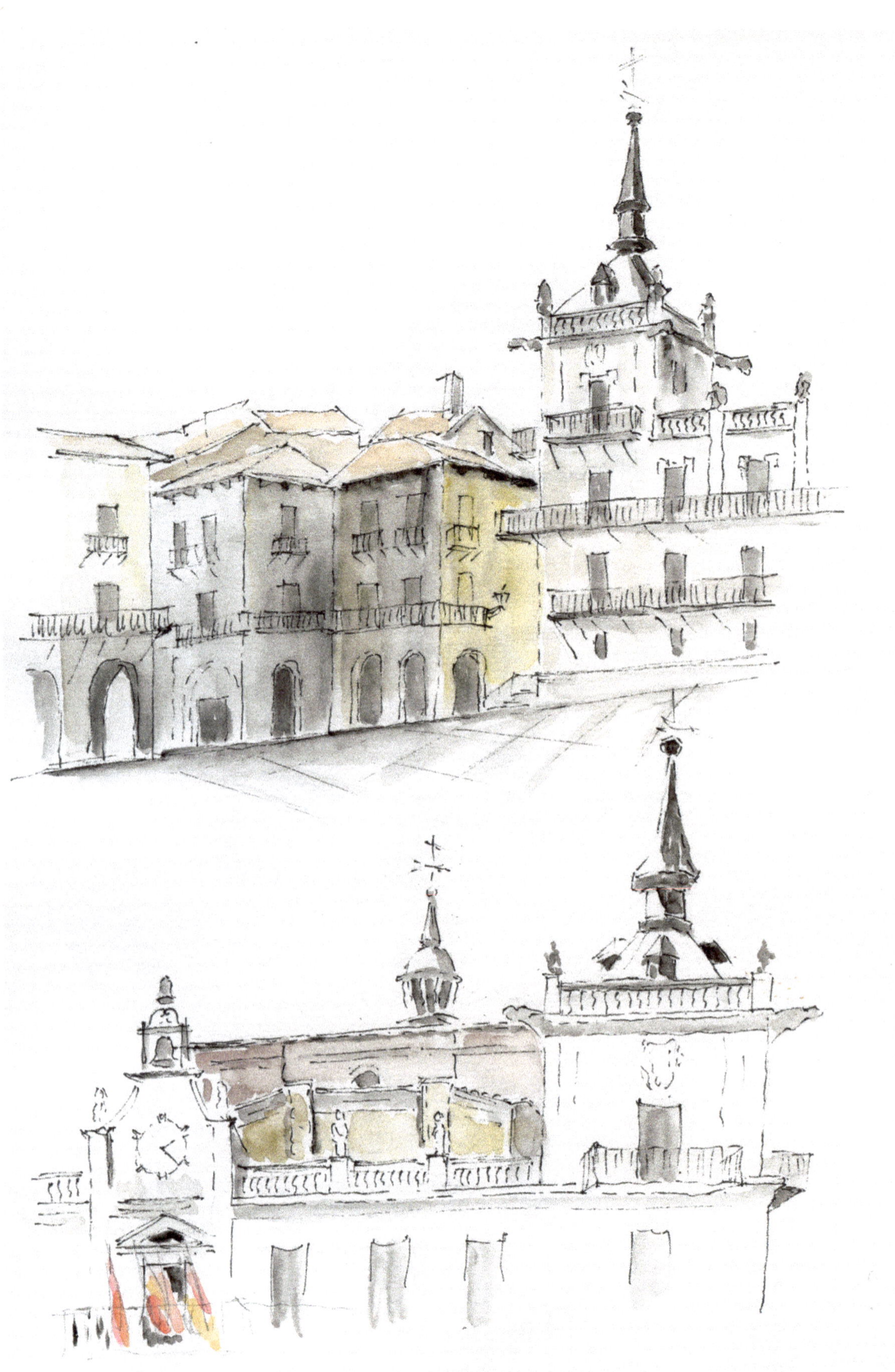

15-05-2015
TWO VIEWS FROM PLAZA MAYOR, LEÓN
WITH IGLESIA PARROQUIA DE SAN MARTIN BEYOND.

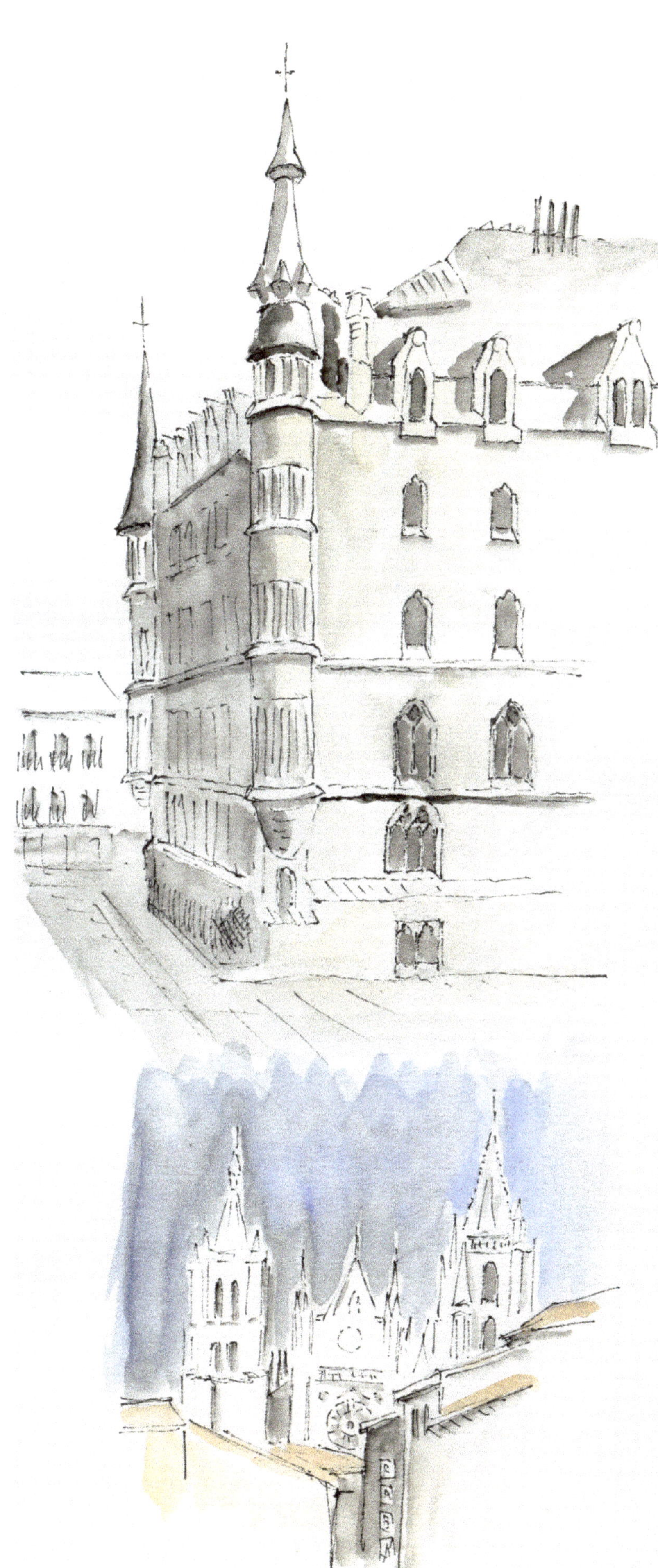

15·05·2015
TWO VIEWS FROM THE
MURALLAS ROMANAS ADJACENT
TO C/EL CID.
ABOVE GAUDI'S ~~PALACIO DE LOS GUZMANES~~ CASA DE BOTINES.
+ BELOW.
EVENING SUN ON THE WEST FACE
OF CATEDRAL DE LEÓN

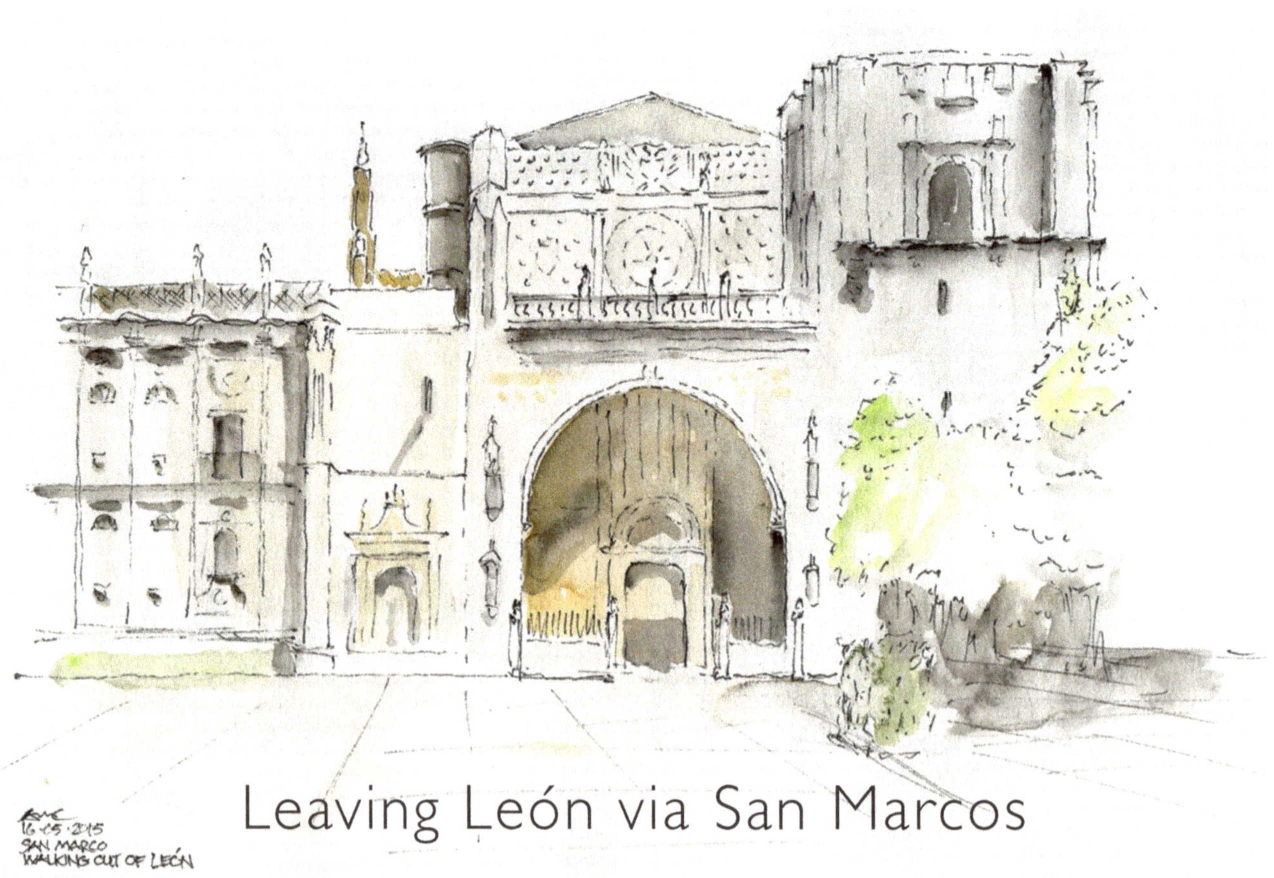

Leaving León via San Marcos

On my first Camino, in 2014, I stayed at a small *Pensión,* just a few hundred yards from *San Marcos,* but the city centre lay in the opposite direction, so I didn't walk to it.

A Pilgrim had told me that her German Guidebook advised that when leaving León, to take the bus from Plaza San Domingo, to La Virgen del Camino and thus avoid walking 8 to 9 Kms of tedious urban ribbon sprawl! Consequently, I didn't walk out, so missed *San Marcos,* In 2015 I again took the bus, but walked to the bus stop via *San Marcos.*

I sat on a bench with my rucksack and drawing kit spread out to my side. Since it was relatively early, and there were numerous empty benches, I was not depriving anyone of a seat. Although concentrating on drawing, I could see the early trickle of tourists, families, and Pilgrims, spread thinly across the enormous Plaza, wandering up and down, admiring the splendid Renaissance facade, photographing, making their way to the *Museo* entrance. A young girl alone, in a bright red dress, stood out from these. She meandered aimlessly here and there, stopping looking around, but seemingly not a glance at San Marcos. Lost again in drawing, the bench suddenly jolted, and looking around the girl sat on the bench which backed onto mine. Odd I thought, grumpily, with dozens of empty benches she should choose that one. Turning back to the drawing, I felt another jolt, and another as she shuffled along the bench to sit immediately behind my things. I turned *"Por favor,* estar *inmóval"* A blank look, so I impatiently gestured, keeping an eye on her. She sullenly rose, and walked away, and as she did so, a guy with a very long lens on his camera approached, his index finger pointing to his eye, and then at the red dressed girl, and then with another unmistakable gesture indicated I should be careful with my things, as he made a sharp lifting movement, nodding in the girl's direction.

It would seem there is always someone watching out for you on the Camino.

La Virgen del Camino to Villar de Mazarife

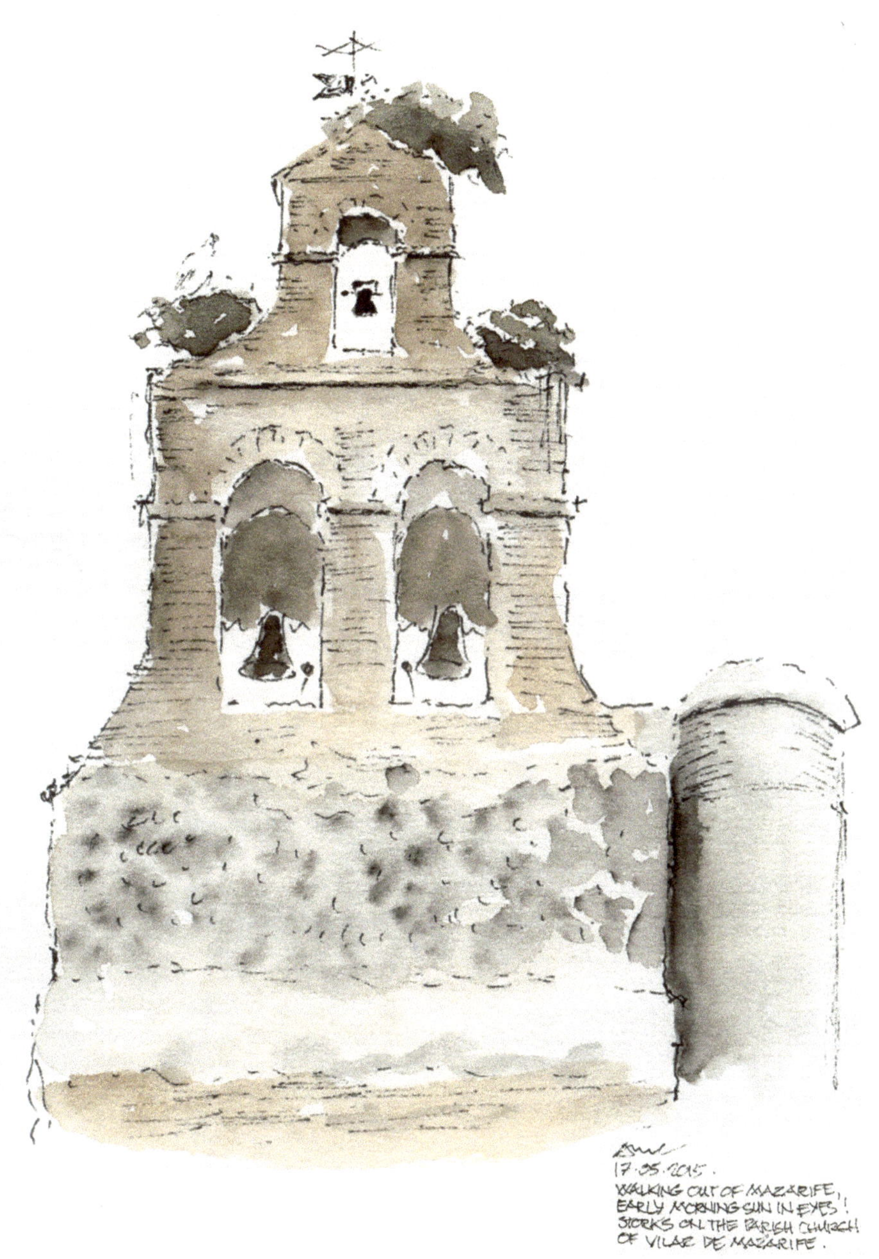

After sketching at San Marcos, I found conflicting information of bus times, probably being a Sunday contributed to the confusion, so I didn't catch a bus until 14.30. On reflection, it really would have been quicker to have walked, however depressing I find ribbon development!

Consequently, I made a relatively short walk to Vilar de Mazarife and stayed at a pleasant albergue on the edge of the village. It was an enjoyable communal dinner, meeting again some pilgrims, and others for the first time that I would see again along the Way.

Before dinner on the terrace I met two charming Canadian ladies writing up their journals. Barbara and Betsy were thrilled with the Stork nests they had seen along the Way, and asked if I had sketched any of them.

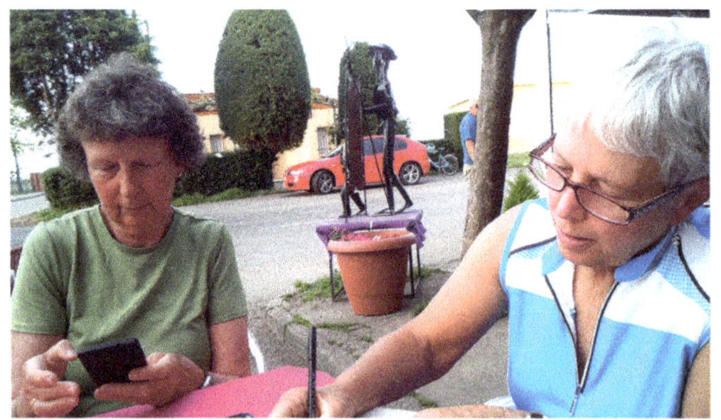

They asked if I knew of the Canadian fiddler, Oliver Schroer, who had recorded himself playing in Churches and Cathedrals along the Way. I was unaware but I have since listened to some of it on YouTube and found it as I suspect these ladies had, both moving and hauntingly beautiful.

As I walked out of the village in the morning, passing the church, I recalled the conversation. The tower had three mature nests, each complete with incumbents! I put my kit down on the narrow footpath, leaned against the rough adobe wall, and sketched the church, *Iglesia de Santiago*, squinting into the morning sun, as is always the case drawing a West Front early morning. The façade had sections of exposed coursed cobbles within the adobe mud, something I had first seen whilst sketching the *Ermita de la Vigen de Perales*, just before Bercianos Real Camino.

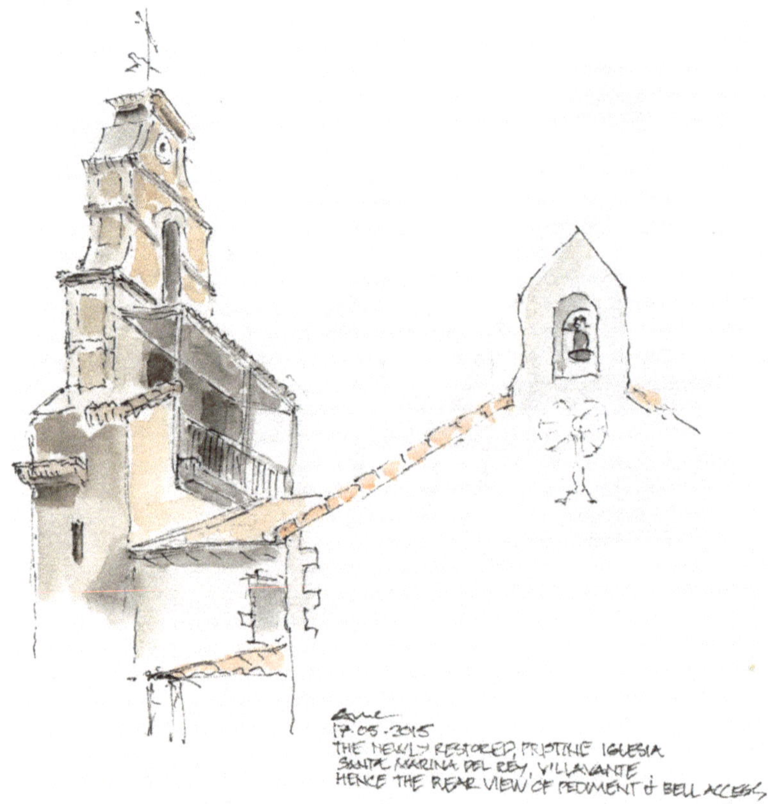

At Villavante, the church, *Iglesia Santa Marina del Rey* had been recently restored. A classic case of the Spanish tendency to over restore, as it would appear the Spanish Authorities "Restore" rather than "Conserve" In the process losing the charm of antiquity, destroying the patina of age. Consequently I sat on a step opposite the South door, and sketched the rear of the Tower, showing access to the belfry. It had, I thought, a little more interest, than the pristine West Façade!

Unbeknownst to me, Tracey the Pilgrim on the right had taken a photo of me drawing in Mansilla. Sitting next to her, Annemiek had done the same as I sat in front of one of my favourite churches, drawing in Villasirga.

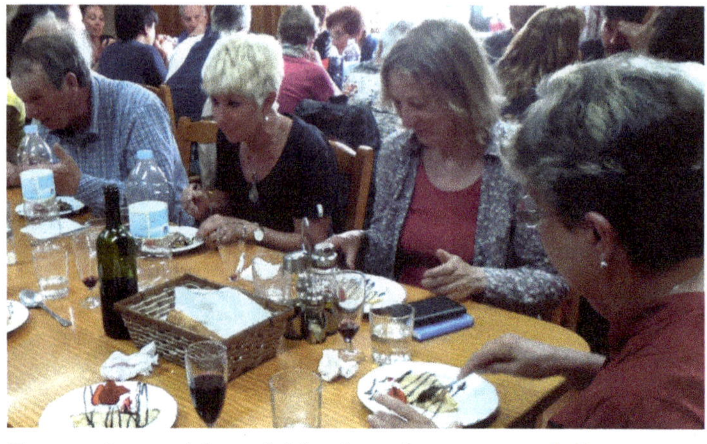

Tracey, Annemiek, and friends at the communal dinner.

Hospital de Órbigo

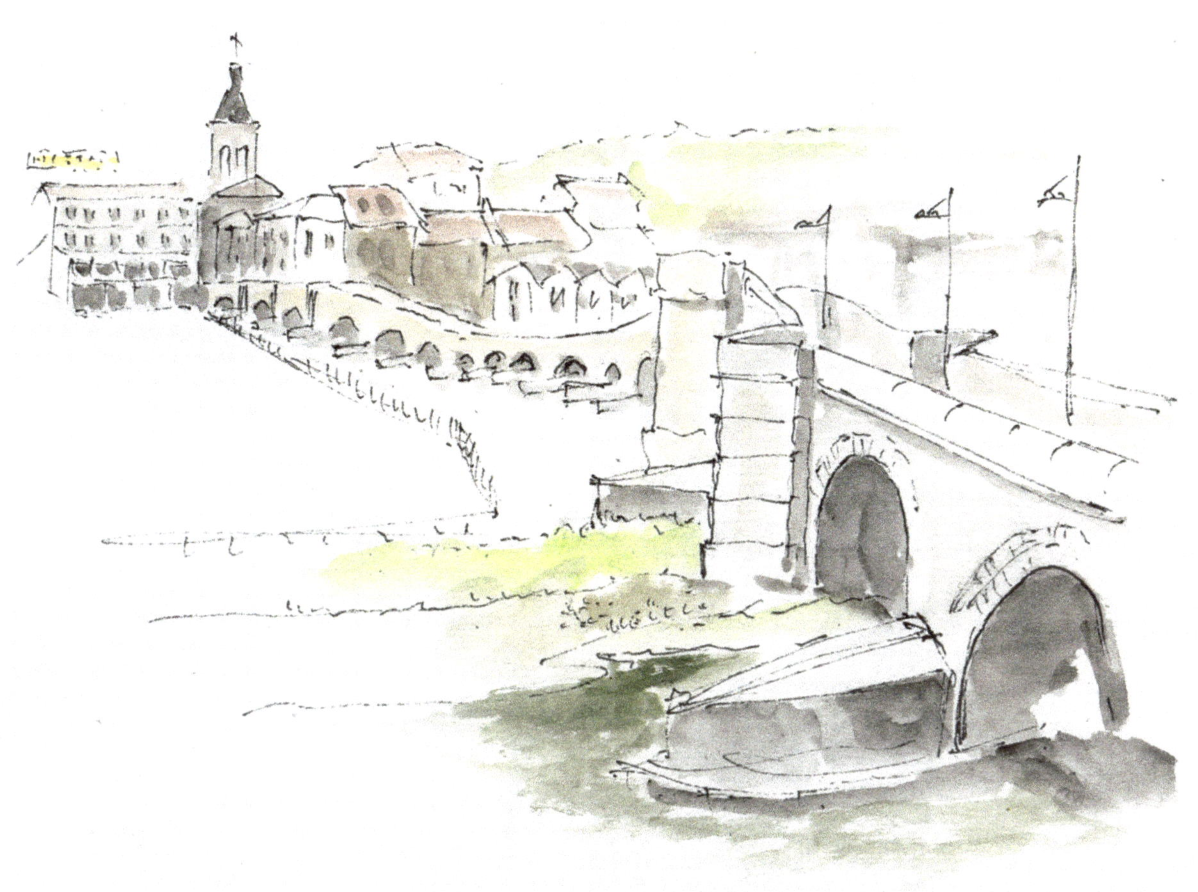

17·05·2015.
VIEW ON ENTRY
TO HOSPITAL DE ORBIGO

& BELOW,
LOOKING BACK FROM THE
BRIDGE, AT IGLESIA
DE NUESTRA SEÑORA
DE LA PURIFICIÓN.

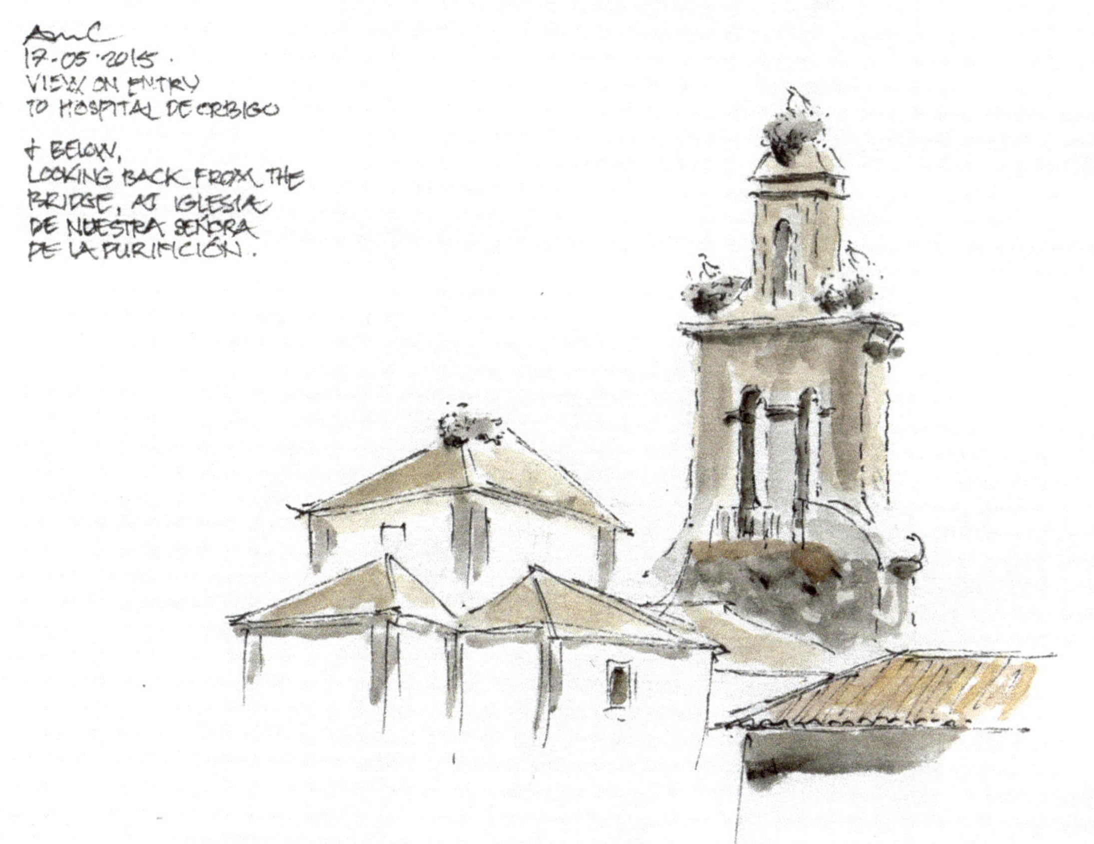

In 2014 I walked through Hospital de Órbigo, across the stunning bridge, and on to Astorga, regretting not being able to spend more time there. I made amends in 2015, arriving early afternoon, so allowing time for exploration, and sketching.

After checking into the albergue I walked back across the bridge, to capture the view that greets as you walk in. The bridge, stretches out like a giant caterpillar to the opposite bank stopped by the tower of *Iglesia San Juan Bautista.*

Whilst there, I was approached by a charming Korean couple, drawn into conversation, photographed, admired. Yes! Hard to believe, but I had met many Koreans along the Way, and invariably they seem particularly delighted, some youngsters even excited, by someone sketching in line and wash.

It's one of Spain's best preserved Gothic bridges. Which thankfully, sensitive restoration due to flood and military damage, has remained faithful to its medieval design and retained a homogeneity despite, as one looks at the sketch, the first two arches are C19, as are the last two on the far side. Then there are three, obscured by the passing space buttress, which are C13, and the others, are C17.

Looking back as I re-crossed the bridge, I stopped to sketch *Iglesia de Nuestra Señora de la Purification*, bedecked with four enormous Stork nests, each complete with resident families.

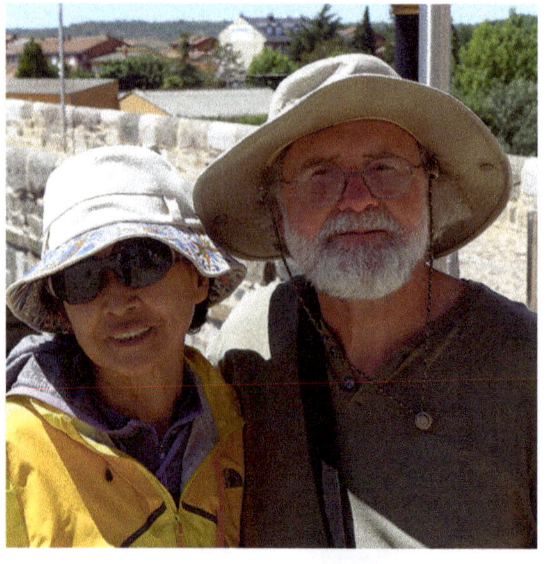

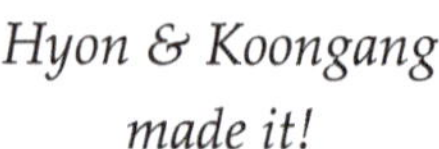

Hyon & Koongang made it!

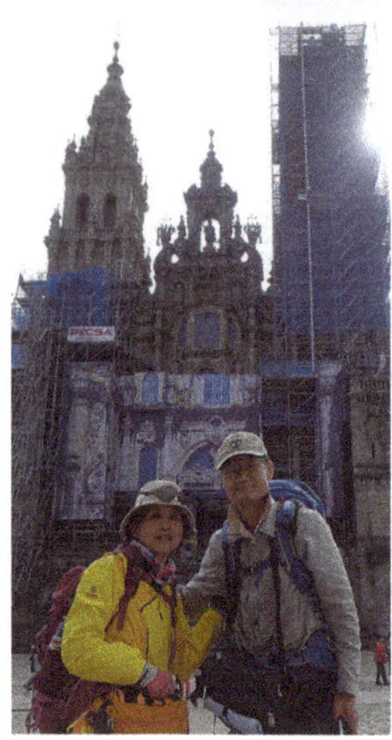

KIMHYON

Astorga

ASTORGA
ENTRANCE TO
PALACIO EPISCOPAL (GAUDI)
FROM BENCH IN PLAZA CATEDRL.
30/04/2014

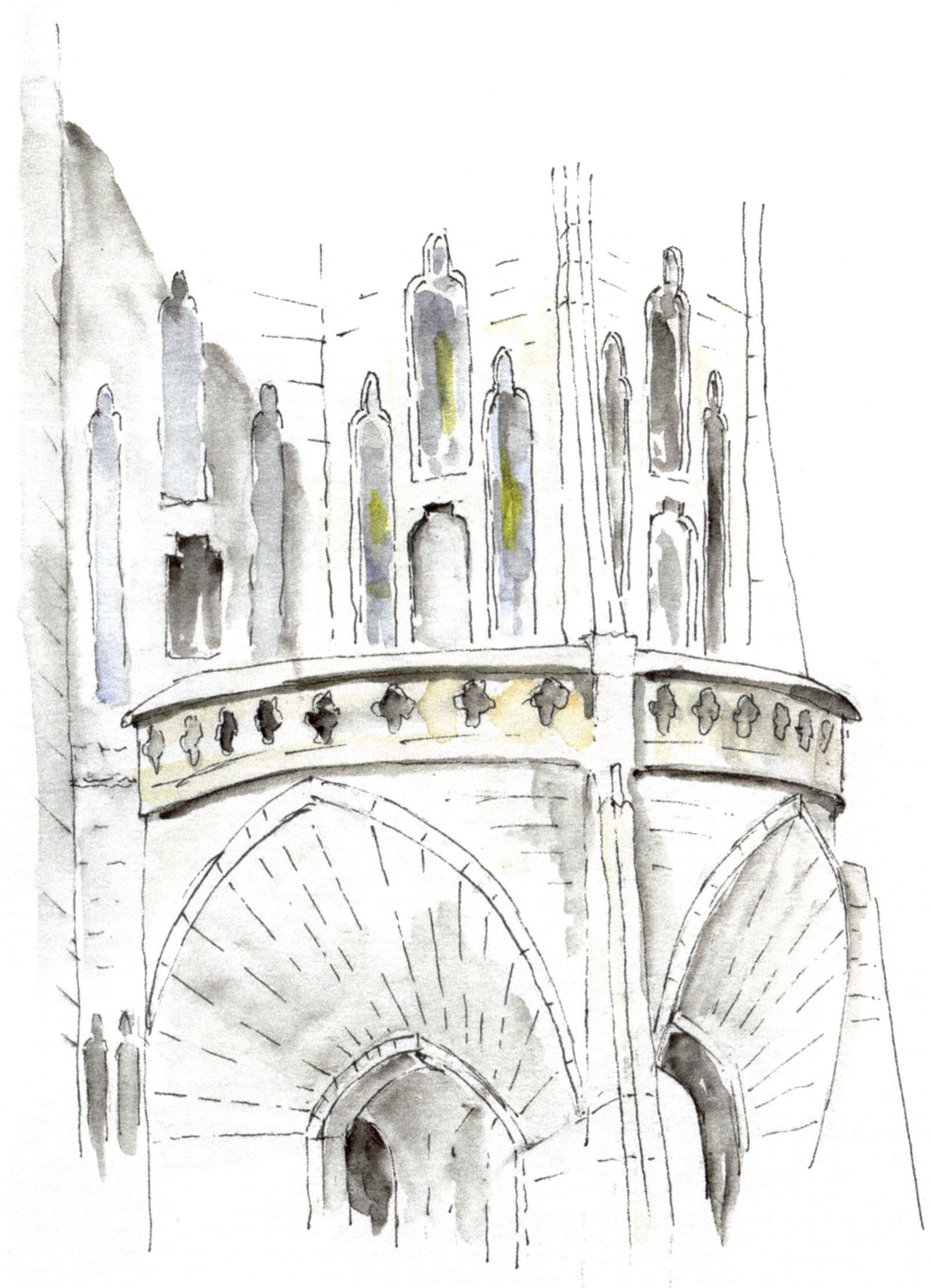

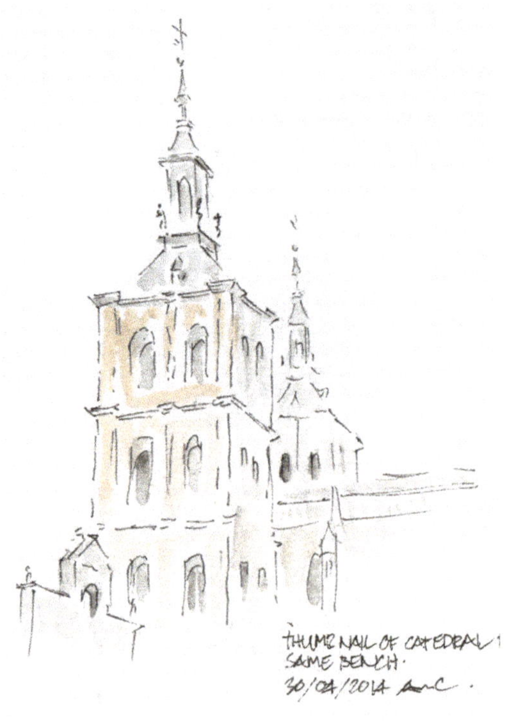

To allow more time for scribbling in Astorga I'd extended the walk from León, and stayed in Villavante, which made for a relatively short walk the following day.

Consequently I arrived in Astorga mid afternoon, but for some reason on that day I was unusually weary. I sat on a bench in the Plaza Catedral, opposite Gaudi's *Palacio*, half dozed and drew part of the entrance, then, still sitting in the same place, I swivelled round and did a thumbnail of what I could see of the Cathedral.

I then walked down behind the Gaudi, through the Walls and sat behind two or three vino tintos in the window of a bar, across the road from the Parque below the Walls, admiring the view, mentally planning tomorrow morning's sketch, resting and passing time before dinner

By chance Monty had seen this lady drawing, as he dined in a restaurant by Burgos Cathedral. After his meal he went and spoke with her. She explained she had been inspired by a *"kind English gentleman!"* (Her words apparently, I don't recognise the description!) Monty replied, he too, and comparing notes found by coincidence it was one and the same guy; me!

Just two steps through the door, I paused, trying to adjust from the bright crisp morning light, to the cosy gloom of the bar. My glasses had steamed up, and I could see little, but from a misty corner, I heard a drawled "ARRRStin! Am I glad to see you, I have a note for you, from one of your girlfriends!" I recognised the Texan drawl, it was Monty whom I'd met walking into Los Arcos, and last seen in Navarette. He fiddled with his pack and eventually from a pile of papers, pulled out a page, torn from a small notebook. Scribbled on it was, an email address, and below, "Thank you for inspiring me to draw" signed Sarah.

By chance Monty had seen this lady, from a restaurant by Burgos Cathedral, whilst she was drawing, and after his meal, went and spoke with her. She explained she had been inspired by a "kind English gentleman!" (Her words apparently, I don't recognise the description!) Monty replied, he too, and comparing notes found by coincidence it was one and the same guy; me!

As she was leaving for home that day, he took the note from her, promising to pass it on if we met, and failing that he had my email address.

So the story comes full circle! He still draws bridges, but laments the lack of antiquity in so young a country, and this lady too still draws.

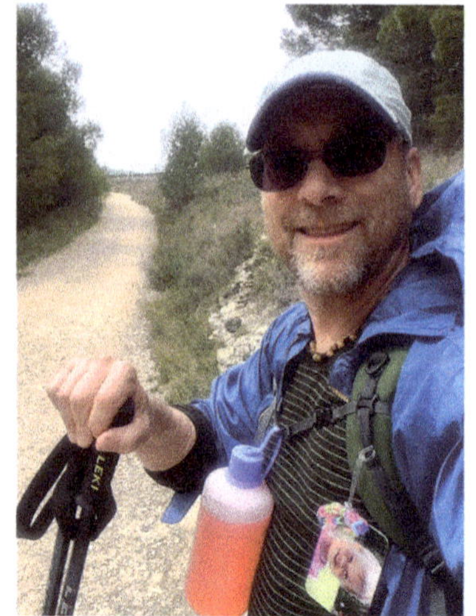

MONTY PELTO

Monty, my partner in crime from Los Arcos! with his Granddaughter.

Astorga 2015

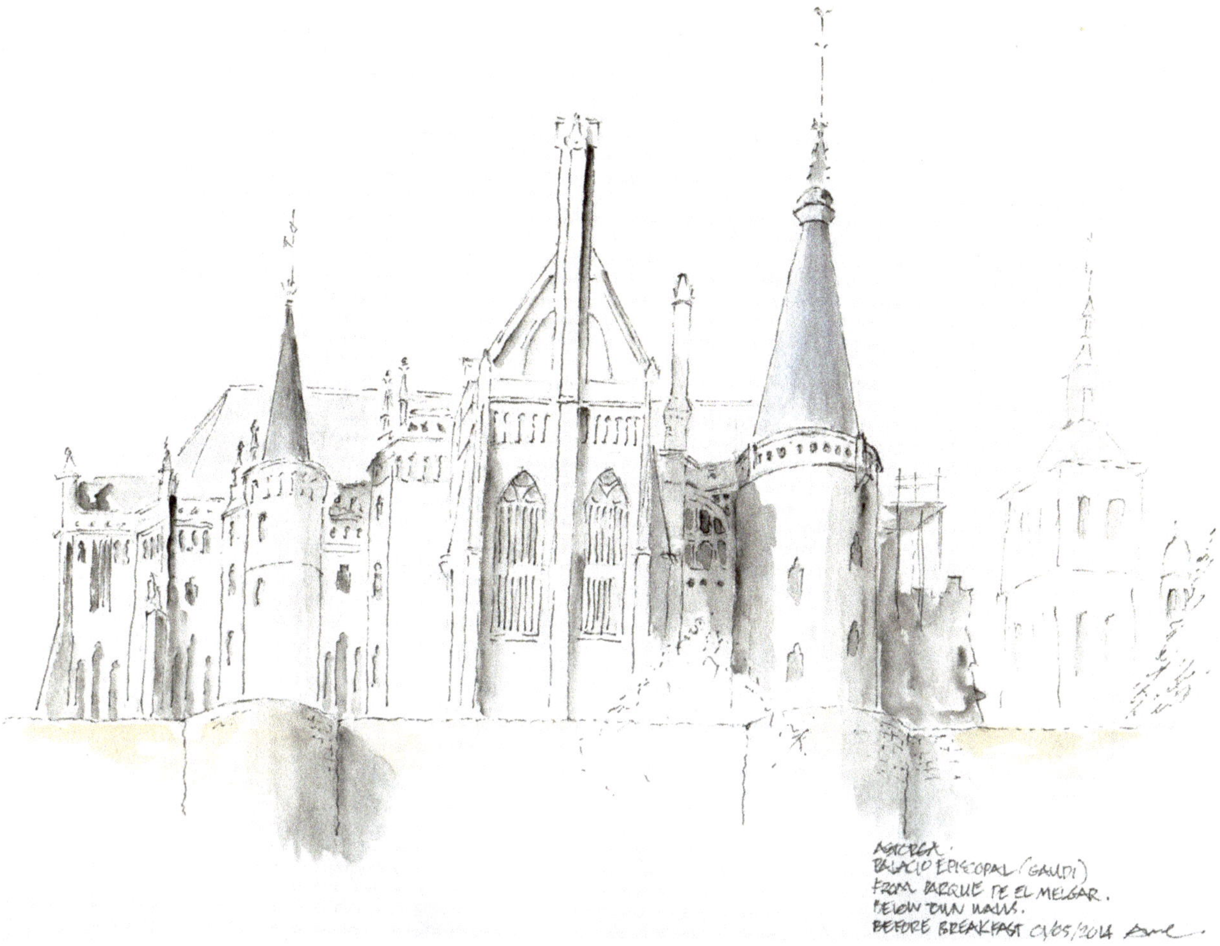

ASTORGA.
PALACIO EPISCOPAL (GAUDI)
FROM PARQUE DE EL MELGAR.
BELOW TOWN WALLS.
BEFORE BREAKFAST 01/05/2014

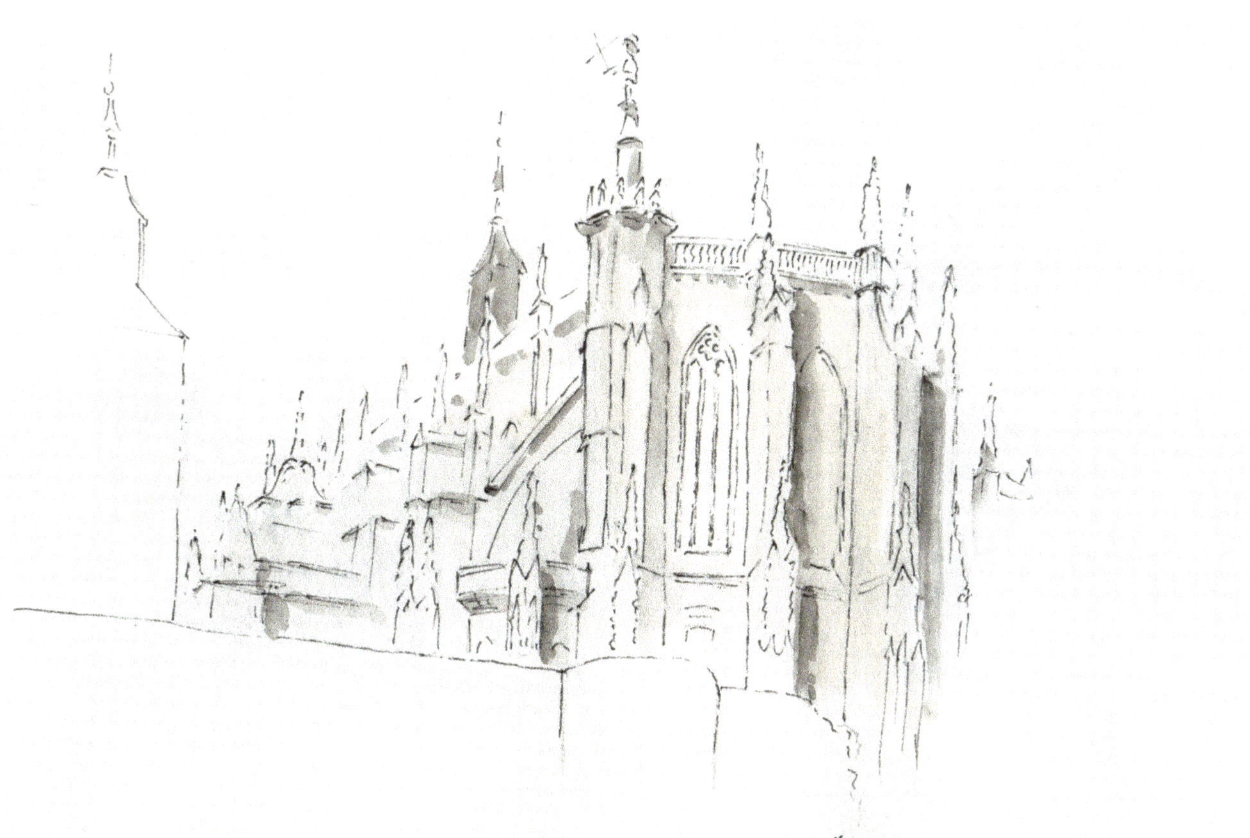

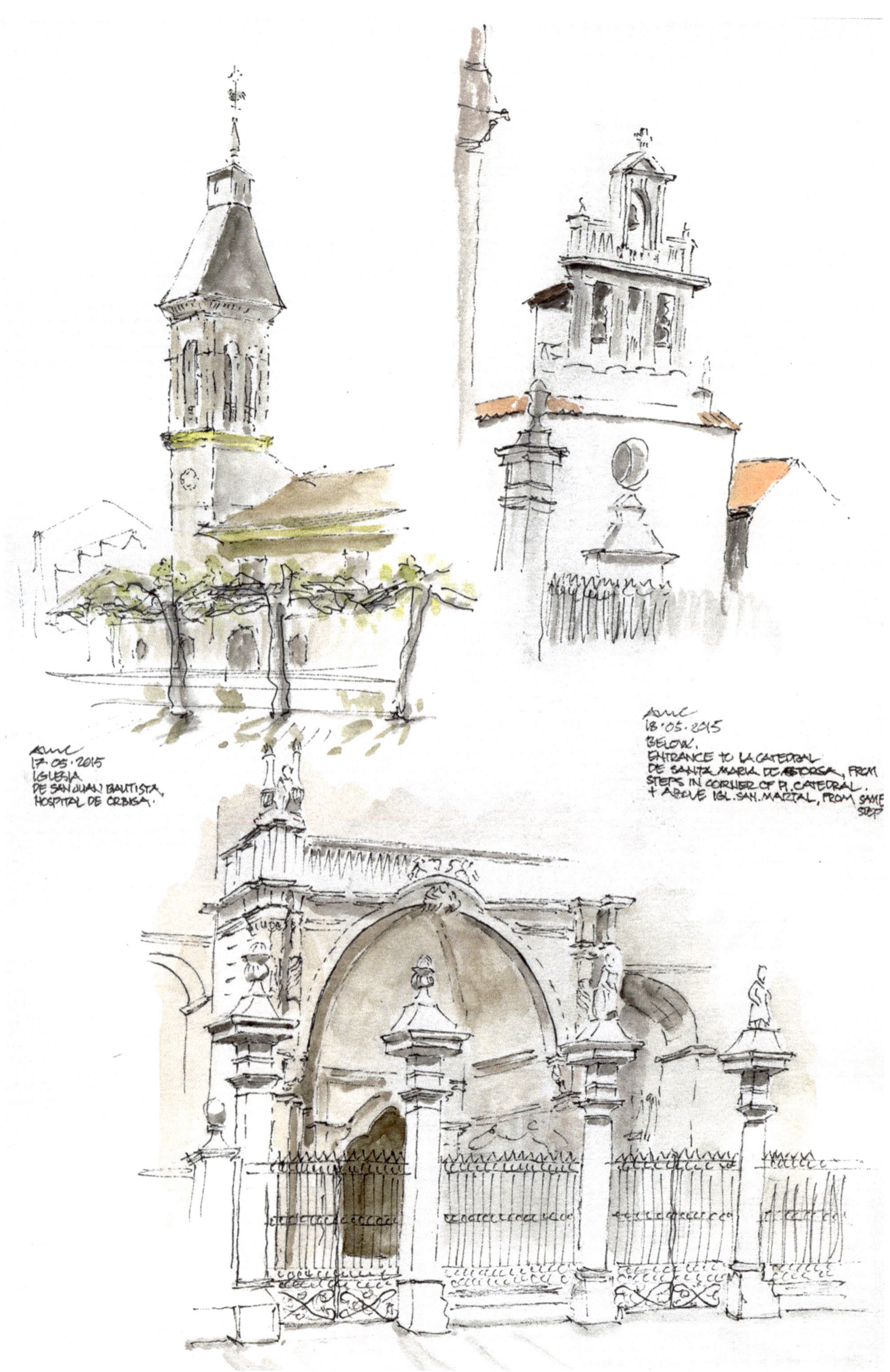
17·05·2015
IGLESIA
DE SAN JUAN BAUTISTA,
HOSPITAL DE ORBIGA.
18·05·2015
BELOW,
ENTRANCE TO LA CATEDRAL
DE SANTA MARIA DE ASTORGA, FROM
STEPS IN CORNER OF PL. CATEDRAL.
+ ABOVE IGL. SAN. MARTAL, FROM SAME
STEP

Two weeks had passed, when I arrived in Astorga, since the American Pilgrim, Denise Thiem had gone missing. There were posters in every shop window, bar doorway, and seemingly everywhere. It cast a cloud over my Camino, as I'm sure it did for many others, particularly I imagine women, many of whom walk alone.

In 2014 I had neither the time, nor the energy to see inside Gaudi's Palacio, so, along with a better Cathedral Sketch, it was on my list of 'To do' in 2015, but somehow, I contrived to be in other parts of the Town during opening hours. However, I did manage a couple of sketches of the Cathedral.

I investigated the possibility of sketching the West Front. Lovely Baroque Façade, which can't fail to bring a smile; a smile of joy! The Nave is expressed by the central Gable, flanked by twin towers, and separated from them by balustered flying buttresses. I walked around, searching for a vantage point, but, just couldn't get far enough back to capture the whole.

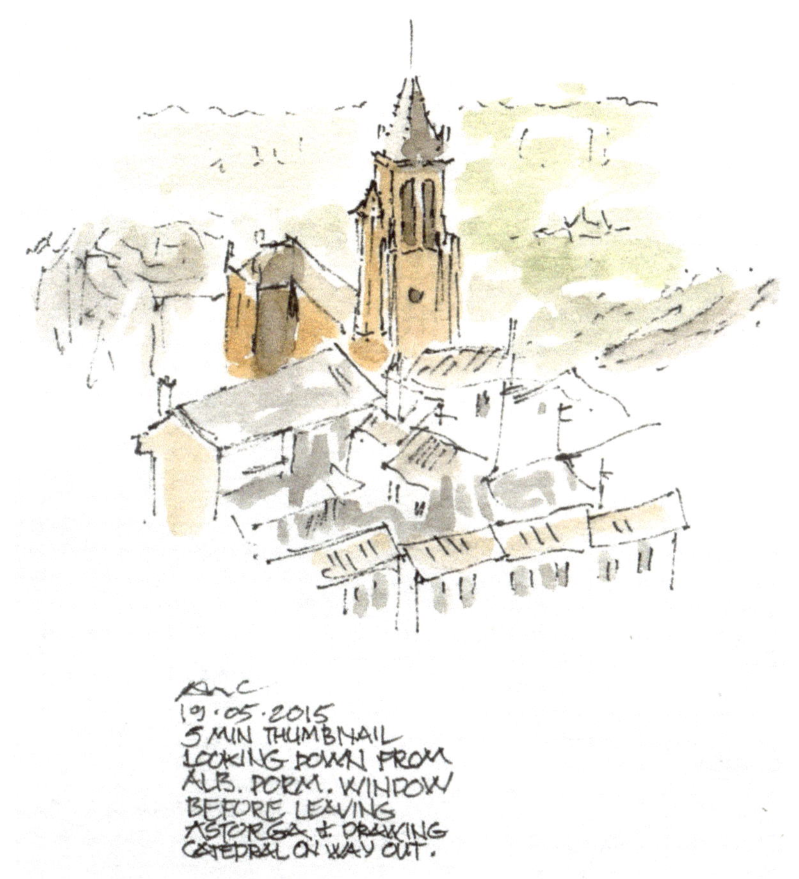

I walked down C/Leopold Panero, looked back, wondering if I might draw a part of the Façade framed by the buildings each side of the Street, as I had done in Pamplona, and León. But, the road is just one vehicle wide, with only token narrow footpaths. As it would require standing in the middle of the road to draw, it was impractical due to the traffic.

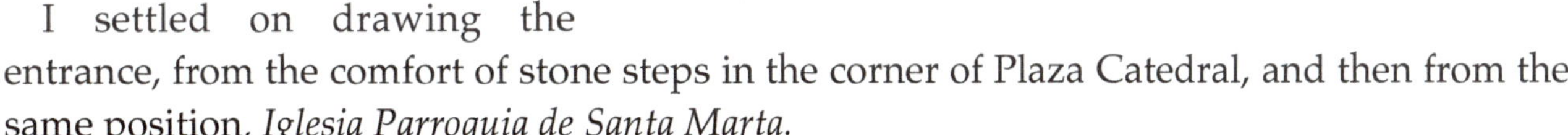

I settled on drawing the entrance, from the comfort of stone steps in the corner of Plaza Catedral, and then from the same position, *Iglesia Parroquia de Santa Marta.*

The following morning, before leaving the albergue, I drew a 5 minute thumbnail from the dormitory window, looking down the escarpment at the rooftops and unknown church below.

Afterwards, I made my way to the *Parque* below the walls, where in 2014 I had sketched Gaudi's Palacio, and from a similar position sketched the apse at the East end and the Gothic buttressed and pinnacled South façade. It was still early morning, and half remembered from the previous year, elderly ladies still walked their dogs at a stately pace, up and down, up and down; always in deep conversation with one another.

From there I walked to the same breakfast bar I had used previously. But this year, no messages!

Rabanal

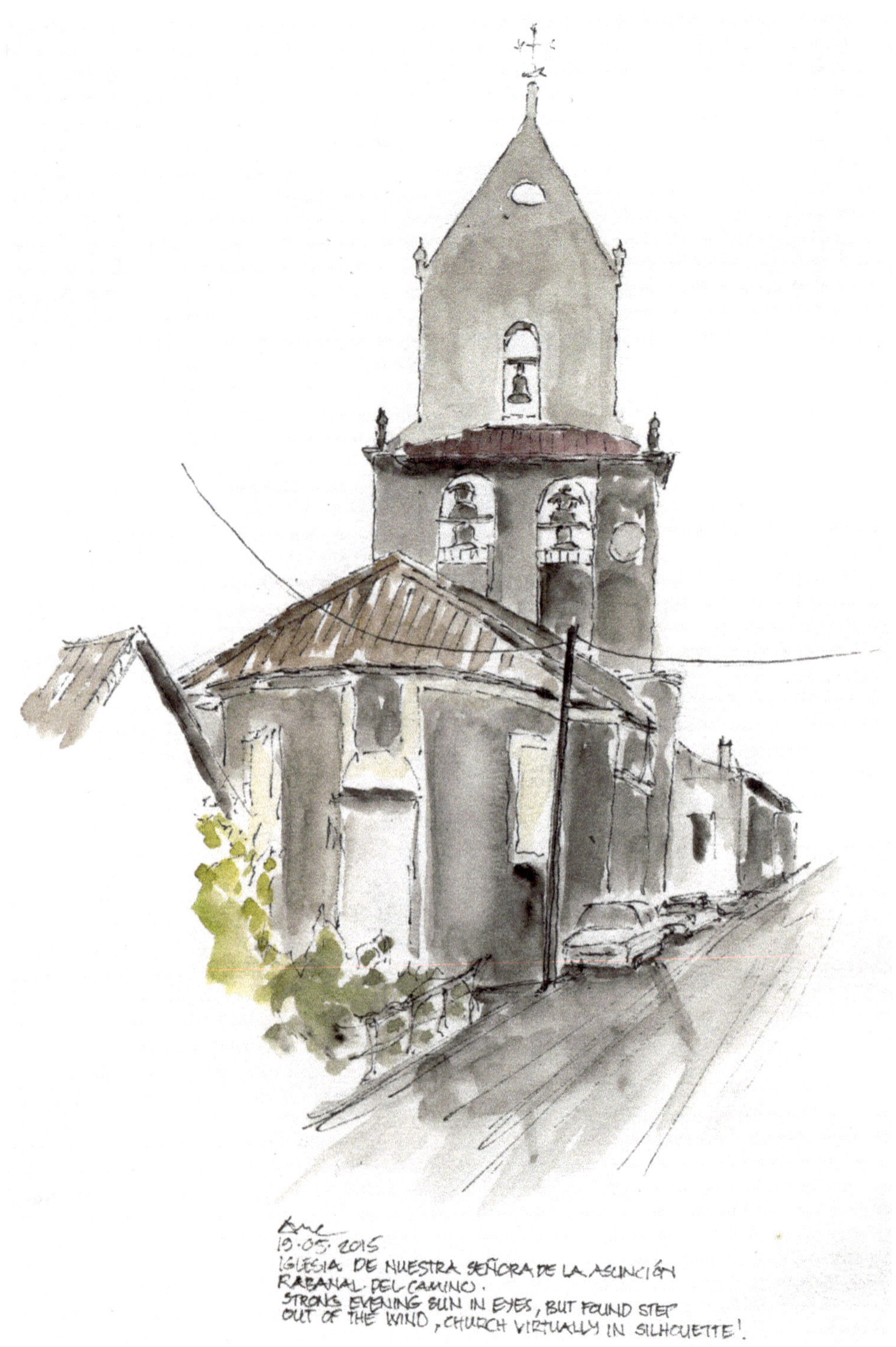

As I was exploring the village, I bumped into Nicola, and we arranged to meet for dinner after Vespers at the church, *Iglesia de Nuestra Senora de la Asuncion*.

Passing through the arcaded porch I took a while to adjust to the dimly lit interior. I was early and sat alone in silence, enjoying the simple Benedictine Romanesque interior. Others began to arrive, and soon the church was almost full. The service was conducted by the monks in Gregorian chant. It was though very cold and I was pleased to meet up with Nicola in the warmth of the bar.

Entering the village in 2015, I had tried a couple of albergues, but they were *completo*. I walked up the hill, to where the village gives out, and sitting in the sunshine opposite the bar where I'd dined in 2014, was the lady I'd left recuperating in El Burgo Ranero. She sat beside a guy of about my age, Canadian I think, who was an artist. He had he said, underestimated the physical and mental drain of the days walking, often leaving one just too weary to paint, and had only managed about half a dozen sketches thus far. I knew exactly how he felt, but also knew I was unlikely to pass this Way again, particularly since I was on my second Camino, and either subconsciously or consciously had developed a sense of guilt, if I sat resting without drawing! In other words, as the Spanish gentleman said in Los Arcos, I must be *loco!* The drawing I was to do later of the Church in Rabanal, would be my 80th in 2015!

It was a bright sunny evening, although with a strong chill wind. I was fortunate to find a stone bench in sunshine to sit on, and thankfully sheltered from the wind. I was reminded of just how chilly it felt that evening, by one of those serendipitous happenings.

As I walked out of Samos, I met briefly with a Swedish lady, Gun who was walking with a French guy Roland at the time. We met again in Sarria, as she walked out of the town, and I was scouting around for somewhere to draw. The French guy was evidently a keen photographer. Gun later emailed his Camino photos to me. Out of interest I glanced through them, recognising places, buildings, and searching faces for Pilgrims I may have met. I only recognised one, Gun, and a couple of shots of me all wrapped up in Rabanal. I had been completely unaware of his presence then, and by the time we had reached Samos, he had most likely forgotten about me.

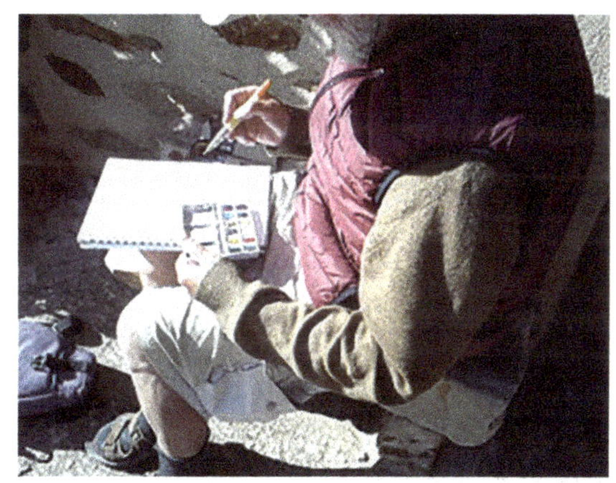

ROLAND MAYERL

As I left, I breakfasted at the bar I'd dined at on both my Caminos. It was empty, bar for an elderly local guy, just there for the warmth and company it appeared, and a young Korean girl sitting alone at one of the tables. As I collected my coffee and croissants off the counter, she gestured for me to join her. A pretty girl, full of life, she insisted on taking several photos of me with a miniature Sony camera, a sort I'd not seen in Europe. I remember as she told me her name was Sunny, pronounced as the camera.

We finished breakfast and I stood preparing to leave, I waited a moment and she said to go on as she needed the bathroom. With Astorga still fresh in my mind, and knowing that the mornings walk to be wild and often lonely scrub heathland. I walked slowly for the first mile or so. looking back, at stretches which offered a distant view, but I could see no sign of Sunny's distinctive red coat. I continued at a normal pace, hoping that she found company.

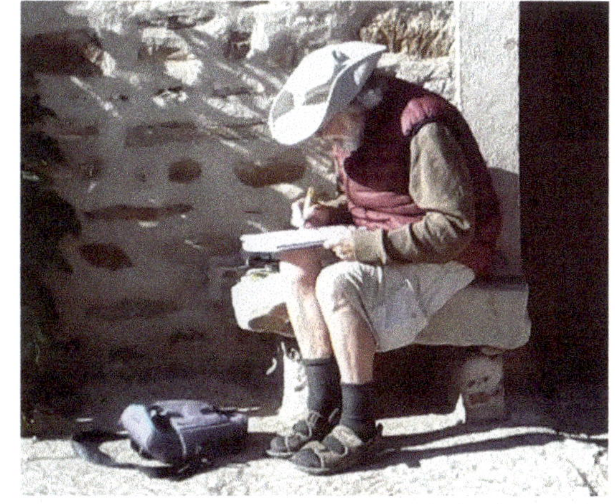

ROLAND MAYERL

El Acebo

On the rocky and at times steep descent from *Punto Alto*, a young girl skipped passed me with the lightness and surefootedness of a mountain goat! It made me feel old, well, at least my age, as I picked my way carefully between the rocks, recalling that used to be my preferred downhill method, much easier on the knees if you have good sense of balance and strong ankles.

The path wound down the steep slope around an acute bend suddenly opening up a view of Acebo spread out below.

In the bar terrace as one enters the village the young girl was sat at a table with the Scottish couple, he was of course sitting comfortably! I joined them, remarking to the girl that she had made me feel very old.

When I reached the same point in 2015, it was just starting to spit spot with rain. A guy I'd seen from the path above, and had hoped to take a peek at, was now hastily folding his easel and packing up his kit, so I didn't wish to delay him.

El Acebo is just a one street village, the Way runs through it. After I settled in my albergue at the bottom of the village, I ventured out, walking back up the hill, drawing and taking shelter under the distinctive balconied village houses, characteristic of El Acebo. I was there for much of the afternoon, and saw many Pilgrims passing by, but not Sunny.

As I was staying in the municipal albergue I had to take dinner at the bar up the hill. As I entered the dining section of the bar for my evening *Menu* I was about to sit at a vacant table when I noticed a lady sitting alone. Rather than take two tables at a busy time, and because it's more fun to have company, I asked if she would mind if I joined her.

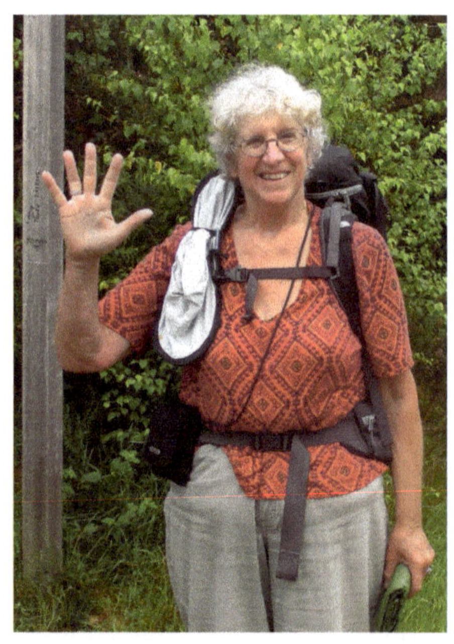

CHRISTY DAY

Christy the biscuit lady

She was an American lady, pleasant, interesting, and good company and we were soon in conversation, after a few moments, something about this lady seemed familiar, and then it dawned, I said, *"You are the biscuit lady!"* and we both laughed.

Towards the end of the meal, during which I'd mentioned that I was concerned about a young Korean girl I'd met in Rabanal, I heard a voice calling from the entrance, and in burst Sunny, all smiles, greeting people she knew at an adjacent table, and then the American lady, whom she had also met, and finally me. I was both pleased and relieved to see her, safe and well. I said as much to my companion. As the *vino tinto* seemed to have evaporated whilst we were deep in conversation, I suggested we repair to the bar so I could introduce her to the delights of Spanish Brandy!

She had apparently never tasted it before, but became an instant convert!

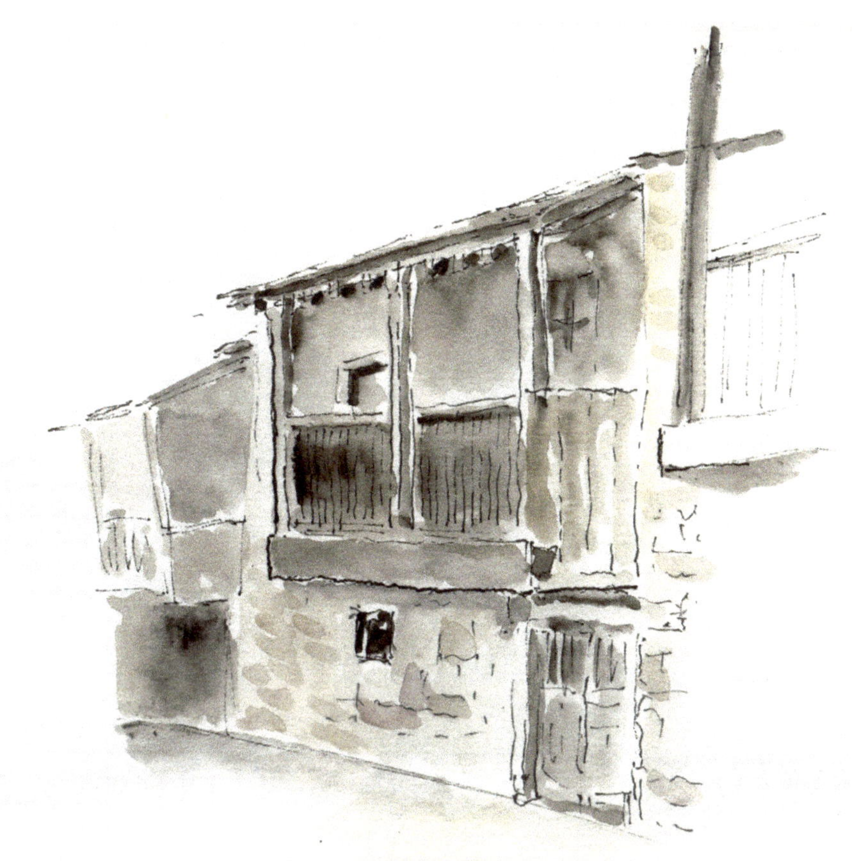

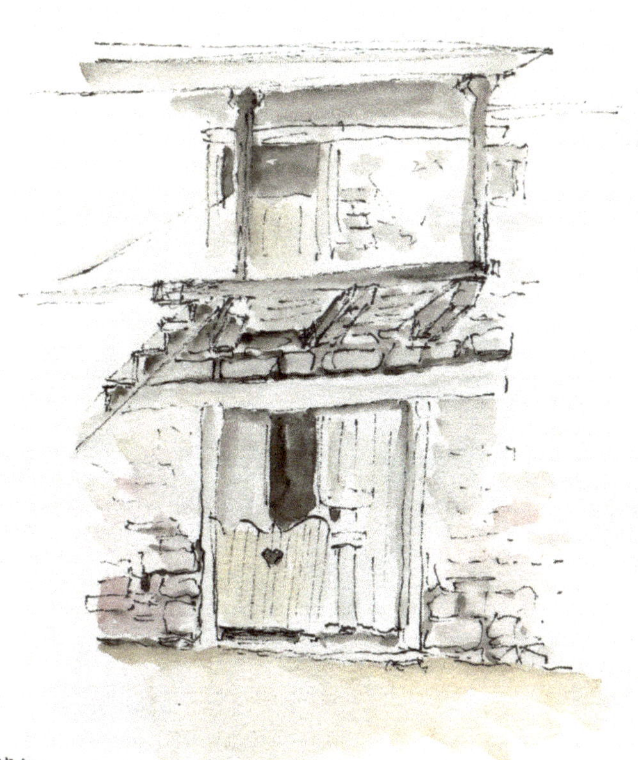
20·05·2015.
ACEBO.
BETWEEN LIGHT RAIN
SHOWERS.

Ponferrada

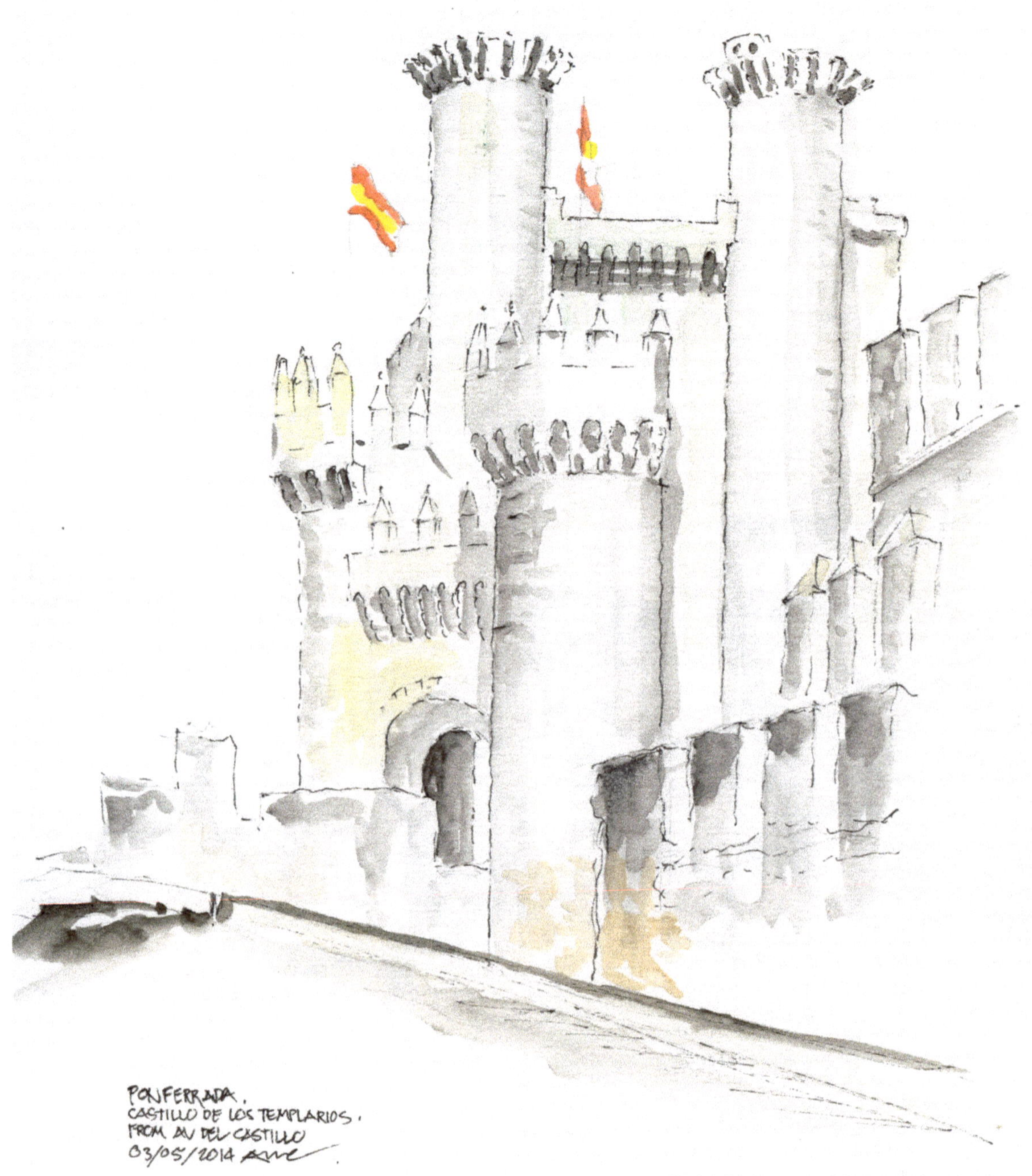

It was just a short walk into Ponferrada from Molinaseca, so I arrived quite early at the top of the hill opposite the *Castillo de los Templarios.* I found a tree to lean against at the kerbside, whilst drawing, and then took an exploratory amble. I got a Town Map from the *Officina de Tourismo*, and then sat just below, beside the Castillo on the low, slate capped wall, rather uncomfortably heated by the fierce sunshine, and drew again.

I thought it was time to find the albergue and had only walked a little way when I noticed further down sat on the low wall the young German lady who had made me feel so old, on the downhill approach to El Acebo. We moved to the shade, at a bar table opposite. She was passing time until catching a bus to Santiago, in the late afternoon.

Seeing I still had my rucksack with me, she insisted on guiding me to the Alburgue, as she had stayed there on a previous occasion. It has a pleasant garden and she said it would be a good place to wait, and take a taxi to the Bus Station, from there.

I said good bye, wishing her a safe journey, and left her sunbathing in the garden.

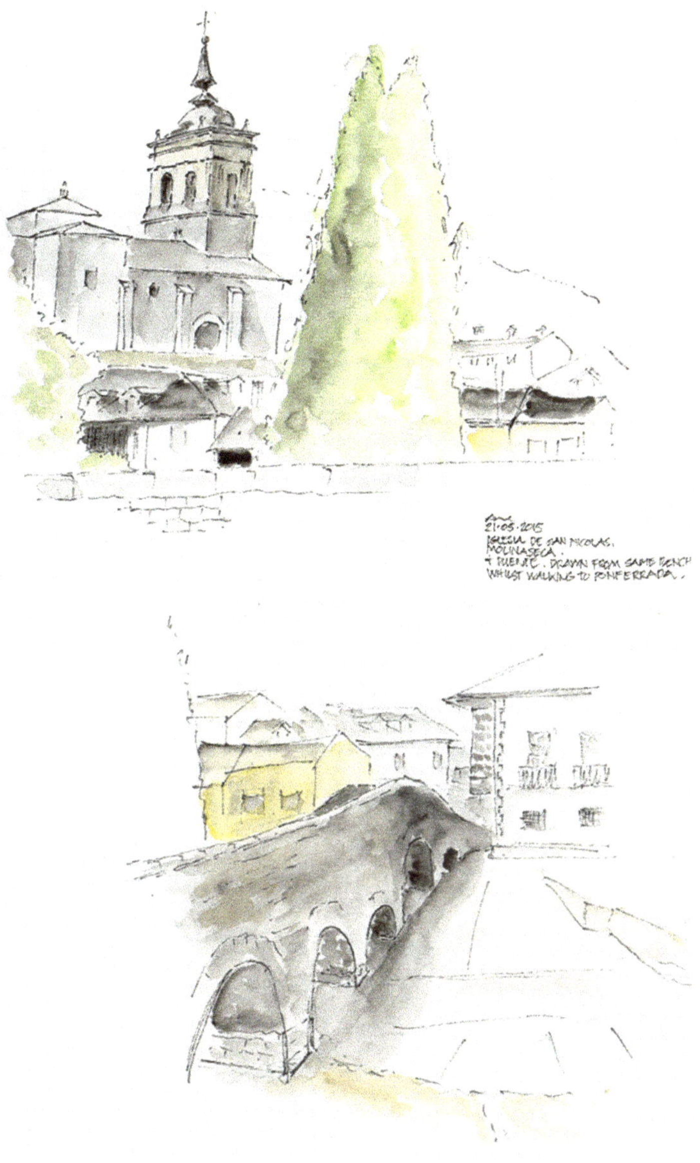

After checking, the first task was to catch up on my laundry. The washing facilities were situated at the end of the garden past the South face of the *Iglesia San Nicolás de Flue*. Walking back the adjacent shower block was empty, and I'd noticed the facilities in the albergue seemed very busy. As I continued through the garden section, a couple of ladies were just finishing a conversation. I thought I'd heard the one lady comment on the shower, and stopped to talk with her. I had been mistaken in what I'd heard, but we had a wide ranging and interesting conversation. Karin was Canadian, widowed, and had an ambition to create a commune of similar independent ladies, of a certain age.

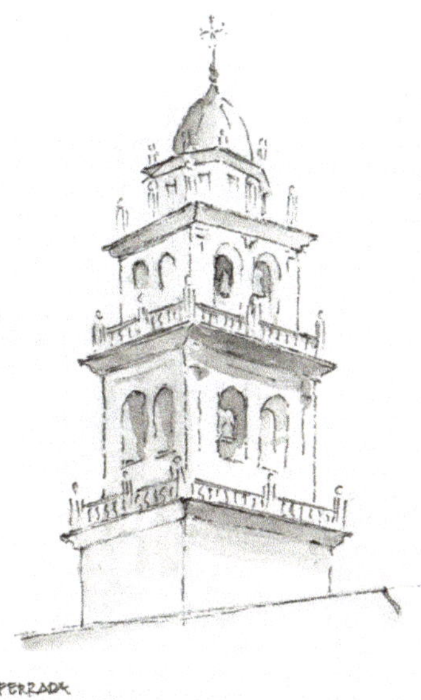

I tried the shower by the washing facility. I was the only one there; I stripped off, went into one of the cubicles, and found out why I was the only one. No hot water, so just a cold shower!

Across the road from the Albergue was a large car park, and beyond that a main road, with two or three bars visible. A couple of them had enterprisingly put sandwich boards with their Menus displayed just outside the albergue entrance. As I was reading the menus, I was joined by a young girl doing likewise. She was from the U.S. and told me she was feeling lonely and blue, as her friend had left earlier in the day. As the conversation progressed it transpired that her friend was Dilek, the young lady who had walked me to the albergue. So in an attempt to cheer her, I suggested we dine together. We sat outside the bar, and in between fending off the odd stray football, kicked by two lads, I listened to her ambition to become a writer. She was preparing a piece on her journey along the Way, as part of her College course, for when she returned.

I stayed in Ponferrada again in 2015. I walked along the Av. El Castillo and found a bench just a little way down the hill which offered a different view of the *Castillo* from my sketch the previous year.

It was a beautiful sunny day, and as the morning wore on, my peace was disturbed as coach loads of French tourists arrived. As one party left, another arrived; they stood around, whilst the tour guide struggled for their attention. I seemed more interesting than the *Castillo,* and various groups in front of me, behind me, literally peering over my shoulder. I can only conclude that they thought I was an item of street theatre, laid on by the Tour Company for their amusement, as a number of them became quite cross that I wouldn't pose to order!

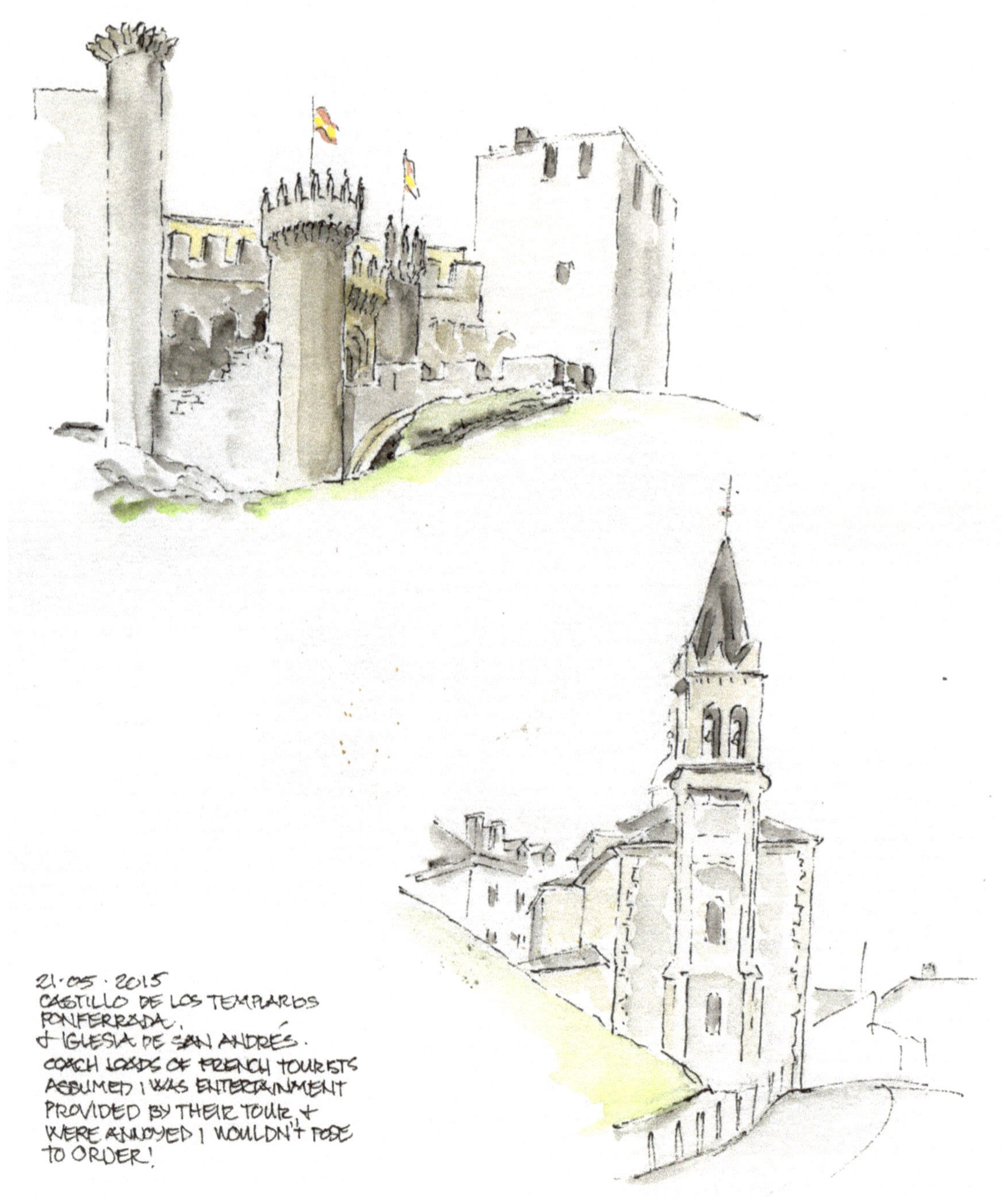

Villafranca del Bierzo

Cacabelos a village strung out along the Camino. As one enters the street is mainly residential, jetted houses, many of which I imagine started life as overhanging balconied dwellings as in Acebo, and over time have been filled in.

I stopped to sketch the *Capilla San Roque,* leaning against a wall up a side street opposite. I was out of sight of the many Pilgrims passing by, or entering the chapel, until a smiling Ann Marie, my Dutch friend with a French accent came by. She deliberately turned, anticipating I'd be there, and called out, that as she approached the chapel, she knew that I'd be sketching it.

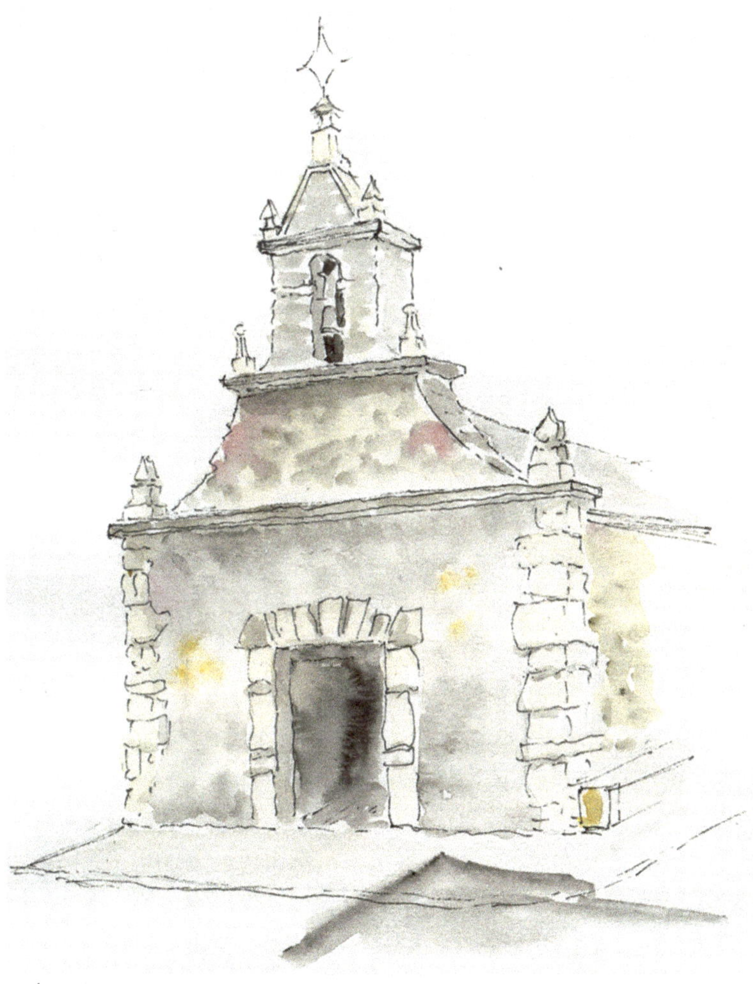

Further on the street narrows into the older and commercial end of the village, and just before the river I was tempted to stop for lunch at a bar with tables set out on artificial turf, under a deep green blind affording shade.I sat at a table, rucksack on a spare chair, and my front sack with my kit I laid down on the grass. Aaaagh! when I picked it up to leave, the turf had been watered and the bottom of the sack was soaked. It's only a cheap sack, light and quite flimsy, so I usually kept my pads in a plastic bag against such an eventuality, sod's law I hadn't that day.

Fortunately I only had a light lunch, and so the water had just penetrated and softened the cardboard cover, with damp creeping up from the bottom and only just beginning to affect the front and back pages.

The Way into Villafranca winds down from the *Alto* along a narrow high hedgerowed lane until the welcome sight of the Municipal Albergue appears below on the right. It looked new, and in a pleasant setting, but it was closed! I walked on a short distance and booked into an albergue just below the *Iglesia de Santiago de Villafranca.*

It was a fine sunny evening, and as I had no idea how far the centre of the village lay, or whether it would have a bar or bars, I elected to take the communal dinner at the albergue.

The upside was it gave me time to sit on the step of the North Portal of the church and Sketch. Miracles do happen along the Way, the church was open! and has a nice simple Romanesque interior.

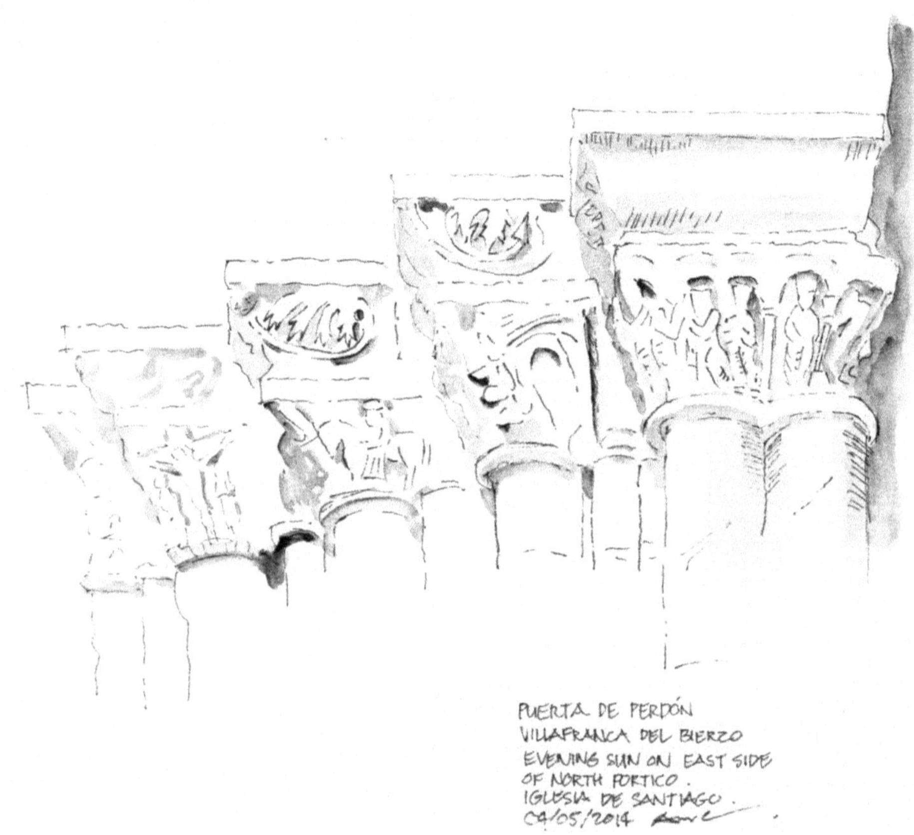

Dinner was memorable only if one had a riveting interest in rustic bread baking in the U.S. I haven't! The guy I sat next to was a baker, who droned on and on about the minutia of his craft. Just when I thought, well, that's it, some earnest Australian guy across the table, would ask another question, and so the monotony continued throughout the meal. The puzzle to me was, although this guy never seemed to shut up, how he still managed to consume 90% of the wine within reach, and beyond!

In 2015, I eschewed the delights of that albergue, and walked into the village with the thought of staying there. I didn't see any signs of albergues, and as I wasn't feeling too tired, I decided to press on a further six or seven Kms up the Valcarce Valley to Pereje, and thereby shorten the remembered hard days walk up to O'Cebreiro.

Arriving there relatively late had its advantages, as the basement dorms had been filled, and the Hospitalera opened up a street level room at the rear that was unexpectedly luxurious. The dorm had just a dozen or so single beds, and access to a balcony running the full length of the dorm, overlooking the garden, and the wooded hillside across the Valcarce Valley. Splendid!

O'Cebreiro

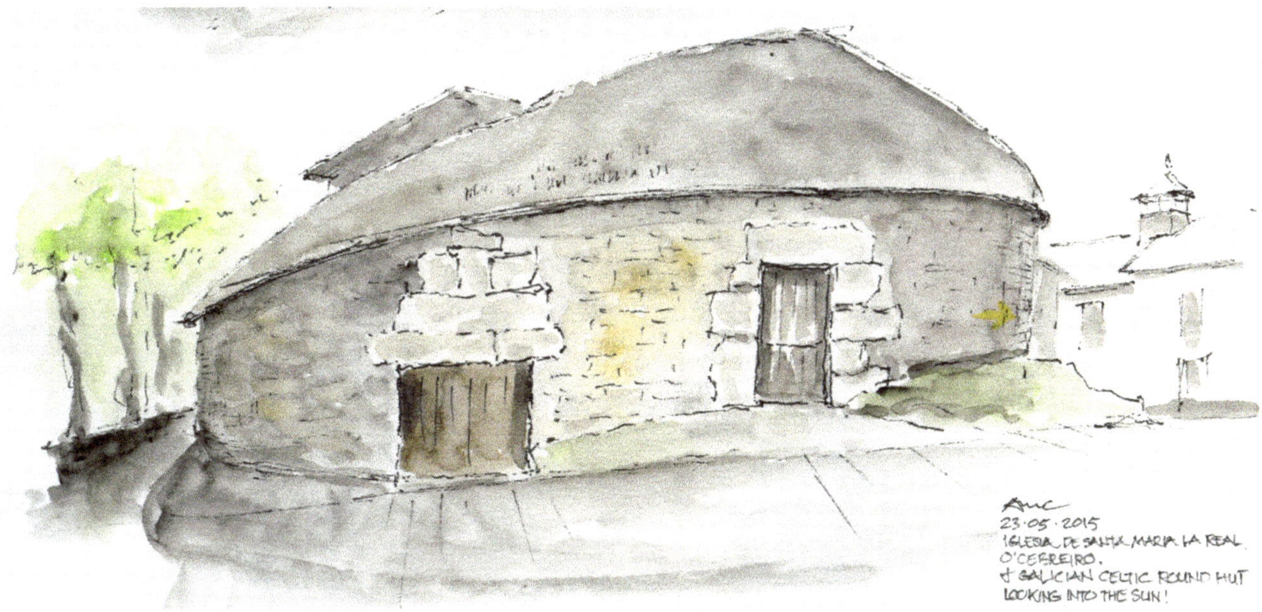

I was unable to find anywhere out of the wind, something to lean against, or sit on, which would have afforded the possibility of a sketch, and after the stiff climb into O'Cebreiro, I was too weary to stand and draw.

As I entered a bar for dinner, I heard my name called. I looked around, and there with tables pushed together to form a makeshift refectory table, sat a dozen or more Pilgrims, at the centre, I should say both physically, and of attention sat Karin! "Come and join us Austin" she said.

Introductions followed, I was she said, the friend she had mentioned, who drew. It was difficult to remember the names of those present at the time, however, I have an eye and memory for faces, and by chance seeing photos on Facebook groups, and other Camino items on the internet, I have identified half a dozen or so.

Karin wanted me to pass my sketchbook around, but at that stage, I had become very possessive of it. I carried it everywhere, not wishing to let it out of my sight, so I definitely did not fancy the prospect of it passing around a food laden table, navigating by sloshing glasses of vino tinto. I am fond of vino tinto, but not tinto on my sketches.

I confess on that evening, probably a little too fond, at least from the point of view of a Californian lady, who joined me as I sat alone twiddling a near empty glass, after Karin's party ha left. Erin was dining late, and her meal came with a bottle of wine, most of which I drank!

Having started out from Perje in 2015, I arrived a little earlier, and in rather better shape. I had to queue to book into the albergue, but then walked back through the village to draw. First I called in the bar by the church for a cool drink. A couple of young American girls came in, enquiring the cost of a room, as the albergue was now completo. I could see by the expression on their faces, it was an unwelcome expense, and could hear the cogs whirring as they calculated whether to afford it.

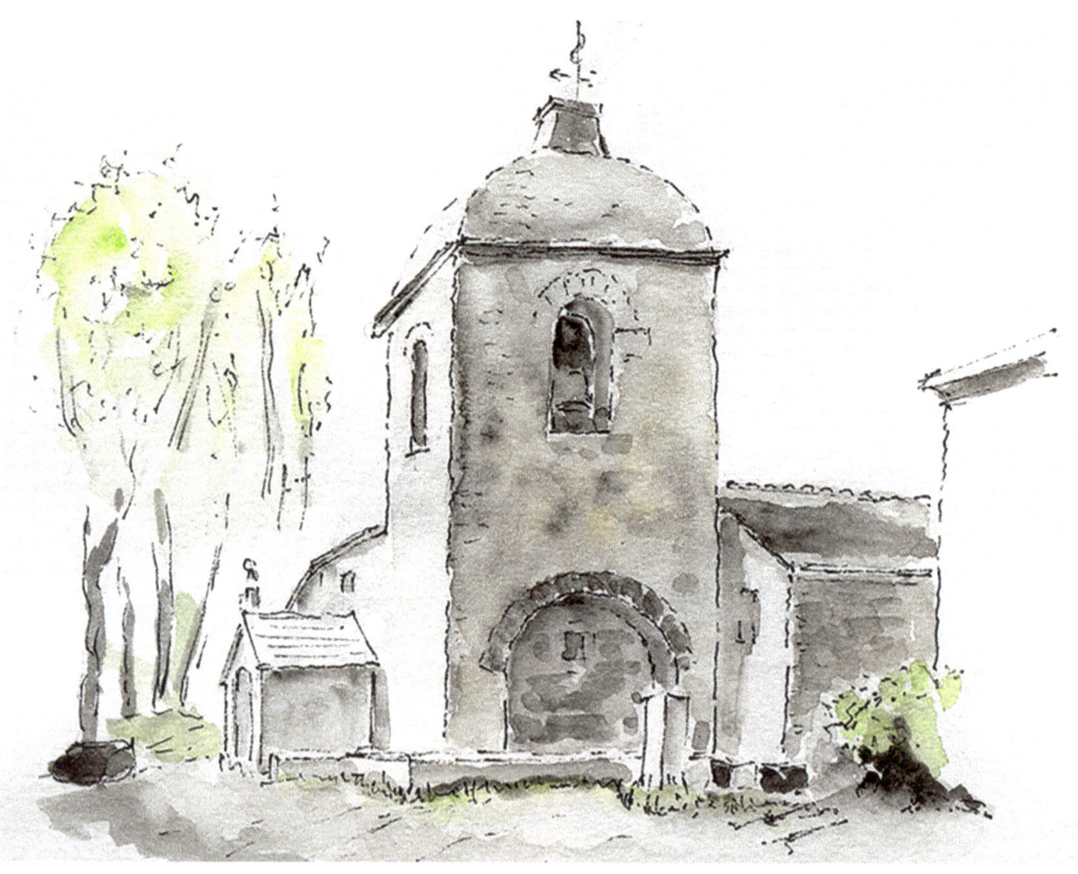

I left the bar, walked across the crazy paved street come square and passed through two fat round stone piers into the church yard. I took my pad, pen and watercolours, leaving my bag and the rest of my kit on a stone bench beside the bar's bedroom annexe; and leant against the stone boundary wall of the churchyard. As I did so I heard the rattle of a window catch, and the creak of a seldom used French window as it opened out onto a small balcony. I recognised the two girls from the bar, they were obviously determined to get their monies worth, in and out admiring the view, and as I was finishing the sketch, they began to put some laundry out to dry.

I crossed the yard, back to the bench, and sat beside my kit taking a rest in the afternoon sun. I was rudely shaken from my reverie by a trickle of water dribbling to the side of me, fortunately away from my kit. Jumping to my feet and looking up I saw a girl wringing some laundry. She hadn't noticed me until I stood. She apologised, and we both laughed. It struck me as funny, as last year I'd been careful to avoid spilt vino tinto on my sketchpad, only to have a near miss of soapy water this year!

I left O'Cebreiro in a light short lived drizzle and arrived in Samos in the late afternoon. I mooched around what I could see of the Monastery church, but the C18 Baroque façade somehow didn't inspire. So made a quick sketch looking across the river, on leaving in the morning.

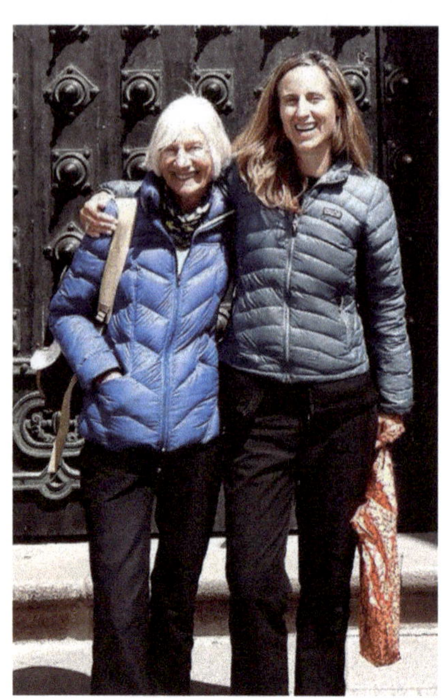

ERIN PRZBYLINSKI

Erin with Mom Eileen reached SdC

Samos

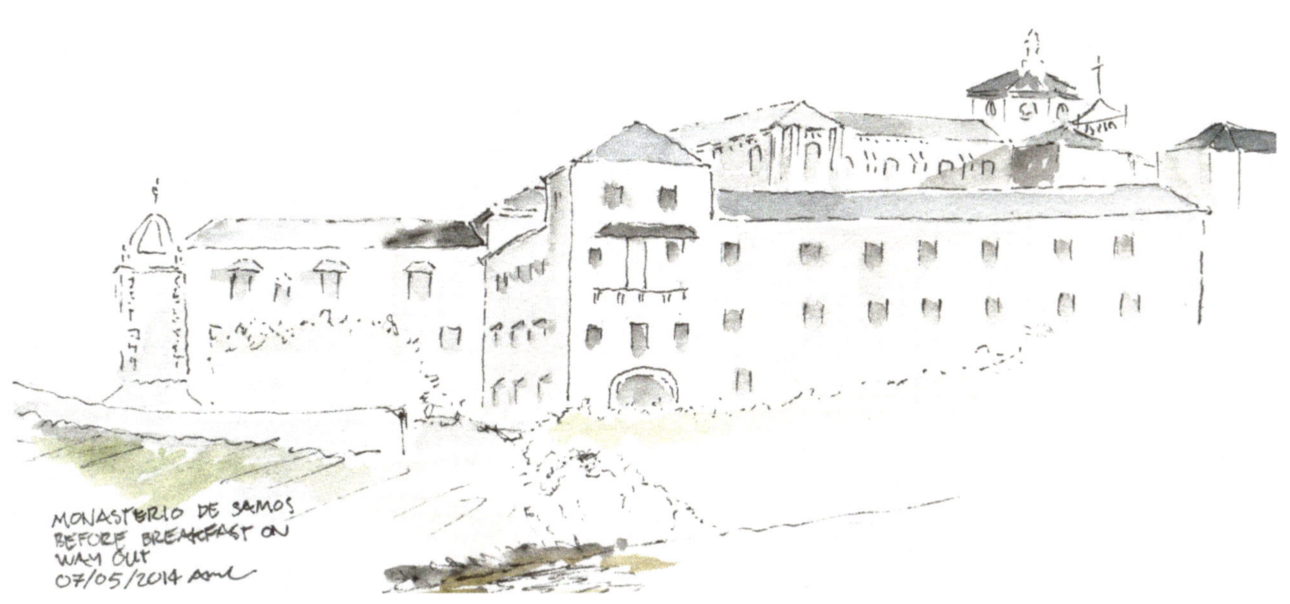

I had booked in at the quaint albergue Monasterio de Samos. Very basic, but what it lacked in amenities it made up for in charm. The dorm had a barrel vaulted ceiling, with the beam soffits painted in a decorative scroll and floral pattern, and murals on the walls in a rather fun naive style. Another memorable feature was the petrol pump outside the entrance door, which appeared to be the only access, so one hoped there wouldn't be a fire!

Conveniently there was a bar across the road which I headed for after leaving Mass in the church half way through as after the heat of the day the church felt icy cold. When I entered the bar I saw Karin sitting at one of the tables where I joined her with a vino tinto to thaw out. She corralled me into another of her wonderful impromptu communal dinners.

Unlike 2014, as I left O'Cebreiro in brilliant sunshine, cloudless blue sky, and a feeling of being on top of the world, quite literally as the rolling hills and valleys to the North were obscured by a sea of fluffy white cloud. I stopped at Triacastela and in the morning approaching Samos en route to Sarria I made a quick thumbnail as the path from San Cristobo descends and the monastery suddenly comes into view.

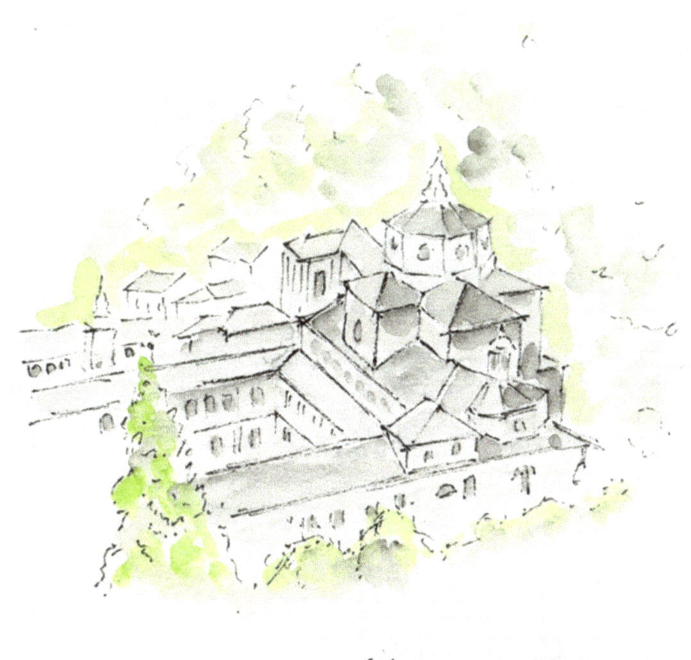

Towards Sarria

24·05·2015
WALKING FROM O'CEBREIRO TO TRIACASTELA.
IGLESIA DE HOSPITAL DE LA CONDESA.
HAS, AS IN PREV VILLAGE LIÑARES, STONE VAULT CAP AS O'CEB.

It was my custom to try and phone home each evening on my old Nokia, which is just one step up from a cocoa tin and string. It was also the limit of technology I could manage, that is if, as my Son is wont to remind me, I remembered to switch it on!

I had foolishly left my Continental adapter in an albergue in Frómista, so as I walked into Sarria I knew my battery was running pretty low; and the phone battery too! It had lasted so long as I only let the phone ring out a couple of times, ring off, and wait for Ann to call me back. Ever the optimist, I felt sure I would pass a shop window full of adaptors, which might serve to remind me to buy one. I didn't.

In Samos the night before, I had warned Ann of the problem, So Sarria was hopefully to come to my rescue. I had noted it was a reasonably sized grey splodge in my Brierley Guide, so I was hopeful.

The people responsible for siting *Officinas de Tourismo* seemed to have strayed from their normal practice in Sarria. It was sited prominently and conveniently just as one enters the Town, and not hidden away so as to be left undisturbed; and, wonder of wonder, it was open!

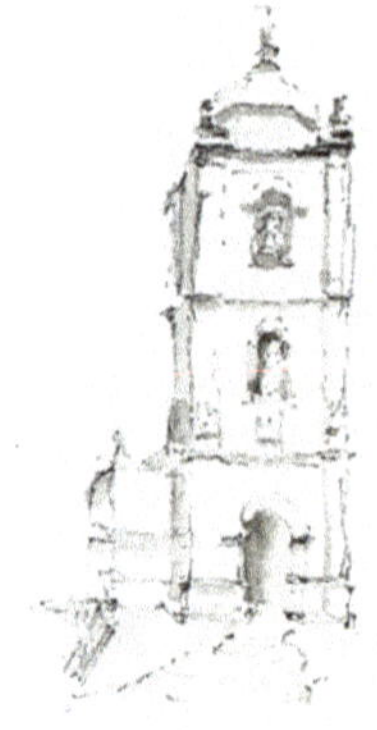

Inside, a very helpful lady gave me a map, telling me of, and marking sites of architectural interest, as I had explained my habit of drawing along the Way. And then another map, this time marked with positions of four shops, she felt might have an adaptor.

I set off map in hand in search of an adaptor. I found the first shop she had marked; it was the kind we rarely see any more in the UK. No stylish window dressing, the shop seemed to sell everything, clothes clocks bags, even furniture, and examples of their stock were crammed into the window without the slightest nod in the direction of aesthetics.

I spoke in my stilted Spanish to the two young women behind the counter, but of course my vocabulary did not extend to Continental adaptors, and I had to resort to English, hand waving, and an English person's last resort, speaking English louder! All met with blank stares and shrugs. I then had an idea, I drew a socket an adapter and the cable to my phone., held it up, and one lady disappeared for a few moments, and returned smiling, holding up a polythene bag with a dozen or so adaptors visible.

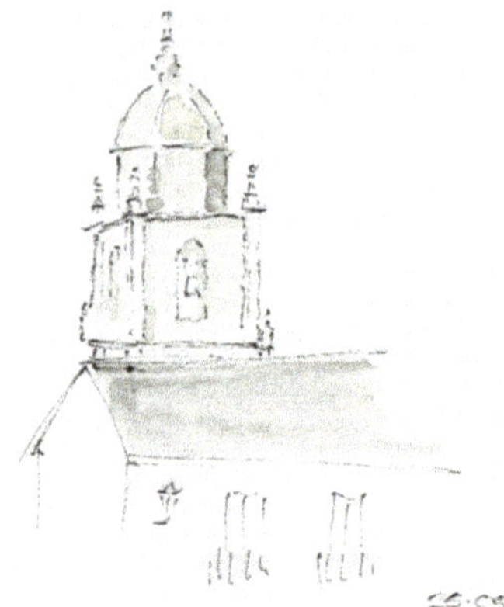

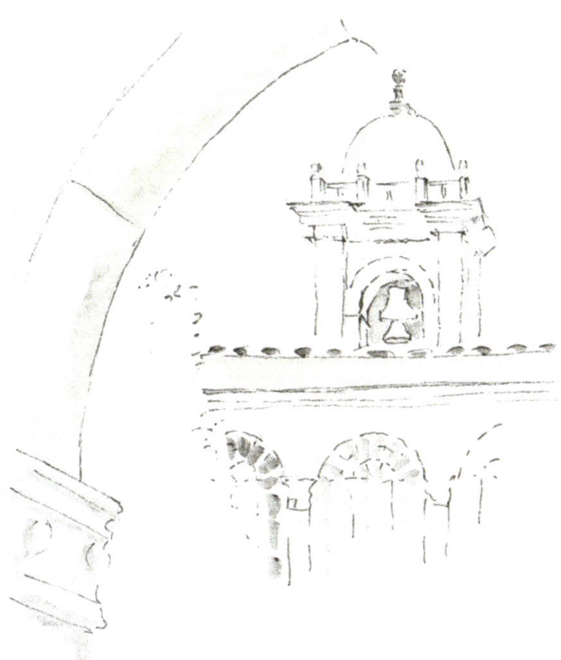

Feeling relieved and rather pleased with myself I continued to follow the Way marks and booked into a pleasant and airy albergue half way up a series of steps leading to the old town.

After dropping off my kit I walked through the town to *Convento de la Madalena* as literature given to me at the Tourist Office suggested the cloisters were worth a visit. I arrived about forty five minutes prior to the 4 PM opening time. Just before four, an elderly guy I'd passed on the walk up the hill walked down and through the door.

I waited patiently till four, and rang the bell. No response. I rang again, and again, still no one appeared. I sat on the wall for a few more minutes and tried again. In the pause following my third attempt, the old guy came to the door, and rather grumpily let me in. Before my eyes had adjusted from the bright glare of the afternoon sun, to the gloom of the hall, he had disappeared, leaving me to explore.

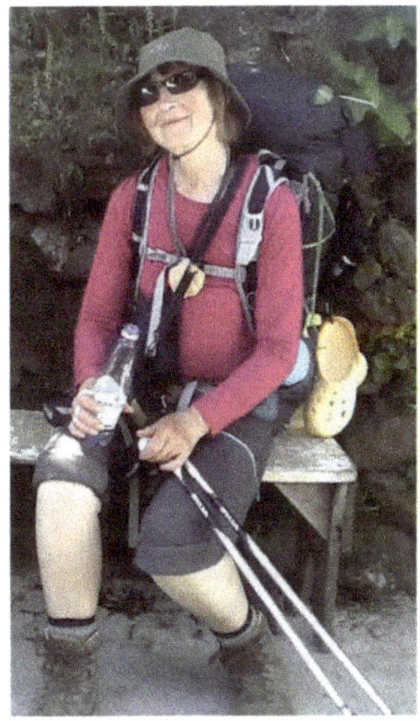

ROLAND MAYERL

My friend Gun

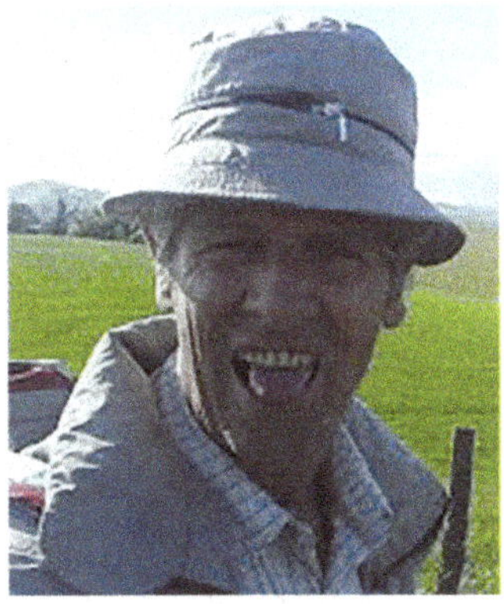

ROLAND MAYERL

The unseen Roland!

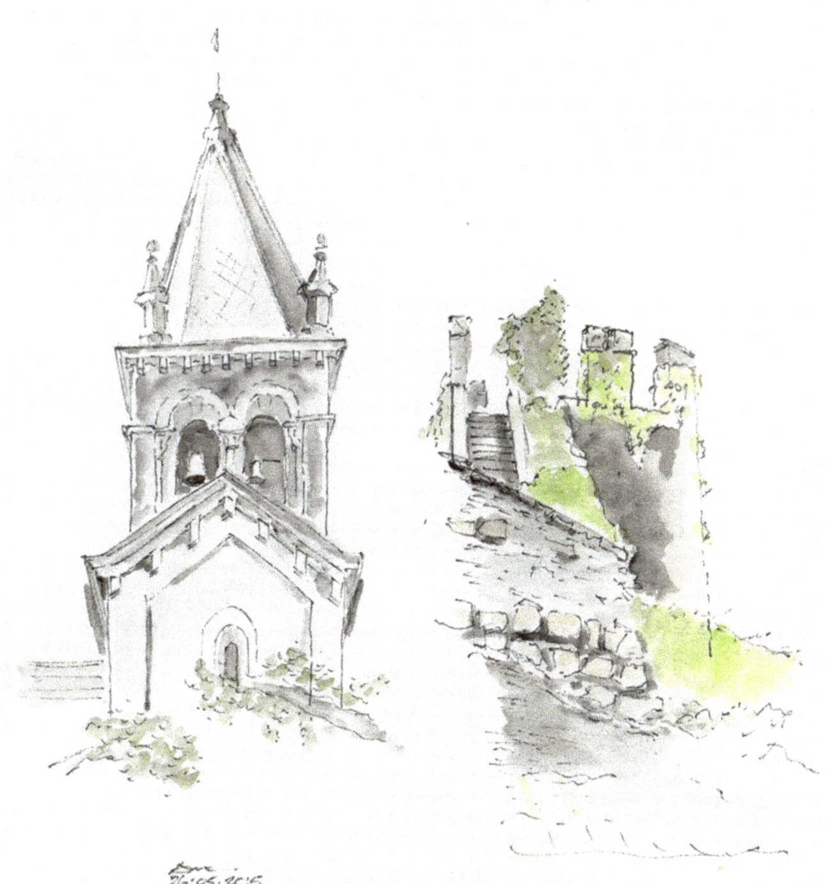

The cloisters were something of a disappointment, but I enjoyed the cool shade, and made a little sketch looking across the garth.

On the way back into town I sat on a low wall below a hedge in the evening sun and sketched the campanile of my favourite church in Sarria. Sadly it was closed, and even sadder, in 2015 the dreaded Spanish Restorers were gutting the place, the roof stripped, scaffolded and hoarded off, no doubt stonework to be replaced. Sigh! If I were to walk that way again, and could bear to look, I would see a pristine exterior, totally devoid of any patina of history.

In 2015, the dorm at the albergue there were just five of us. A rather glamourous lady of about my age, who had greeted me as I first entered, pleased she said to hear an English accent. She had apparently left England at an early age to pursue a career in films. Her husband, I think Canadian, a retired Opera bass, their son and his partner. Since I was the only non-family member, I might have felt uncomfortable, but they all were most welcoming, and great fun.

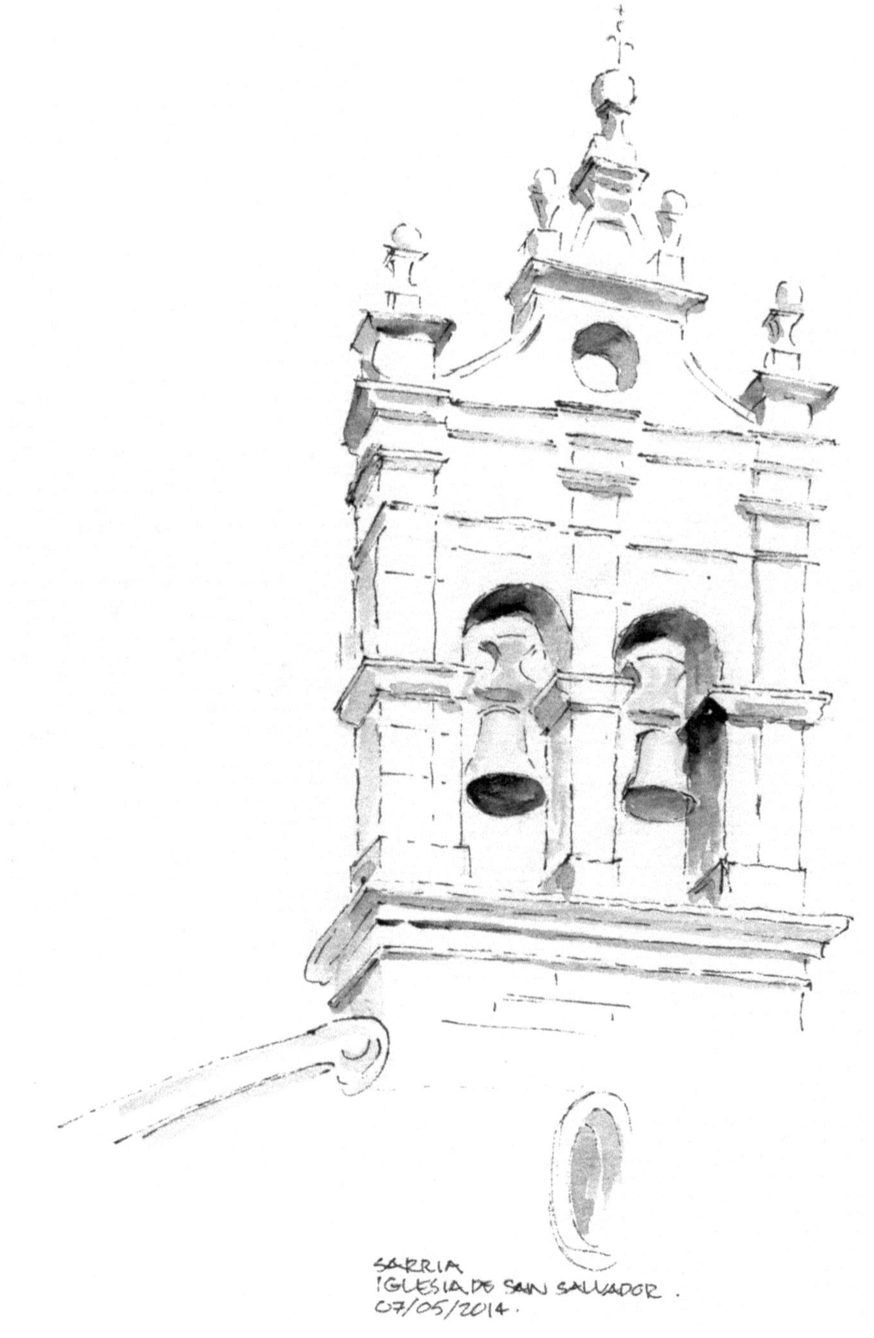

Leaving Sarria to Portmarín

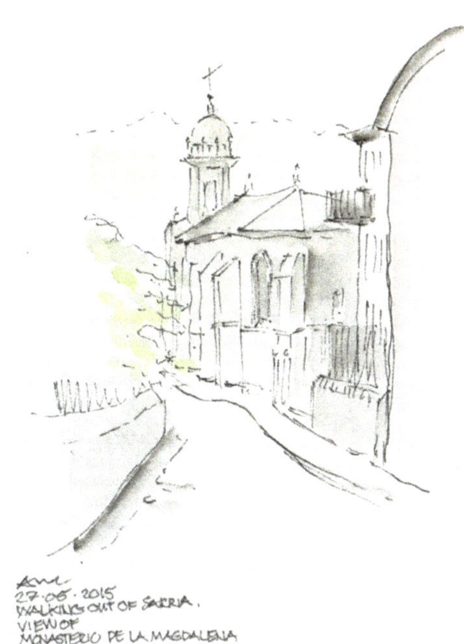

As I was walking back down into the town in the evening, after drawing the *iglesia San Salvador* I saw a Pilgrim I'd seen off and on since San Bol. He was from Alaska and walking with his sightless Son. His passion was ornithology, which apparently was as time consuming as drawing, and hence we seemed to keep pace with one another, staying in the same villages. But that was the last time I met with him, although I did chat briefly with his Son who was enjoying a pint in Santiago.

Setting off for Portomarín in the morning I stopped a short while to sketch the Monastery, just beating the traffic jam of Mom's and Dad's taxis dropping off their children at the school.

On both Caminos, I stayed at the same albergue in Portomarín. In 2014 I mooched around, not finding a sketch that caught my imagination, so settled for a beer at a bar across from the church. I had apparently missed Mass, as whilst I sat there Pilgrims spilled out of the South Portal. I wasn't too disappointed as four Irish ladies, sisters I'd seen along the Way spoke to me, they were frozen and glad to be out in the warm.

Leaving in the morning, I saw the illusive sketch I'd failed to find the night before. On my second visit, though I paced up and down the hill, stopping and peering at all angles, frustratingly I was unable to find it again.

Feeling a little dejected I continued down the hill into the *Praza* (now being in Galicia) and drew the dour 13th.C. Fortress church of the Knights of St John sitting on the steps of the *Ajuntamiento*.

The church was rebuilt stone by stone, when the valley was flooded in the 60's.

Returning to the albergue, I found my biscuit lady was also booked in, so I had enjoyable company for dinner.

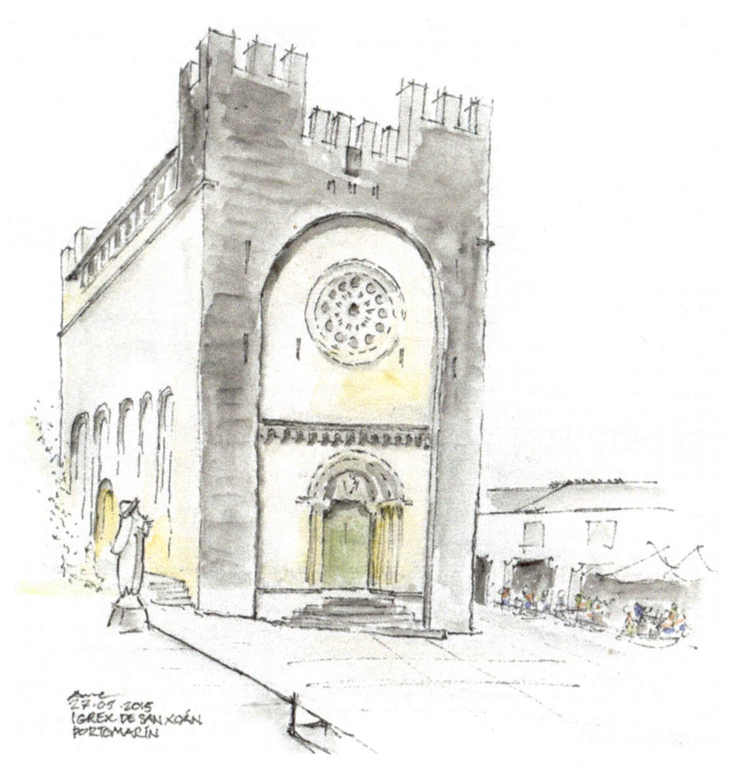

Portomarín to Eirexe and Palas de Rei

It was another splendid day leaving Portomarín. I had one Euros worth on the internet back at the albergue, checked my emails and was delighted to see a message from Caroline; she was hoping to reach Santiago for dinner the evening before my flight back home.

My shin splints had all but disappeared and with the news from Caroline I felt as if I was walking on air.I had dropped down the hill from Ligonde and was climbing up the other side, passed a bar set back from the road with tables spread over the grass, busy with Pilgrims. I recognised a couple I'd met previously and raised an arm in acknowledgement. Still climbing, I had gone another couple of hundred yards, when a cricket ball hit me very hard on my right calf, halting me abruptly in my tracks. I looked around, no cricket ball, but an excruciating muscle cramp. In hindsight, it was probably my own fault through not drinking enough water.

I limped on very gingerly, frequently stopping to rest. A few minutes passed, and amazingly, or so it seemed at the time, in the middle of nowhere I came across a bar set back on the left, and a modern looking albergue opposite.

After resting at a bar table for an hour or so, trying weight on my leg occasionally, it became obvious I was not going to be able to walk the 8Km to Palas de Rei, which had been my intention, so opted for an early night in the albergue opposite.

In the morning I still didn't feel able to walk any distance, and after considerable soul searching, I arranged for a taxi to the Bus Station in Palas de Rei. The Bus Station turned out to be a lay-by, or rather an indentation into the footpath, adjacent to the *Ayuntamiento.*

I crossed to a bar opposite situated at the bottom of an alley, and judging from the arrows painted on the road next to the crossing, the alley probably lead to an albergue.

I took my time over breakfast, testing now and then my leg. The guy behind the bar carefully wrote the times of buses for me, and standing in the doorway pointing to the Lay-by across the road.

As part of my preparation for the Camino, I carried a note book, with possible albergues, gleaned from the Eroski site, and importantly for me, sites of interest I wished to visit, and possibly draw, noted from my Gitlitz and Davidson. The *Iglesia Santa Maria de Melide,* was one such, so I caught the bus to Melide, thinking if I have to rest, I may as well draw.

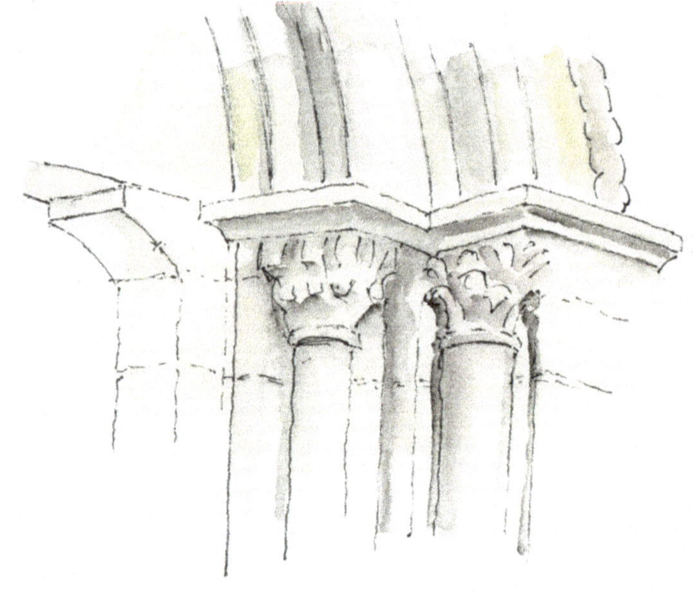

I limped slowly from the bus stop, to a *Farmacia* and bought pain killers. Disappointingly, I found the church was over a Km distant from the centre, and I hadn't the confidence that I could manage that far and possibly back again to obtain accommodation in the Town.

In 2015 I walked carefully up the hill into Eirexe, and enjoyed the prospect of walking over new ground. Passing through Portos, I bumped into Biscuit Lady who I had dined with the previous evening. She was just coming out of the albergue garden where she was staying.

We walked a short distance together; she was going to Vilar de Donas. At the junction we chatted a while, she saying I should accompany her as I would appreciate the monastery. It is one of the few regrets I have of my Camino, that I didn't join her. In 2014 from my Gitlitz and Davidson I had included in my notebook, to take the detour to the *Monasterio de San Salvador,* but I had omitted to transfer it to my 2015 notebook, and for reasons I can't explain, I failed to remember.

Instead I continued to Palas, and found there was not much more to it than I'd previously seen limping across the road and back again.

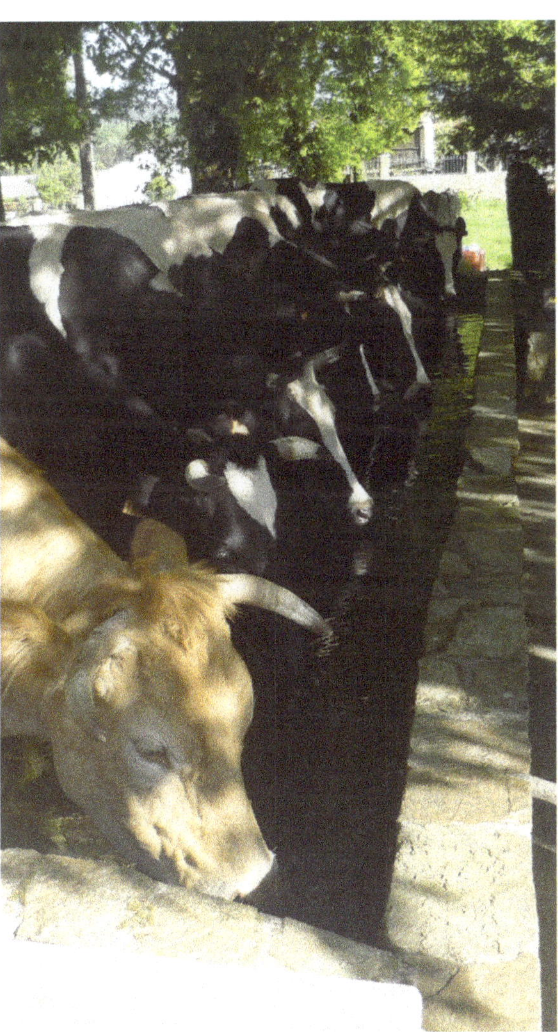

My drinking companions at the bar in Eirexe

Walking from Palas de Rei 2015

It was new walking territory again and we were well into *Horreos* country, and had been since Portomarín. Arriving in San Xulián del Camino there was a splendid example at the side of the road, and somewhere to sit for a while. As I sketched I heard behind me, a lady calling encouragement to cattle she was moving for milking. I was sat on a plinth in the middle of the road, and the herd split, passing very close either side of me. A number of the more curious stopped literally peering over my shoulder, although none passed a comment

Approaching Melide, I was tempted to stop at bar with an attractive courtyard set with a number of busy tables. I joined two Italian ladies, and had been there but a few minutes, when Biscuit Lady arrived, taking the remaining vacant seat at the table.

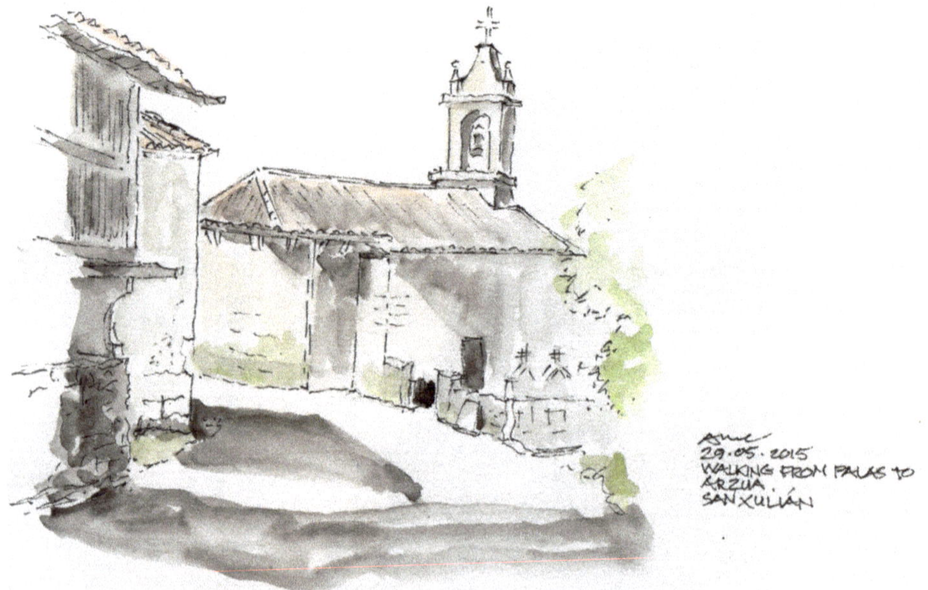

It was pleasant to see her again, and we walked together into Melide, where she wished to stay. We had enjoyed one another's company, much nicer to dine with someone, rather than alone, so we tentatively arranged to meet up in Santiago. Sadly, although I waited at the appointed meeting place, she failed to turn up. I was to learn from correspondence afterwards, that she was just too tired.

I'm an old grump, never satisfied. I moan because the majority of churches along the Way are closed, and I found the church I would like to have drawn the previous year, open. But they were holding some sort of event, and folk milling around everywhere, making it difficult to find a peaceful spot to draw. Having grumpily given up I entered the church, my grumpiness soon dispelled and spirits lifted by the wonderful 15th.C frescoes.

Making the right decision seemed to have been beyond me at that period. I had inexplicably missed the opportunity to visit the *Monasterio de San Salvador, Vilar de Donas* the day before. Now, although I had previously found Arzúa to be probably the most boring town along the Way, I walked through Ribadiso, the albergue in an idylic setting in the river valley. Pilgrims sun bathing on the grassy banks, some dangling feet in the cool water, and braver souls paddling, yet continued and again stayed in Arzúa.

Arzúa

The bus stop in Arzúa was at one end of the town, the wrong end for me. A town strung out along the main road. Fortunately, the pain killers bought in Melide were now kicking in, and I was able to limp along continuously, without constant pauses.

After booking in I limped back to the square, and sat at a bar table and did a thumbnail of the modern church tower, through the pollarded Plane trees. I passed the time there, until it was time to go in search of a *Menu*.

It was a Saturday evening, approaching nine o-clock, but even so the street was virtually deserted, when I saw a strange sight. It was Angus, walking toward me! One of the very few times I saw him, 'not sitting comfortably'. Like most Pilgrims by this stage of the Camino, waist lines have shrunk, and trousers are in danger of falling around ankles! He had just purchased a pair of trousers and was wandering around whilst his tailor made the necessary alterations. I should add, still wearing the old trousers.

I was amazed that he had found such a service at such a late hour, in what appeared to me a one horse town.

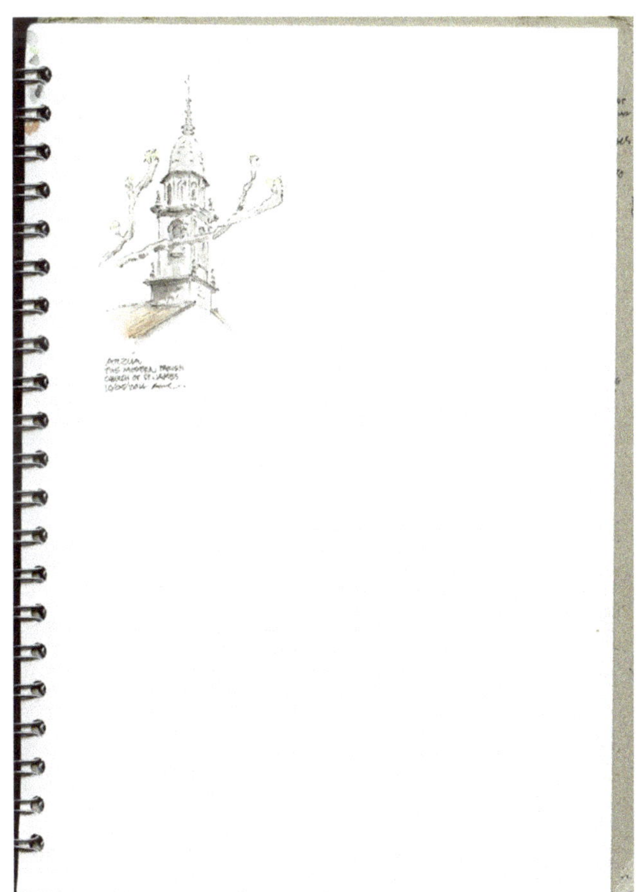

Arzúa was much as I had remembered from my first Camino. I recall sending an email to my friend Caroline, telling her where I had got to, and was making the most of what the town had to offer. I mentioned, standing watching the *Farmacia* sign go, green cross, date, time, temperature. Green cross, date, time, temperature. Green cross….. and so on, and then turned my attention to the traffic lights, red, amber, green. Red, amber, green…..All pretty heady stuff in Arzúa!

The page from my sketchbook sums up how I felt about Arzúa at the time!

In fairness to the town, I suppose my grumpiness from a painful calf may have influenced my judgement! I should add the albergue I stayed at on both occasions was very comfortable, with excellent facilities. And the food was good too where I ate my *Menu* on both occasions, although there was not much of an alternative.

I recall I had 'stiffed' peppers which were splendid, and explaining to the lady that we spell it with a 'u' Although she may have been better advised to leave it, as like me, others might choose it to find out what 'stiffed' peppers were.

Walking from Arzúa, the final stages

What I found, of my two Caminos, is how they reflect a life in miniature. One starts out at SJPdP, full of energy and enthusiasm, as in childhood, you feel you could climb a mountain, and you do! Then you mature, as in life, you grow by experience, you meet, meet again, say goodbye to, or not to friends made. You walk with those you have come to love, carefree, enjoying the day, and before you know it, it seems like only yesterday you walked into Pamplona, but there you are, a day or so from Santiago, and the end!!! Just as in life, like me, I 'suddenly!' find myself in my mid-seventies, and I suppose the end too, not that far away!

The final few stages were for me the least enjoyable of the Way. As one nears Santiago, whilst there are admittedly attractive stretches of countryside, and the odd interesting hamlet, the towns increasingly become dormitories and are devoid of any architectural interest. Pilgrim numbers too, are swollen by those wishing to obtain a Compostela, but with only the time and or energy to complete the last 100Km from Sarria. Many walk in groups, insular and detached from the Way and other Pilgrims, and something of the comradery and benevolence of earlier sections of the Way is lost.

Reaching Arca do Pino in 2014, I just about managed to pass the *Tanatorio* which was next door to the albergue. Arca is a small dormitory town, with a good deal of new development, some of it only loosely connected to the existing, creating a semi-rural patchy urban sprawl.

In the evening, I walked to the church. I had glimpsed the tower across fields in gaps between new developments. The church and the small cluster of dwellings surrounding it are separate from the new, and the earlier 20th.C ribbon development, strung out along the main road to Santiago. A simple, rather sad building, but its tower must have presented an elegant silhouette and focal point in earlier times.

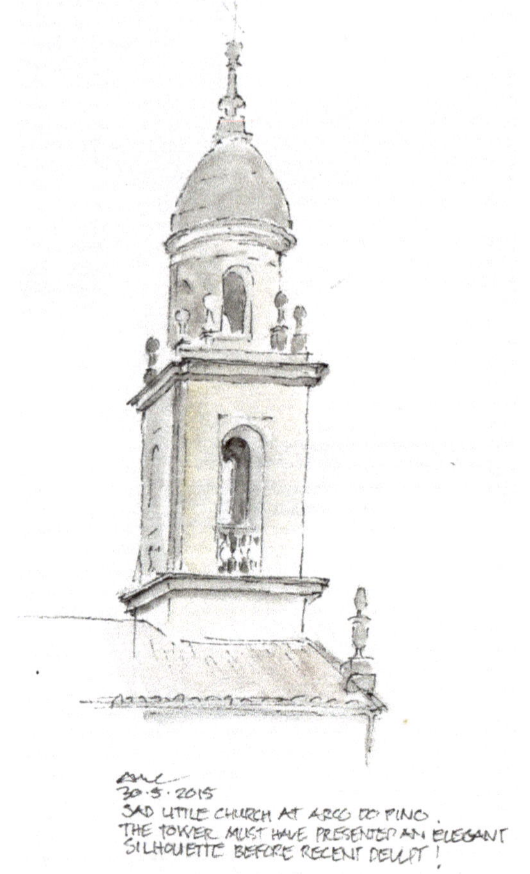

As I sat drawing I saw for the last time three young girls, I suppose in their twenties, whom I'd seen on numerous occasions along the Way. One of the girls was in a wheelchair, and I'd seen her two companions struggle up steep, stony paths, refusing offers of assistance from other Pilgrims. It seemed a real pilgrimage, in the true sense of the word. Bless them.

My first Camino, the journey along that stretch was enlivened by tightening the string on my cocoa tin, searching the darker recesses of my memory to recall the semaphore alphabet from my scouting days, and pinching blankets from the albergues, to send smoke signals from the hilltops, all to relay messages to Caroline of my progress, as I neared Santiago; and of course scanning the horizon for her replies.

I was overjoyed that Caroline was hoping to be in Santiago the day before I was due to leave, and had suggested meeting up for dinner. I had thought Nicola would have been well ahead of me, but I learnt that she was behind. I was disappointed to have missed her by just a day, but as I wrote to her afterwards, my sadness was somewhat assuaged by the prospect of having Caroline's company all to myself.

I seem to have lost my bearings in the euphoria of reaching SdC. It was of course the NORTH TOWER, which was scaffolded and nettted when I was there in 2014.

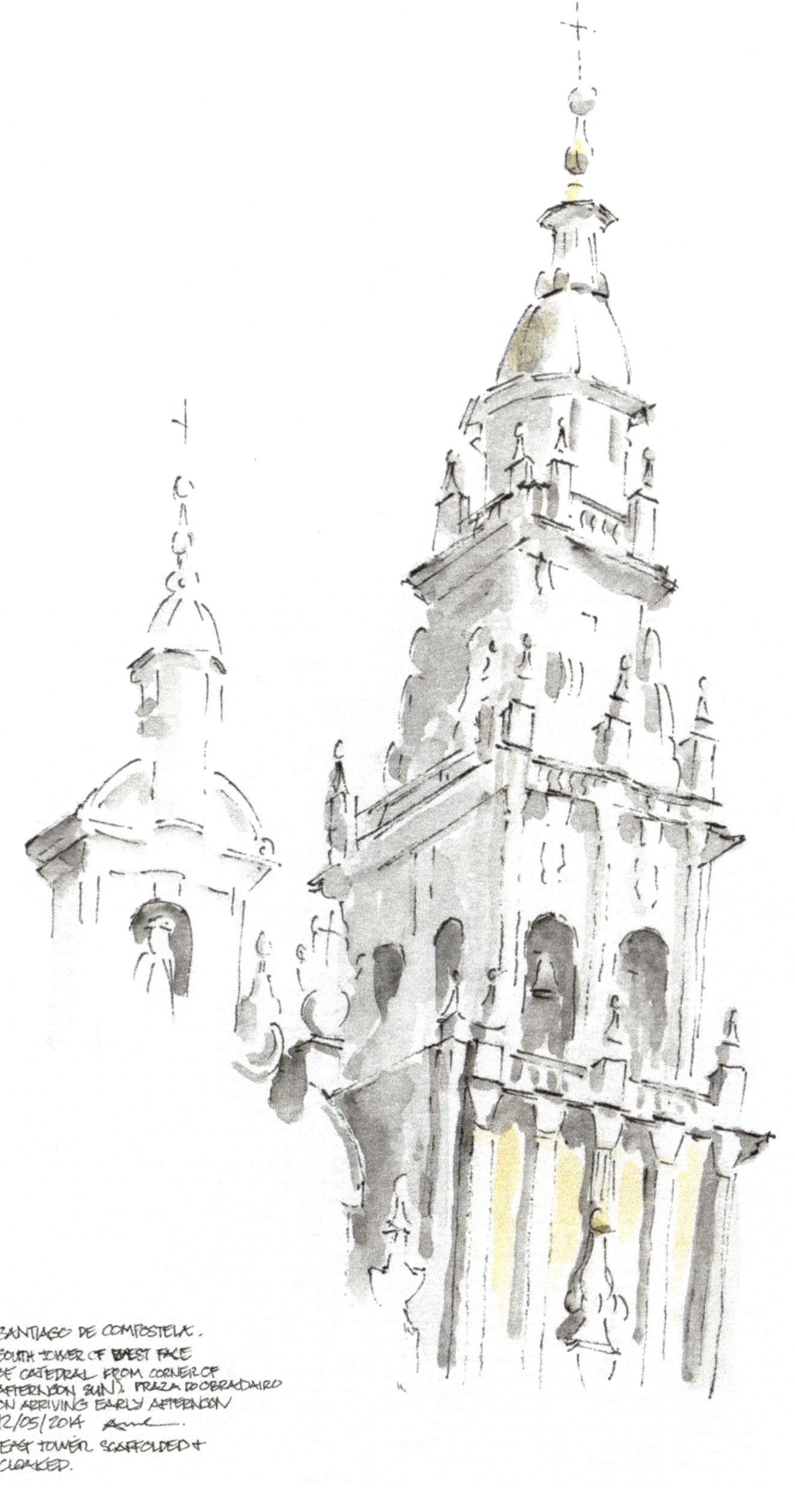

Santiago de Compostela

I had been to Santiago on a motoring holiday with my wife some years ago. So I felt privileged to have seen the iconic West Facade of the Cathedral unadorned with scaffold and netting. At that period too, we gained entry by the Baroque steps from the Plaza Obradoiro, into the Narthex, and not being a Pilgrims at the time, squeezing passed the queue of Pilgrims in the *Puerta de la Gloria,* awaiting their turn to touch, and contribute to the centuries of hand polishing, on the marble *parteluz* (mullion) supporting the statue of St James.

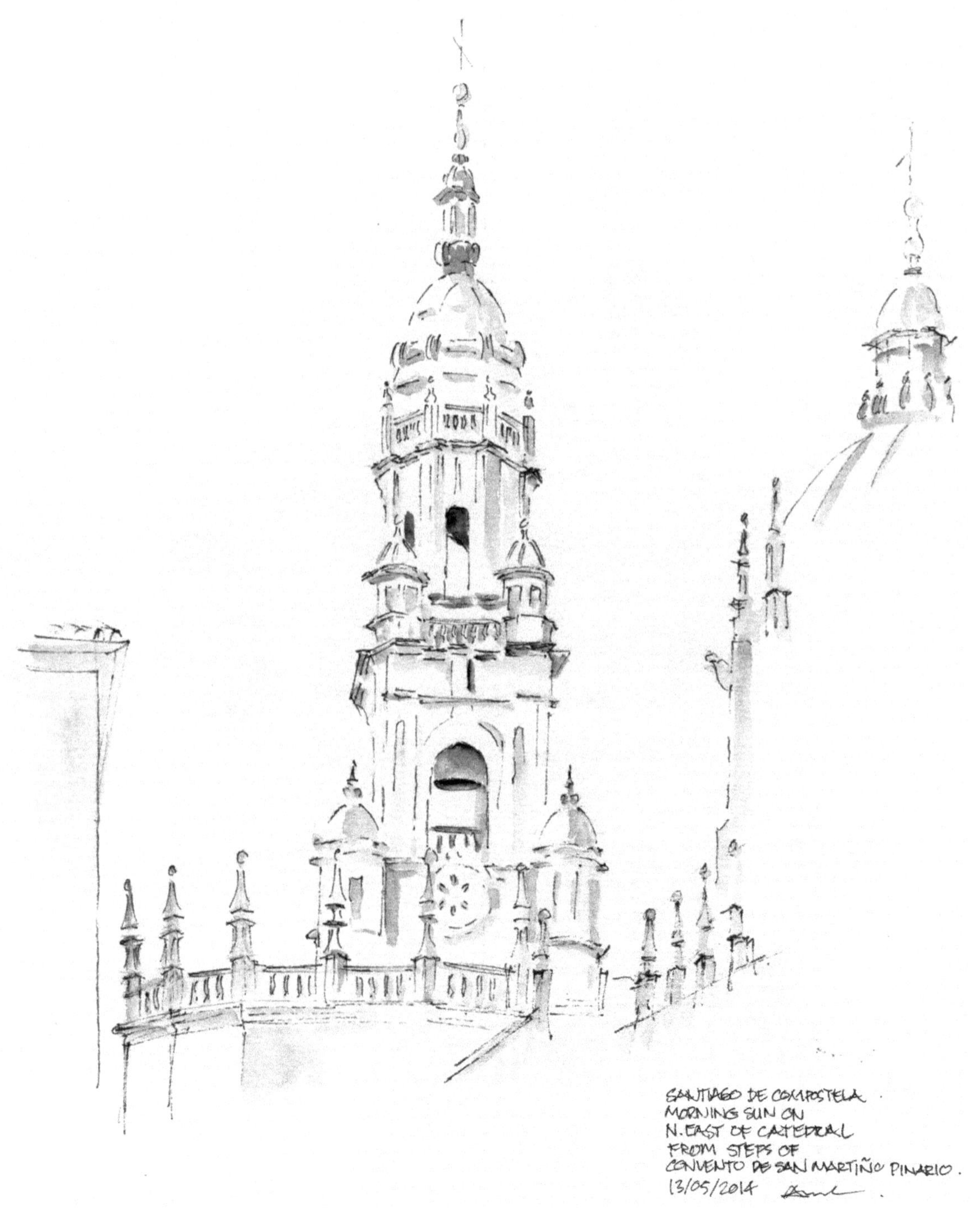

Having entered by either North, or South Transept doors on my Caminos, I'm not sure if this Pilgrim ritual is or will be re-introduced, as I believe it has been caged like a zoo animal, for restoration work

Very often during conversations along the Way with Pilgrims, they were not aware that these works would see the North Tower in 2014, and South the following year, scaffolded and netted, albeit with a printed image of the tower on the netting. As some of them seemed disappointed, I learned to comment that they would be privileged to see a unique aspect of the Facade. One, hopefully, will not be seen again for hundreds of years.

Although I had memories of Santiago as a tourist, I was surprised how different it felt walking in on my first Camino. Santiago was wonderful. There was an energy about the place derived from the aggregation of achievement, dreams and hopes of all the arriving Pilgrims. Euphoria hung tangibly in the air. Joyful faces everywhere, painful limps mostly forgotten! Pilgrims sat and lay in the *Praza do Obradoiro* soaking up the sun, with others to whom they have become extraordinarily close, and from whom they would soon be separated.

I bumped into Angus and Grace, walking toward me, he not sitting comfortably, but sartorially elegant in his newly tailored trousers. They were having a last walk around before catching a flight home, and were happy that whilst doing so, thought they had bumped into virtually all the Pilgrims they had known along the Way.

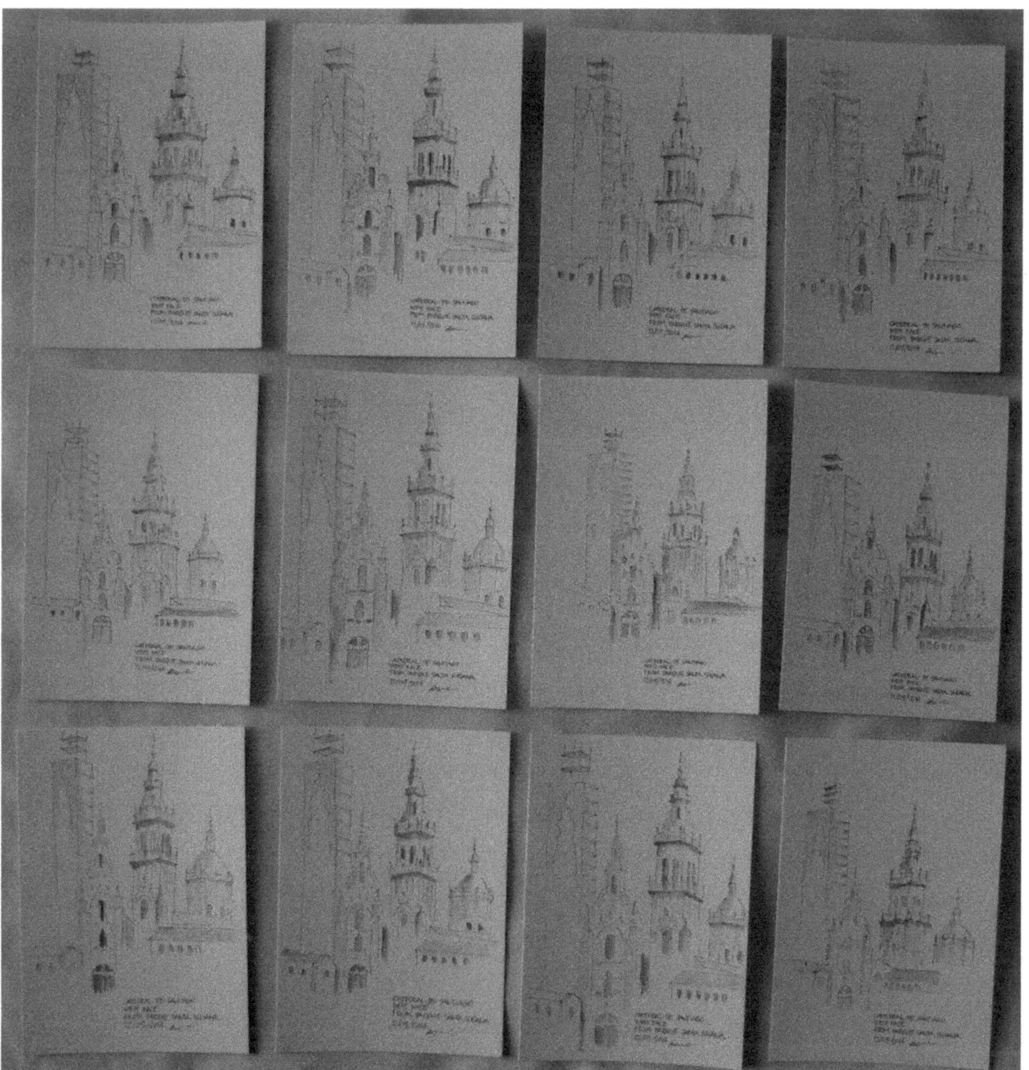

I did the odd drawing, filled my sketchpad, then resting on the stone bench in front of the *Parador* in the corner of the *Praza* I drew for family and friends, twelve blank post cards, Ann (my wife), had bought for me from the Tate. As I progressed I did think that this was not such a good idea, and vowed to seriously reduce the numbers in future! Lazily unwilling to pack up and move to a different vantage point my mind wandered as I repeated the same sketch, over and over, looking up from time to time to scan the skyline for smoke signals to monitor Caroline's progress as she neared Santiago.

I abandoned Albergues in Santiago, for the relative comfort of a small Pension.. Whilst booking in, there was an American lady, who had just arrived prior to me. We exchanged pleasantries, and she explained she was catching a train back to SJPdP to start her Camino. (No I couldn't understand the logic either!) As I had just completed my Camino, she remarked, could I offer advice etc.

We went to a bar and over a glass of Rioja talked do's and don'ts, things to see, places to miss, detours worth the effort. Afterwards we walked back to the Pension and at her suggestion, to her room for a discussion of what to take, and what to cull from the contents of her rucksack.

From my point of view, her most useless and weighty item which she insisted she could not do without; a travel immersion water heater. To make coffee in Spain! I told her, in my experience, from smart City restaurants, to scruffy village bars in the middle of nowhere, I have never been served with anything less than excellent coffee. She would not be budged, although I suspect the walk from St Jean to Orrison would prove more persuasive.

She then asked to see my rucksack, and its contents. Oh Lord, you can imagine how tidy my room was! But as I glanced around, her room was not much tidier, so we crossed the corridor to my room where she tested the weight to see how it felt, and I showed her how to adjust the straps. Would I show how to adjust the straps on her rucksack, she asked, so off we went back across the corridor to her room again.

I should add at this point, this lady though not that much younger than me, was very attractive, and like many American ladies of a certain age had impeccably applied make up, and coiffure, and, how can I put it, an outstanding figure! As you might imagine, adjusting straps can and does involve close physical contact.

I adjusted her straps and explained where the weight of the sack should sit, for both comfort and efficiency. That completed, I wished her a safe journey the following day, and of course *"Buen Camino"* and as I made for the door I felt myself offering paternalistic advice to this lady. Saying she needed to be careful, and aware such trusting friendliness might be interpreted by some males along the Way, as an invitation to rather more than a discussion of the contents of a backpack!

When I recounted this story over dinner to my friend Caroline, she said, "Austin, did it not occur to you, that is exactly what she was offering you!" Ahh, more follies of an old man. I think not, but an amusing anecdote against myself!

Judging by queues I'd seen, both before, and after visiting The Pilgrims Office to obtain my *Compostela,* I had fortuitously timed it well. There were no queues in the yard, and I only had to wait behind a couple of Pilgrims at the desk. Whilst waiting, I rather cheekily asked a lady who had just obtained her *Compostela* if I could take a peek at it.

Later whilst drawing the lady recognised me and we chatted. She knew of a book by a Swiss guy who had published an illustrated guide book, and sent me details. I managed to track it down to a bookshop in Germany. The book had such a snappy title I just couldn't resist it, it was nineteen words long! Obviously the text is in German, but as an added challenge to my long forgotten school German, it is in hand written script.

My arms were aching from sending semaphore messages, but I had tightened the string on my cocoa tin and consequently had managed to arrange a time and place to meet up with Caroline. My last day of my Camino, well, in Santiago, would have been tinged with sadness in other circumstances, but with the evening to look forward to, I was like a child on Christmas Eve!

I felt incredibly privileged that Caroline chose to meet up and dine with me. We met at the appointed place, oddly enough, where I had drawn the day before. It was again a fine balmy evening and after dinner we strolled around enjoying the atmosphere. Earlier, knowing of my interest in drawing a lady in the Tourist Office had told me the *Parque Alameda* was a good place to observe the Cathedral as darkness falls, shadows change, colours mute, and lights begin to show

We walked along the Ria do Franco, yes, much as I like Galicia and its people, as an old romantic lefty I'm saddened the area was pro Nationalist in the Civil War. We passed the arcaded *Corroeos* where earlier to buy stamps for my drawn Post Cards, I'd spent a fruitless twenty minutes in what I thought was the queue, only to find I needed to have taken a ticket on entry and await it's number showing above the counter, meandered through milling crowds along the narrow street, lined with tacky souvenir shops and seemingly overpriced restaurants, and ladies offering samples of goodies. The street opened out and lead to a pedestrian crossing to where we could see the broad avenued path into the park.

We passed by the awful sculpture, Las Marias, well we thought it so, but I gather many love it! and found a bench with a view over the pan tiled roofs glowing orange in the evening sun, where we sat talking. I wishing the still clear blue sky would continue to hold back dusk, stop time. Caroline probably wondering what she was doing there, commenting that we must seem like teenagers! A pretty close description of how I felt, at that moment, as Shakespeare put it, 'My glass shall not persuade me I am old' ha ha

Inevitably dusk gathered, colour washed from the stonework, pantiles earlier glowing bright orange in the evening sun sank to deep vermillion, shadows deepened, the odd light in the West wing of the cloisters began to show; imperceptible at first but shining more brightly in the gathering gloom. Caroline suggested it was time to walk back; just as well as no doubt I would have continued sitting there. Walking her back to where she was staying, the elation I had felt throughout the day slowly began to ebb. I had said goodbye before, thinking that we would not meet again, but this time there was no doubt. I was flying home the next morning, and she planned to walk on with Nicola, to Fisterre and Muxía, before travelling home.

It's strange, after so brief a friendship it can feel with some Pilgrims met along the Camino that you've known them for a lifetime. So it was with Caroline, as I mumbled my goodbyes that evening stood outside her door, it seemed like bidding farewell to an old friend. We exchanged a brief hug, and she walked the few paces to the door, and was gone.

Apart from rain on the evening, and early morning in Burgos, I had experienced wall to wall sunshine, even in Galicia where it expects rain one day in every three. Sadly for the girls, the weather changed after I left, and they experienced rain, hail, sleet, thunder, they got lost, and Nicola twisted her ankle. I had an email from Caroline, it read that she was sitting in a bar in Lires, and never wanted to take another step! I felt quite guilty at being just a fair weather Pilgrim.

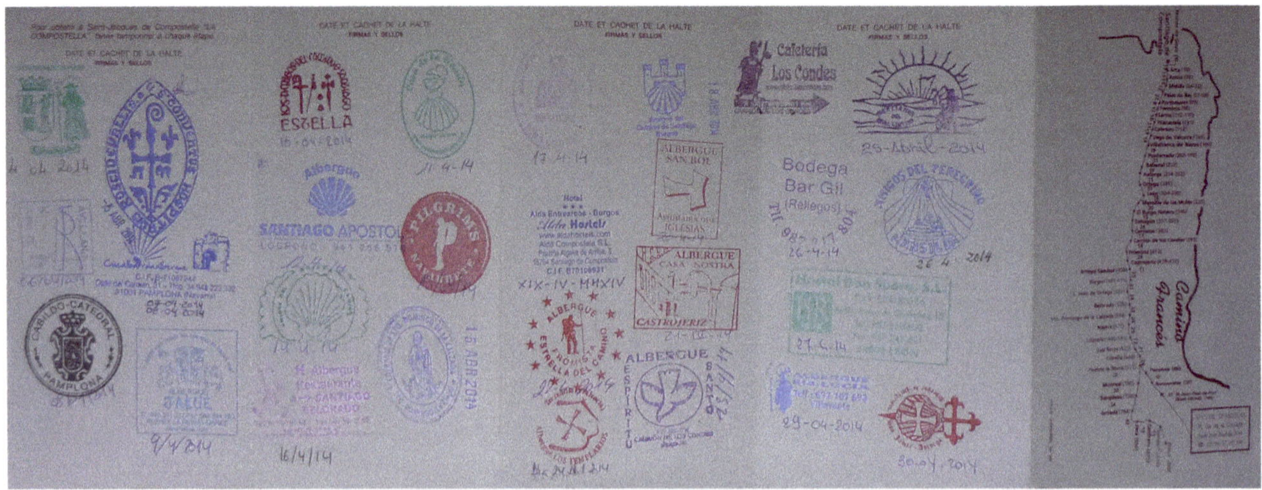

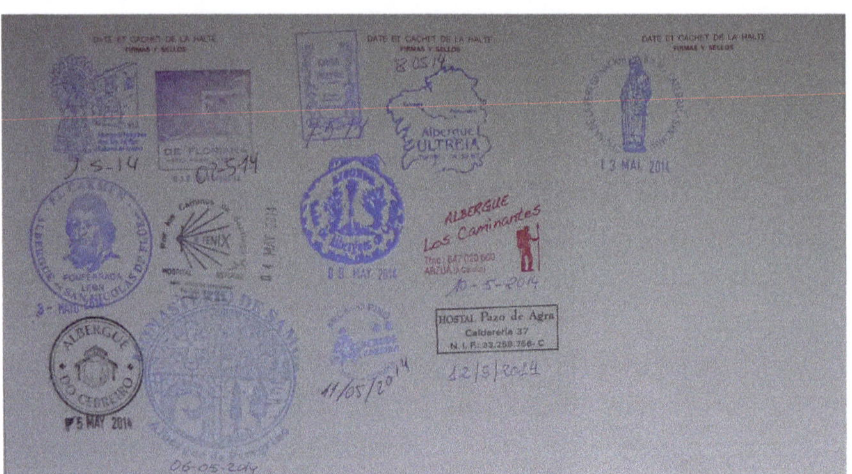

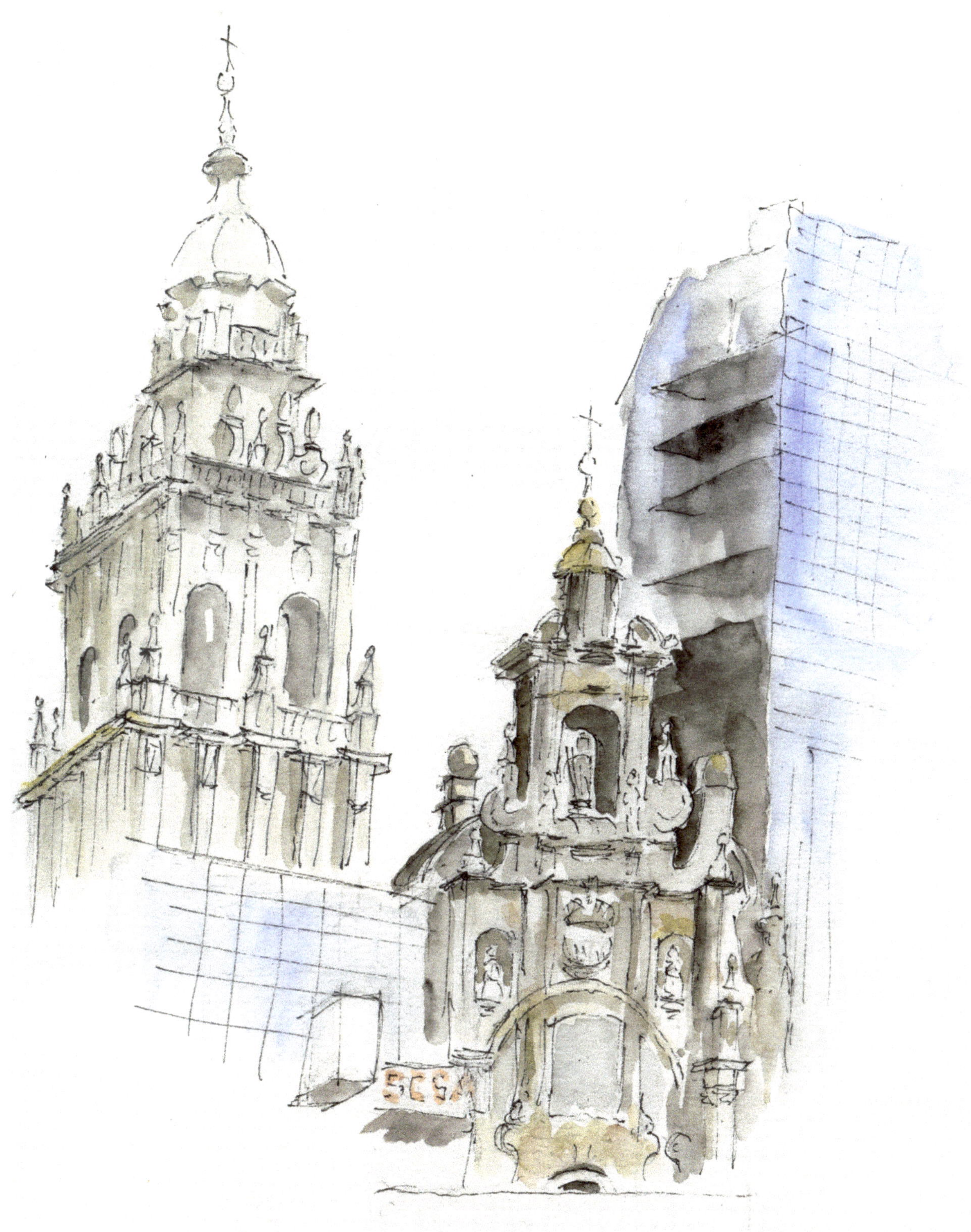

01·06·2015
CATEDRAL DE SANTIAGO DE COMPOSTELA
FROM FAR CORNER OF PRAZA DOOBRADOIRO
SCAFFOLD BEING STRIPPED FROM NORTH TOWER
BUT THIS YEAR, THE SOUTH TOWER IS
SCAFFOLDED.

Santiago de Compostela 2015

I didn't feel the same buzz of excitement, but then the first time is always special. On reflection too, the prospect of meeting again with Caroline probably played a significant part in the euphoria I had felt!

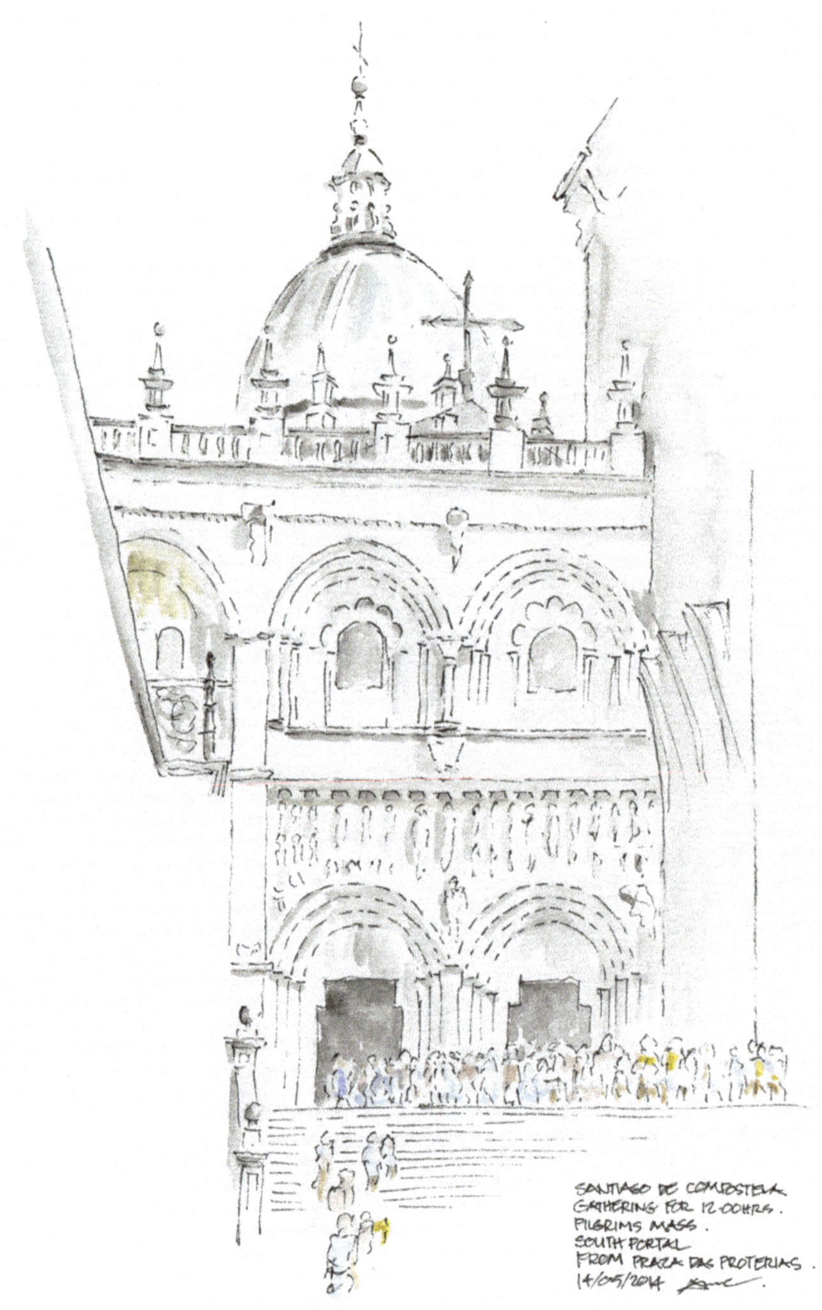

In 2014 this was the last drawing in my sketchpad. I leant against the stone wall of a rather expensive souvenir shop, with my butt on the handily placed plinth. I was so engrossed in drawing that I missed the 12 noon Mass I'd planned to attend, it was ten minutes past the hour, and I would have felt uncomfortable entering late. So I waited till the following year to attend. I need not have worried as people wandered in and out all the time, seemingly odd behaviour from my Anglican's viewpoint.

Whilst drawing two Australian Guys spoke to me. They had been at Karin's dinner party in Samos. They were sat down at the far end of tables pushed together refectory style, so we never spoke then. I think they may have recognised me more for what I was doing, rather than my face. But having said that nearly two years down the line, Facebook threw up a face of someone I might know. It was one of these guys. I have a memory for faces.

At the Mass I attended they did not swing the *Botafumeiro*. I had assumed, like those around me, that it was the custom at a Pilgrim's Mass. I would have been interested and enjoyed the spectacle no doubt but I am slightly asthmatic and incense catches my breath; so a little disappointed, but relieved not to have to suffer incense. I felt sorry for those around me for whom it was a real disappointment. Obviously no money changed hands on that date.

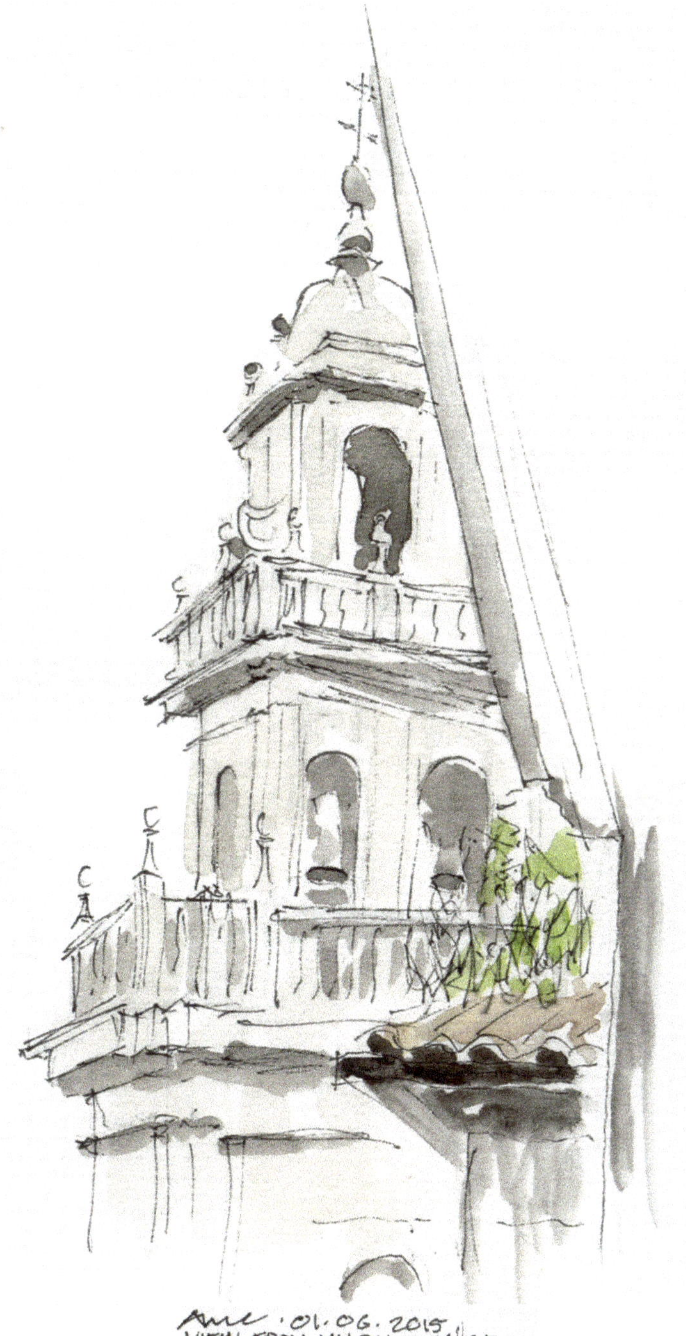

I stayed in the small Pension I'd stayed previously. I had a similar room on the second floor with French windows opening to the usual small balcony. I am not comfortable with heights and ventured timidly onto the stone slab, trying the weight one foot at a time, and grasping and testing the wrought iron balustrade. Eventually I had confidence, or at least convinced myself I wasn't about to crash to the pavement below and made a sketch of what I could see of the University.

It was centrally situated, very lively during the day because of its proximity to the University, but generally peaceful at night. Until, that is, one night. I woke, or was awakened at 1.30 by whoops, singing, shouting, laughter. And between dozes, this went on till 4.30ish!

That evening, I had dinner around the corner, at a bar facing the campus entrance, and whilst eating, was entertained by photo calls of graduation ceremony after ceremony. No gowns, with caps in the air, as here, but a sort of turquoise shawl thrown up enthusiastically. It explained the celebratory noise. The following night was much the same, until I closed the French windows to the balcony.

In the morning as I rounded the corner to the breakfast bar where I'd had dinner, I was met with a heap of sleeping students, on the floor, draped across tables, and some teetering precariously on the edge of chairs.

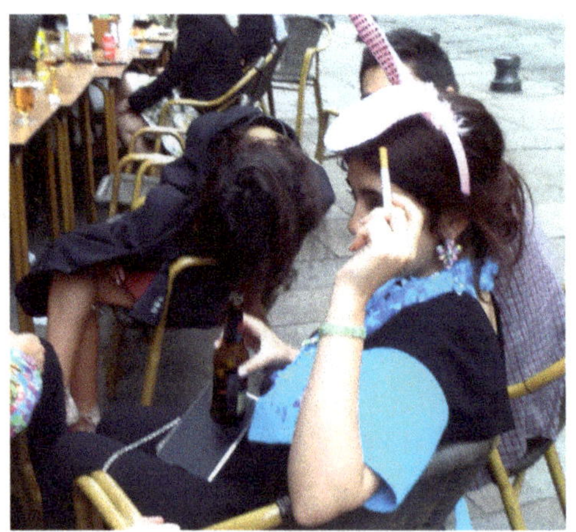

Students, or I should say, Graduates God bless them!

Those still conscious greeted me with a cheer and good humour. Alas one girl smoking, but with the wrong end lit! One rather tubby young man, who had started out the previous evening in a white shirt and black bow tie, had obviously been elected by his peers as waiter for the day. As I made my way to a table inside, I was accosted for my order, which through an inebriated haze, he tried, and almost succeeded in holding onto!

After a while he came weaving between the mostly empty tables, lurching to left and right as if aboard ship on Biscay. My coffee arrived, some of it still in the cup!

I went to the Ministry of Funny Walks, or as some know it, the Pilgrims Office to collect my second *Compostela.* There was a small queue winding around the yard this time, entertained by a young man singing and shouting *"Compostela Compostela"* with great gusto. It was a mixed bunch, some like the young man, I've no idea how far he had come but he was obviously unscathed, and others shuffling forward painfully each time a Pilgrim was admitted into the Office; still others remained seated on benches, whilst others kept their place for them.

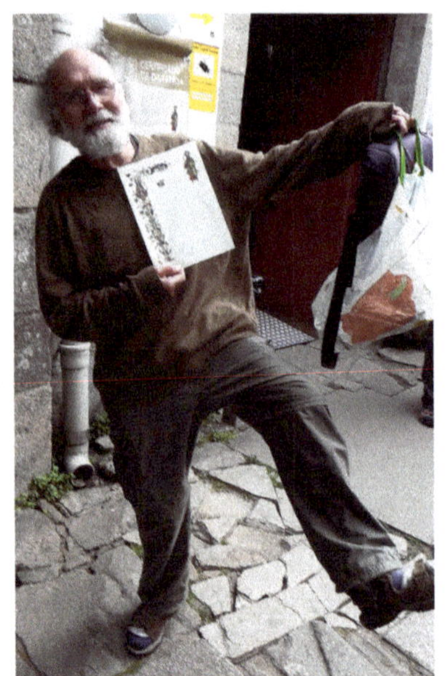

ANNEMIEK LEEKSMA

As I looked along the line I was really happy to see a little ahead of me Ann Marie. I had last seen her ten or eleven days prior, walking by as I sketched in Cacabelos. I was particularly pleased as in optimistic mood I'd drawn a postcard for her, and as I had no contact details, bumping in to her in Santiago was the only way I could give it to her.

As she exited the Office I photographed her, smiling radiantly, holding up her *Compostela.* She kindly hung around and took a photo as I exited clutching my second *Compostela* in one hand whilst hung from the other the small case containing my drawing kit and the well travelled 'Waitrose' plastic bag which contained my sketch pads. It was only as I packed to come home I noticed the wording on the bag, it read:

To the end of the World!

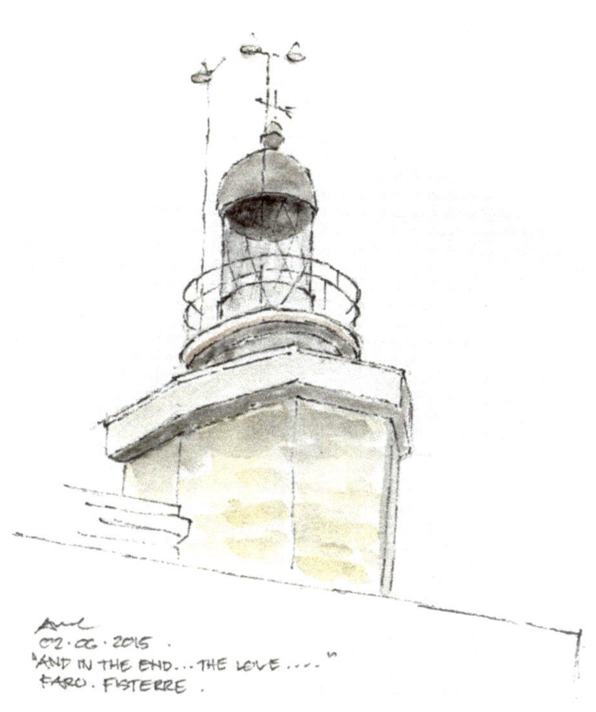

I had considered walking on to Fisterre, but had not properly prepared and had badly underestimated, and was surprised by the distance.

As I had booked a flight a week before whilst still labouring in ignorance, I had to compromise, and caught the bus to Fisterre to walk on to Muxía.

As passengers alighted in Finisterre, accommodation touts milled about, but I preferred to wait and get my bearings first. I stood a while talking to, and saying farewell to an American couple, Jan and Terrill. Our paths had criss crossed since a shared communal dinner in Mansilla de las Mulas. Terrill seemingly some little distance ahead, or behind Jan, indulging his passion for photography. They intended just walking to the Faro and back, before catching a bus back to Santiago in the afternoon.

As I moved off, a lady walked briskly by, calling out, "Rooms" She had a trail of half a dozen or so following. I decided to tag along to see where she led. She led us at a pace through the market, along the front and up steps into the residential area. I had a splendid double room for just €15, and the street lead on to the Faro path as well.

I walked to the Faro in the afternoon. I suppose I must have seen images of it, but I'd forgotten, or put them to the back of my mind. Somehow I expected, or hoped for something more elegant, picturesque, romantic even! But it is distinctly none of those. Non the less I drew it, for fun as much as anything. The rock I found to sit on, was thankfully sheltered from the breeze, and the choking smoke which

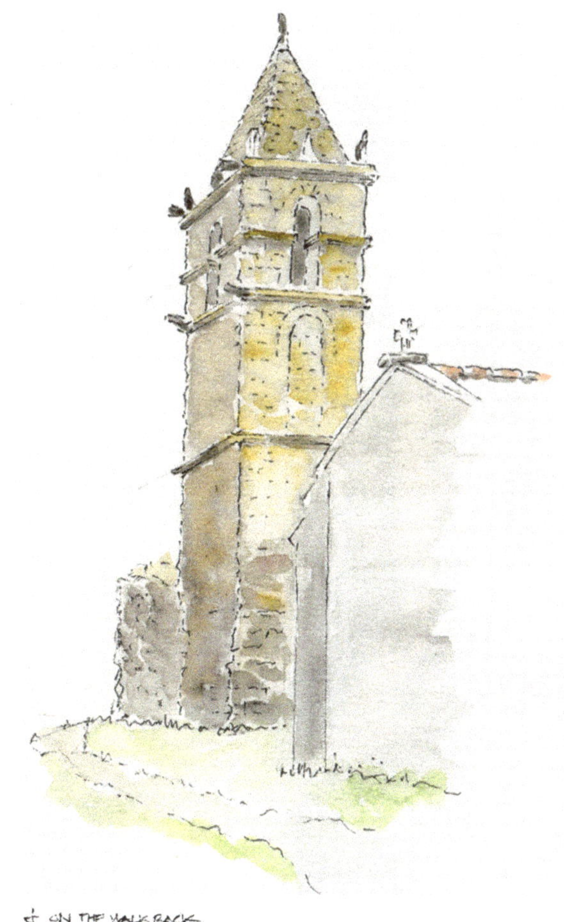

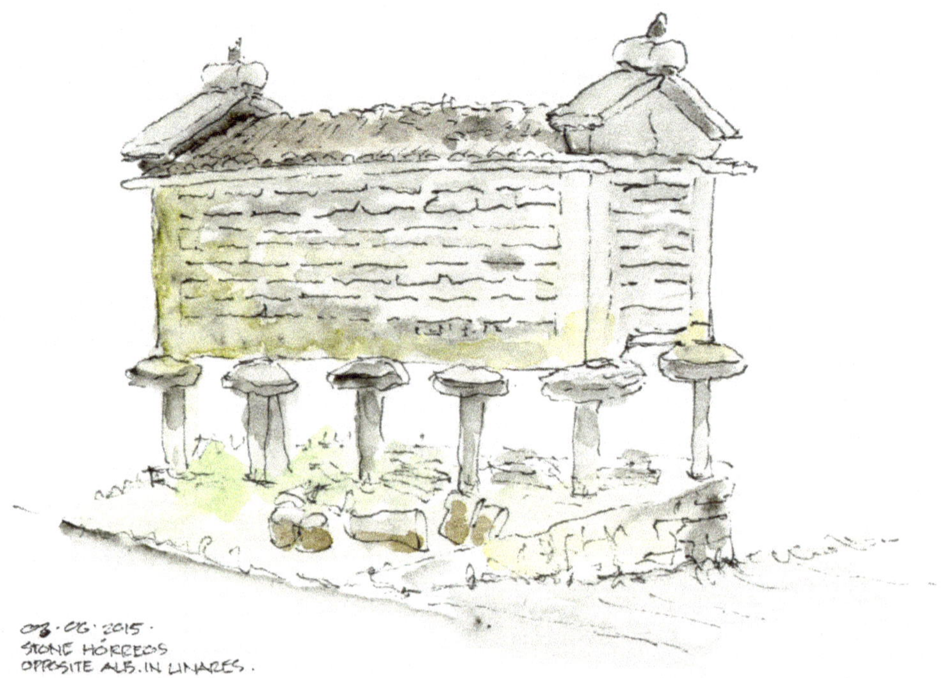

swept up the path from the car park, from, were they Pilgrims, perhaps burning their clothes?

I sat there, reflecting I suppose on the journey, and the folk I'd met. Although I planned to walk on to Muxía, this was an *'End'* of sorts, and the Beatles song came to mind, well as much as I remembered. *"And in the end, the love you take, is equal to the love you make"* The tune though was an earworm for the rest of the day, and much of the day after.

The day after, I had planned it to be a winding down, pleasantly short walk of around 14Km to Lires. I set out in the sun, again blessed with the weather, my mind wandered, enjoying the walk, I had passed through Sardiñeiro and up the hill to a large traffic island before I realised, wool gathering, I had hopelessly missed my way. I was half way back to Cee!

I turned around, oh, retraced footsteps are always the hardest, and after failing at first to find the waymark out of Fisterre, I eventually made it to Lires. My short walk just over 30KM!

My final day of walking arrived in sunshine again. I walked without incident, apart from, searching for a waymark at a junction in one small village; I was misdirected by locals queueing at a mobile fish sales van. It took me in a circular route, back to a part of

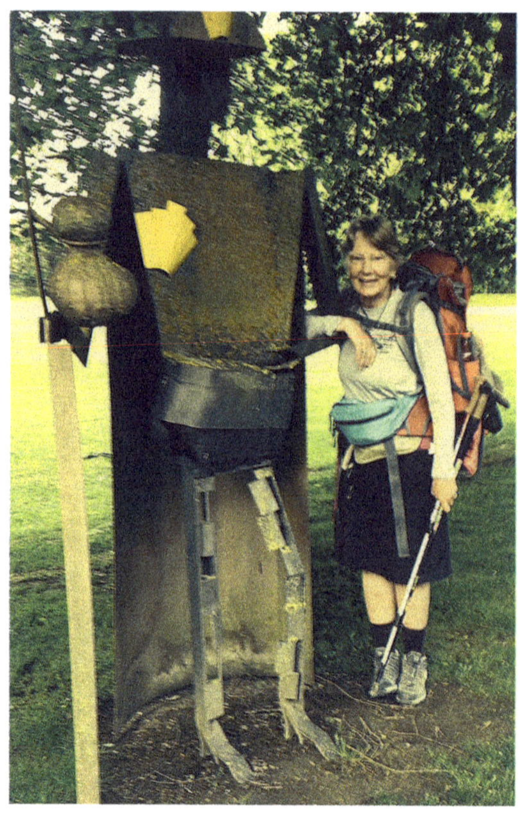

TERRILL FAUL

My friends Jan and Terrill earlier along the Way, Terrill looked much better towards the end!!

the path I fortunately recognised. It probably only added another two or three Km, and I met couple who had taken similar advice, so I can only conclude we were sent deliberately in the wrong direction. So sad.

Nearing Muxía one passes a number of splendid looking beaches with heavy surf rolling in, but with danger signs too. Almost there, the Way joins a narrow undulating road, a shallow gradient descends, and a sea view opens up ahead. Soon a sign, Praia de Lourido, and a splendid vista across a wonderful deep wide bay, sheltered from the Westerlies by the headland. The sweep of fine sand stretching to the rocks below the headland five or six hundred metres off, looked awfully tempting.

It is an idyllic place, spoiled, as only the Spanish could contemplate, by the construction of huge sprawl of a building atop the Head. The beach however was deserted, apart from a local farmer and his tractor harvesting seaweed, and as if Nature read my mind, a sea mist rolled in, drawing a veil over my skinny-dipping No doubt to the relief of fellow Pilgrims passing by on the path above. One lady though, sat on the rocks below the path, watching......the tractor presumably!

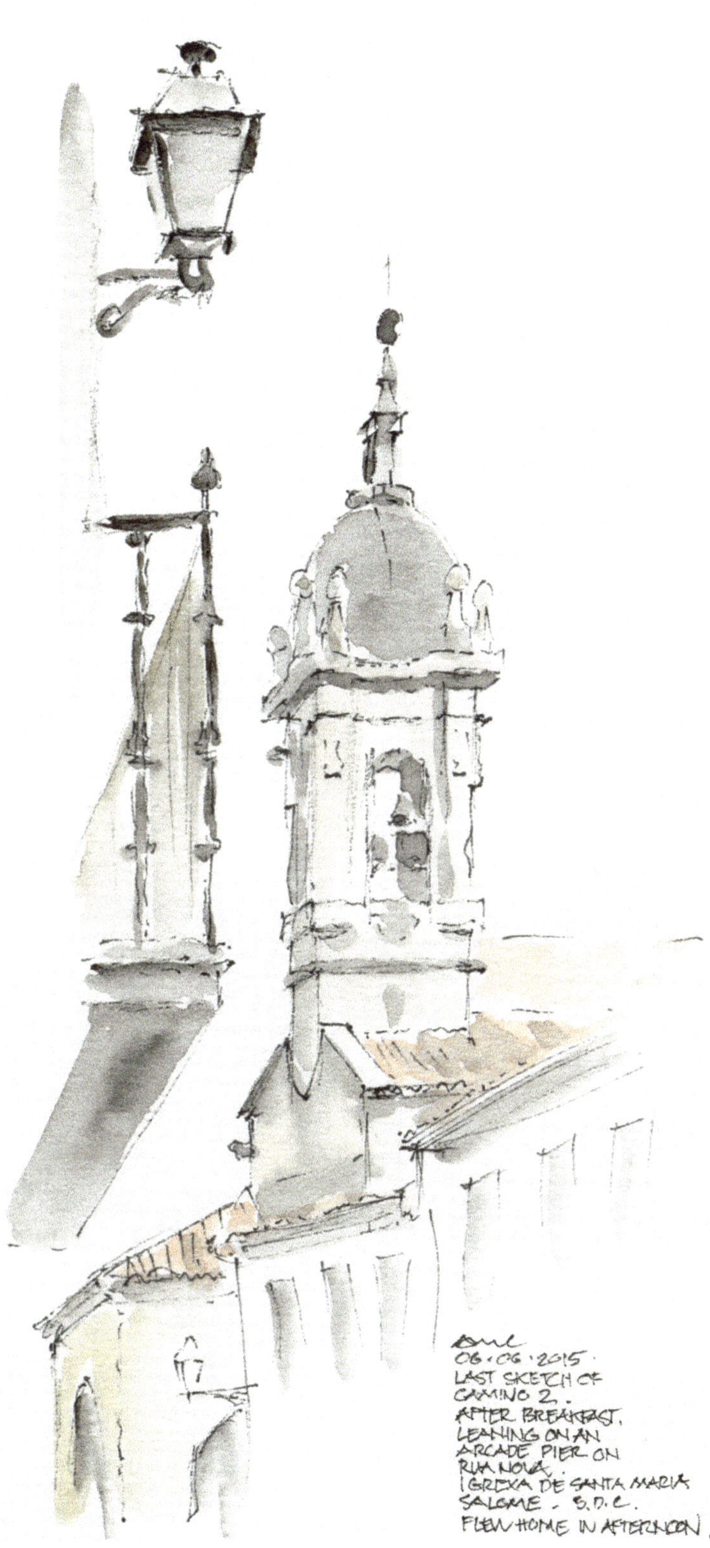

The last sketch of Camino 2, before flying home in the afternoon.

Conclusion

In 2014 I walked the *Camino Francés* from St Jean Pied de Port to Santiago, 496 miles in 33 walking days, a rough average of 15 miles per day, carrying a 15Kg. rucksack on all but two occasions.

I filled my A4 sketch pad with 44 drawings. Sometimes, perhaps surprisingly, it felt like drawing was the most tiring part. I carried a mono-easel, basically a telescopic aluminium tube with a walking stick ferrule and a bulldog clip fixed at the other end to grab the top of the pad. Whilst walking I carried it attached to the walking pole loops on my rucksack. *(See photo of me leaving SJPdP.)* It protruded just above my head, and intrigued many pilgrims behind me. Many were prompted to ask what it was for. "It's a lightening conductor" I would reply, and wait, almost hearing cogs turning, before "No!" or sometimes to my amusement, "Really?"

Back home, yes, I missed the big skies of Northern Spain, the Sunshine, the *vino tinto*, the architecture, both vernacular and the grand; but the joys I found back with the familiar served as something of a balm.

I left at the beginning of April as it was slowly creeping out of winter, with only the odd tentative sign of Spring, and returned in mid-May, it feeling like early Summer. *(I seemed to have brought the Camino weather home with me!)*

The pool I pass on my morning walks, swans had six tiny fluffy cygnets. A little further on a family of Canada Geese trooped by with several goslings in step, and in my minds ear I heard Fats Waller singing *'Your feets too big.'* Yellow Flags teetered at the water's edge, the braver ones had taken the plunge, waving, not drowning.

Grass was tall and lush; trees were decked in their church going Sunday best, boughs gently dipping in the breeze under the weight of pristine foliage. Cow Parsley sprung out at me as I walked passed hedgerows, hedgerows blousy with May Blossom, or as A E Housman put it, dressed in white for Whitsuntide. *(or was it Eastertide for him?)* Thrushes, seemingly aware of my defective hearing, repeated each call, note for note, and phrase for phrase. Cowslips their bright sunny yellow glow just beginning to fade as seed heads formed. The splash of yellow replaced in the meadows by a sea of leggy Buttercups rippling in the breeze, and on the heathlands Gorse shone bright against last year's fading bracken. Whilst below, in woodland clearings, drifts of Bluebells lay like a mist over the ground.

Everything seemed renewed or changed, my Grandson Finley too, he was now 8 months, and what progress I noted in the 6 weeks I'd been away. He now sat up, was very vocal, and if I was not careful, grabbed, and tenaciously clung onto my beard at every opportunity.

My very favourite young lady assistant at my local Waitrose store skipped across the store floor and hugged me on my return. In short, everything was different. I was different, not just a stone lighter, walking the Camino was/is somehow life changing, life enhancing.

And yet, oh I still missed the Camino. I had withdrawal symptoms, or what the lovely young girl who insisted on guiding me to the albergue in Ponferrada referred to as Camino blues. I missed the routine, the walking, the albergues; but most of all the pilgrims I had met, and re-met, said goodbye to, or not, laughed with, walked with, shared pain with, and joys along the moving community that is the Way.

On the first of what turned out to be several goodbyes to my friend Caroline, I suggested we were as ships that pass in the night. Oh Lord, how trite was that! I didn't realise that for weeks afterwards I would be rocked up, and down, in the wake!

As the Seasons turned, late Spring into Summer, hedgerows that had once worn white now as I looked across the meadows, glowed rust, as red Hawthorn berries blended with the dry green leaves.

Horse Chestnuts, their leaves tinged ochre, always among the first to signal Autumn, would soon be reluctantly yielding their bounty to little boy's thrown sticks; or perhaps Dad's and Grandpa's sticks. And as I scuffed through carpets of dry leaves, kicked at the spikey green conker shells, the rawness of Camino blues now blunted by time; I began to contemplate a second Camino.

Initially I had been deterred from the thought of a second Camino by the prospect of walking with the ghosts, or shadows of Pilgrims I had met. As time went by I became increasingly lured by the chance to capture the numerous drawings I would have wished to have made, had I had the time, and or energy. Gradually the idea formed of a second Camino to remedy those omissions, or at least some of them; and possibly, as had been suggested by a number of Pilgrims, produce a book.

I walked again in 2015, and yes, there were moments when triggered by the recognition of places I'd walked through, or bars I'd sat at, when I faced those shadows; but they only evoked pleasurable memories, and of course I met with and made new Pilgrim friends to add to my store of memories.

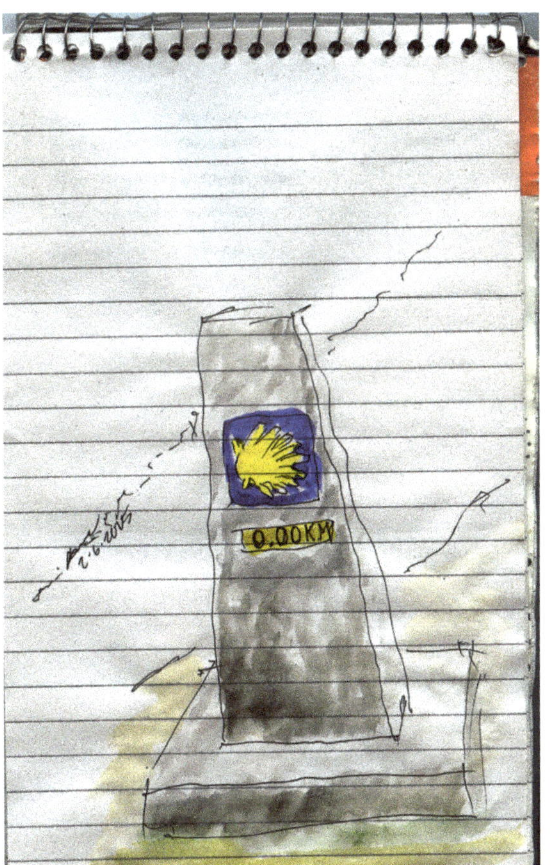

Fisterre

I didn't manage to accomplish all on my wish list, but I filled a further two sketchpads with 101 drawings.

Thankfully I did not suffer Camino Blues the second time around, although I missed all those young, by my standards, ladies whose company I had enjoyed along the Way. I had thought it was down to my natural good looks and charm, but Ann my wife disabused me of that idea, saying "It's the grey beard, it says SAFE!" Sadly I think she may be right! Ha ha.

Would I make a third? I think not, but I have a yen to do the section before St Jean Pied de Port from Le Puy en Velay, and then again, may be the shorter *Camino Portugués*.

The Camino poses challenges, asks questions, test one both physically and spiritually. Some challenges we meet. Some questions are answered, but those tests we fail are the most self-illuminating.

Bibliography

Brierley, John *A Pilgrim's Guide to the Camino de Santiago*
Gitlitz, David M & Linda Kay Davidson *The Pilgrimage Road to Santiago*
Mullins, Edwin *The Pilgrimage to Santiago*

Suggested further reading

Day, Christy. Walking from Here to There, finding my way on El Camino.
Confraternity of Saint James guides.
Camino de Santiago, todas las etapes y albergues. EROSKI. caminodesantiago.consumer.es/

Austin can be reached on:- amcampad@gmail.com

If we met along the Way, or if you have any comments on the book, or maybe you wish to share your experiences of the Camino; I'd love to hear from you.

A selection of the drawings is available as Fine Art, signed, limited edition prints, each complete with a 'FINE ART TRADE GUILD' Certificate of Authentication. Contact me for details.

Notes

www.ingramcontent.com/pod-product-compliance
Lightning Source LLC
LaVergne TN
LVHW070408110826
845147LV00016B/969
9781910864791